Unix®

Your visual blueprint to the universe of Unix

by Michael Bellomo

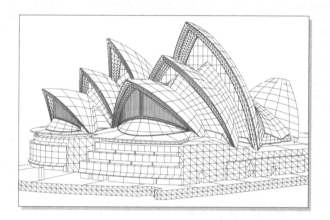

Visual

From
maranGraphics™

&

 IDG BOOKS

IDG Books Worldwide, Inc.
An International Data Group Company
Foster City, CA • Indianapolis • Chicago • New York

Unix®: Your visual blueprint to the universe of Unix

Published by
IDG Books Worldwide, Inc.
An International Data Group Company
919 E. Hillsdale Blvd., Suite 400
Foster City, CA 94404
www.idgbooks.com (IDG Books Worldwide Web Site)

Library of Congress Control Number: 00-107549

ISBN: 0-7645-3480-7

Printed in the United States of America
10 9 8 7 6 5 4 3 2 1

1O/RV/QZ/QQ/IN

Distributed in the United States by IDG Books Worldwide, Inc.

Distributed by CDG Books Canada Inc. for Canada; by Transworld Publishers
Limited in the United Kingdom; by IDG Norge Books for Norway; by IDG Sweden
Books for Sweden; by IDG Books Australia Publishing Corporation Pty. Ltd. for
Australia and New Zealand; by TransQuest Publishers Pte Ltd. for Singapore,
Malaysia, Thailand, Indonesia, and Hong Kong; by Gotop Information Inc. for
Taiwan; by ICG Muse, Inc. for Japan; by Intersoft for South Africa; by Eyrolles
for France; by International Thomson Publishing for Germany, Austria and
Switzerland; by Distribuidora Cuspide for Argentina; by LR International for
Brazil; by Galileo Libros for Chile; by Ediciones ZETA S.C.R. Ltda. for Peru;
by WS Computer Publishing Corporation, Inc. for the Philippines; by
Contemporanea de Ediciones for Venezuela; by Express Computer Distributors
for the Caribbean and West Indies; by Micronesia Media Distributor, Inc. for
Micronesia; by Chips Computadoras S.A. de C.V. for Mexico; by Editorial Norma
de Panama S.A. for Panama; by American Bookshops for Finland.
For corporate orders, please call maranGraphics at 800-469-6616.
For general information on IDG Books Worldwide's books in the U.S.,
please call our Consumer Customer Service department at 800-762-2974.
For reseller information, including discounts and premium sales,
please call our Reseller Customer Service department at 800-434-3422.
For information on where to purchase IDG Books Worldwide's books
outside the U.S., please contact our International Sales department at
317-572-3993 or fax 317-572-4002.
For consumer information on foreign language translations, please contact
our Customer Service department at 800-434-3422, fax 800-550-2747,
or e-mail rights@idgbooks.com.
For information on licensing foreign or domestic rights, please phone
650-653-7000 of fax 650-653-7500.
For sales inquiries and special prices for bulk quantities, please contact
our Sales department at 650-655-3200.
For information on using IDG Books Worldwide's books in the classroom
or for ordering examination copies, please contact our Educational Sales
department at 800-434-2086 or fax 317-572-4005.
For press review copies, author interviews, or other publicity information,
please contact our Public Relations department at 650-653-7000 or
fax 650-653-7500.
For authorization to photocopy items for corporate, personal, or
educational use, please contact maranGraphics at 800-469-6616.

Trademark Acknowledgments

Permissions

U.S. Corporate Sales	U.S. Trade Sales
Contact maranGraphics at (800) 469-6616 or fax (905) 890-9434.	Contact IDG Books at (800) 434-3422 or (650) 655-3000.

ABOUT IDG BOOKS WORLDWIDE

Welcome to the world of IDG Books Worldwide.

IDG Books Worldwide, Inc., is a subsidiary of International Data Group, the world's largest publisher of computer-related information and the leading global provider of information services on information technology. IDG was founded more than 30 years ago by Patrick J. McGovern and now employs more than 9,000 people worldwide. IDG publishes more than 290 computer publications in over 75 countries. More than 90 million people read one or more IDG publications each month.

Launched in 1990, IDG Books Worldwide is today the #1 publisher of best-selling computer books in the United States. We are proud to have received eight awards from the Computer Press Association in recognition of editorial excellence and three from Computer Currents' First Annual Readers' Choice Awards. Our best-selling ...*For Dummies*® series has more than 50 million copies in print with translations in 31 languages. IDG Books Worldwide, through a joint venture with IDG's Hi-Tech Beijing, became the first U.S. publisher to publish a computer book in the People's Republic of China. In record time, IDG Books Worldwide has become the first choice for millions of readers around the world who want to learn how to better manage their businesses.

Our mission is simple: Every one of our books is designed to bring extra value and skill-building instructions to the reader. Our books are written by experts who understand and care about our readers. The knowledge base of our editorial staff comes from years of experience in publishing, education, and journalism — experience we use to produce books to carry us into the new millennium. In short, we care about books, so we attract the best people. We devote special attention to details such as audience, interior design, use of icons, and illustrations. And because we use an efficient process of authoring, editing, and desktop publishing our books electronically, we can spend more time ensuring superior content and less time on the technicalities of making books.

You can count on our commitment to deliver high-quality books at competitive prices on topics you want to read about. At IDG Books Worldwide, we continue in the IDG tradition of delivering quality for more than 30 years. You'll find no better book on a subject than one from IDG Books Worldwide.

John Kilcullen
Chairman and CEO
IDG Books Worldwide, Inc.

VIII WINNER
Eighth Annual Computer Press Awards ≥ 1992

IX WINNER
Ninth Annual Computer Press Awards ≥ 1993

X WINNER
Tenth Annual Computer Press Awards ≥ 1994

XI WINNER
Eleventh Annual Computer Press Awards ≥ 1995

IDG is the world's leading IT media, research and exposition company. Founded in 1964, IDG had 1997 revenues of $2.05 billion and has more than 9,000 employees worldwide. IDG offers the widest range of media options that reach IT buyers in 75 countries representing 95% of worldwide IT spending. IDG's diverse product and services portfolio spans six key areas including print publishing, online publishing, expositions and conferences, market research, education and training, and global marketing services. More than 90 million people read one or more of IDG's 290 magazines and newspapers, including IDG's leading global brands — Computerworld, PC World, Network World, Macworld and the Channel World family of publications. IDG Books Worldwide is one of the fastest-growing computer book publishers in the world, with more than 700 titles in 36 languages. The "...For Dummies®" series alone has more than 50 million copies in print. IDG offers online users the largest network of technology-specific Web sites around the world through IDG.net (http://www.idg.net), which comprises more than 225 targeted Web sites in 55 countries worldwide. International Data Corporation (IDC) is the world's largest provider of information technology data, analysis and consulting, with research centers in over 41 countries and more than 400 research analysts worldwide. IDG World Expo is a leading producer of more than 168 globally branded conferences and expositions in 35 countries including E3 (Electronic Entertainment Expo), Macworld Expo, ComNet, Windows World Expo, ICE (Internet Commerce Expo), Agenda, DEMO, and Spotlight. IDG's training subsidiary, ExecuTrain, is the world's largest computer training company, with more than 230 locations worldwide and 785 training courses. IDG Marketing Services helps industry-leading IT companies build international brand recognition by developing global integrated marketing programs via IDG's print, online and exposition products worldwide. Further information about the company can be found at www.idg.com.

1/26/00

**maranGraphics is a family-run business
located near Toronto, Canada.**

At maranGraphics, we believe in producing great computer books — one book at a time.

maranGraphics has been producing high-technology products for over 25 years, which enables us to offer the computer book community a unique communication process.

Our computer books use an integrated communication process, which is very different from the approach used in other computer books. Each spread is, in essence, a flow chart — the text and screen shots are totally incorporated into the layout of the spread. Introductory text and helpful tips complete the learning experience.

maranGraphics' approach encourages the left and right sides of the brain to work together — resulting in faster orientation and greater memory retention.

Above all, we are very proud of the handcrafted nature of our books. Our carefully-chosen writers are experts in their fields, and spend countless hours researching and organizing the content for each topic. Our artists rebuild every screen shot to provide the best clarity possible, making our screen shots the most precise and easiest to read in the industry. We strive for perfection, and believe that the time spent handcrafting each element results in the best computer books money can buy.

Thank you for purchasing this book. We hope you enjoy it!

Sincerely,

Robert Maran
President
maranGraphics
Rob@maran.com
www.maran.com
www.idgbooks.com/visual

Please visit us on the Web at:
www.maran.com

CREDITS

Acquisitions, Editorial, and Media Development

Project Editor
Pat O'Brien

Acquisitions Editor
Martine Edwards

Associate Project Coordinator
Lindsay Sandman

Copy Editor
Donna Frederick

Proof Editor
Dwight Ramsey

Technical Editor
James Marchetti

Permissions Editor
Carmen Krikorian

Associate Media Development Specialist
Megan Decraene

Editorial Manager
Rev Mengle

Media Development Manager
Heather Heath Dismore

Editorial Assistant
Candace Nicholson

Production

Book Design
maranGraphics©

Project Coordinator
Cindy Phipps

Layout
Joe Bucki, Barry Offringa,
Jill Piscitelli, Kathie Schutte

Proofreaders
Corey Bowen, Joel Showalter

Indexer
York Production Services, Inc.

ACKNOWLEDGMENTS

General and Administrative

IDG Books Worldwide, Inc.: John Kilcullen, CEO

IDG Books Technology Publishing Group: Richard Swadley, Senior Vice President and Publisher; Walter R. Bruce III, Vice President and Publisher; Joseph Wikert, Vice President and Publisher; Mary Bednarek, Vice President and Director, Product Development; Andy Cummings, Publishing Director, General User Group; Mary C. Corder, Editorial Director; Barry Pruett, Publishing Director

IDG Books Consumer Publishing Group: Roland Elgey, Senior Vice President and Publisher; Kathleen A. Welton, Vice President and Publisher; Kevin Thornton, Acquisitions Manager; Kristin A. Cocks, Editorial Director

IDG Books Internet Publishing Group: Brenda McLaughlin, Senior Vice President and Publisher; Sofia Marchant, Online Marketing Manager

IDG Books Production for Branded Press: Debbie Stailey, Director of Production; Cindy L. Phipps, Manager of Project Coordination, Production Proofreading, and Indexing; Tony Augsburger, Manager of Prepress, Reprints, and Systems; Shelley Lea, Supervisor of Graphics and Design; Debbie J. Gates, Production Systems Specialist; Robert Springer, Supervisor of Proofreading; Trudy Coler, Page Layout Manager; Kathie Schutte, Senior Page Layout Supervisor; Janet Seib, Page Layout Supervisor; Michael Sullivan, Production Supervisor

Packaging and Book Design: Patty Page, Manager, Promotions Marketing

*The publisher would like to give special thanks to Patrick J. McGovern,
without whom this book would not have been possible.*

About the Author

Michael Bellomo received a degree in law from the University of California, Hastings College of the Law, in San Francisco. Despite this awful start, he moved into the technical field and became certified in UNIX System Administration at the University of California, Santa Cruz (go, Fighting Banana Slugs!). Michael has written several books on UNIX, Linux, and network management.

Author's Acknowledgments

This book is dedicated to David Marhoffer, whose crystal-clear thinking, philosophical steadfastness, and interest in GUI-free operating systems, has been a voice of reason on this side of Galt's Gulch.

Thanks to both Kathleen McFadden and Pat O'Brien for their expertise in navigating the shoals of the new Blueprint Series. Thanks for keeping us off the rocks!

1) LOGGING INTO UNIX

2) THE UNIX DESKTOP ENVIRONMENT

UNIX:
Your visual blueprint to the
universe of UNIX

3) WORKING WITH FILES AND DIRECTORIES

4) WORKING WITH UNIX FILE PERMISSIONS

5) CREATING TEXT FILES

6) WORKING WITH TEXT FILES

7) WORKING WITH PROCESSES

UNIX:
Your visual blueprint to the
universe of UNIX

8) WORKING WITH SHELLS AND SYSTEM VARIABLES

9) BASIC ADMINISTRATION

10) ADMINISTERING USERS AND GROUPS

11) WORKING WITH HARD DISKS AND PRINTERS ——

12) NETWORK CONNECTIVITY ——

UNIX:
Your visual blueprint to the
universe of UNIX

13) USING NETSCAPE

14) E-MAIL IN THE TERMINAL

15) WORKING WITH ARCHIVED FILES

16) TROUBLESHOOTING

17) ACCESSORIES

UNIX:
Your visual blueprint to the
universe of UNIX

18) ADVANCED SYSTEM ADMINISTRATION

APPENDIX A: VI EDITOR COMMANDS <span></span>

THE GRAPHICAL USER INTERFACE

The UNIX operating system was originally developed without a GUI, or Graphical User Interface. This was mostly was because of the slow speed and high price of early computers. Today, most forms of UNIX use a GUI for some kinds of system configuration and user navigation.

Like Microsoft Windows, the UNIX desktop uses icons and toolbars to display information and allow you to access programs with the click of a mouse. While the exact icons on your screen depend on utilities you choose, your desktop should look similar to the following diagram.

The desktop that provides the background for the windows, icons, and other objects that you work

with in UNIX is called the CDE Desktop Environment. CDE itself stands for Common Desktop Environment. It's the standard offering with most forms of UNIX, such as Solaris.

The toolbar at the base of the screen contains most of the configuration controls for your UNIX environment in CDE. Any aspect of your UNIX machine that can't be controlled from here changes through the UNIX terminal.

Each icon on the toolbar accesses system tools or applications. Click the small arrows located directly above the pictures; the menu options slide like a drawer. Select your choice by clicking on the option.

THE GRAPHICAL USER INTERFACE

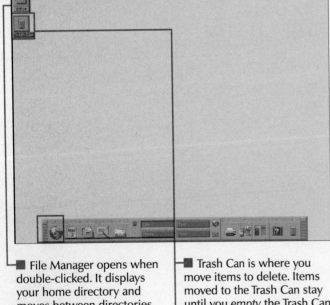

■ File Manager opens when double-clicked. It displays your home directory and moves between directories.

■ Trash Can is where you move items to delete. Items moved to the Trash Can stay until you *empty* the Trash Can.

■ Links controls your Internet access. You call Web-based information and your Web browser from here.

■ Cards activates calendar-oriented objects, such as a day planner and similar tools.

■ Files controls access to the UNIX file system. You can access your CD-ROM or floppy disks from here.

■ Applications starts a text editor for writing documents, or other programs.

■ Mail accesses the CDE-oriented mail applications.

Extra

Typing commands into UNIX

The terminal window allows access directly to the UNIX operating system. This window doesn't contain any icons or toolbars inside of it. Terminals can be opened from the Hosts Button on the toolbar panel, or by right-clicking the desktop and selecting Tools and Terminal from the pop-up menu.

Terminal windows, unlike regular windows, don't have names. Calling additional terminals doesn't allow you to distinguish between each one.

The frame of the Terminal window has pull-down menus for Windows, Edit, and Options. These options allow you to edit the Terminal window properties, such as color and size.

Commands are executed in UNIX from the command prompt. Text or commands typed in are displayed at the cursor in the Terminal window.

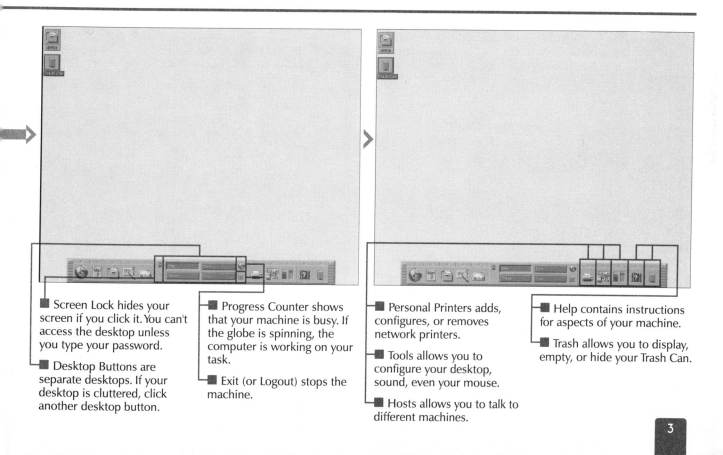

■ Screen Lock hides your screen if you click it. You can't access the desktop unless you type your password.

■ Desktop Buttons are separate desktops. If your desktop is cluttered, click another desktop button.

■ Progress Counter shows that your machine is busy. If the globe is spinning, the computer is working on your task.

■ Exit (or Logout) stops the machine.

■ Personal Printers adds, configures, or removes network printers.

■ Tools allows you to configure your desktop, sound, even your mouse.

■ Hosts allows you to talk to different machines.

■ Help contains instructions for aspects of your machine.

■ Trash allows you to display, empty, or hide your Trash Can.

LOG INTO UNIX WITHOUT A GUI

You can log into UNIX without depending on a *GUI*-style login screen. (GUI stands for Graphic User Interface, and is pronounced *gooey*.) When a computer screen uses pictures, icons, or any other kinds of graphics to help you access the system or the system tools, you're working with a GUI.

Whether you see a GUI-style login screen depends on the type of UNIX software you use. You may not see a special login screen when the machine is finished booting. Instead,

you may see a blank screen with a single line of text asking you to log in, called a *login prompt*. To log in from a login prompt, you follow similar steps as when you're logging in through a login screen — you enter in your user account name and password.

If your UNIX machine doesn't run X Windows, Motif, the Common Desktop Environment, or any other kind of GUI-based desktop system, then you always use this login procedure.

LOG INTO UNIX WITHOUT A GUI

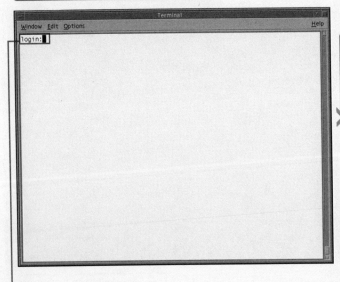

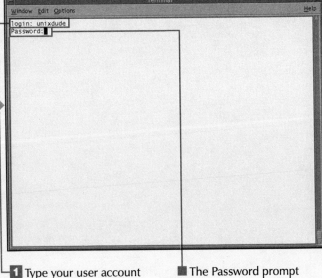

■ Once your computer finishes booting, UNIX displays a login prompt where you enter your user account name.

1 Type your user account name.

2 Press Enter.

■ The Password prompt appears.

Extra

Acting when UNIX doesn't display a GUI-style login screen consistently

Something may be wrong with your UNIX installation. The next time your system boots, watch the system checks that UNIX performs for reported errors.

Also, if you're using an older version of UNIX, you may be able to see a GUI-style login screen by upgrading your system to the latest version of UNIX. For example, you can receive the latest version of Solaris by purchasing it from Sun Microsystems and installing it from the CD-ROM they ship to you. You may also be able to upgrade by downloading the latest software off the Web.

Checking system settings when login name and password are rejected

Check the Caps Lock key. UNIX is case-sensitive, so Caps Lock affects your attempts to log in.

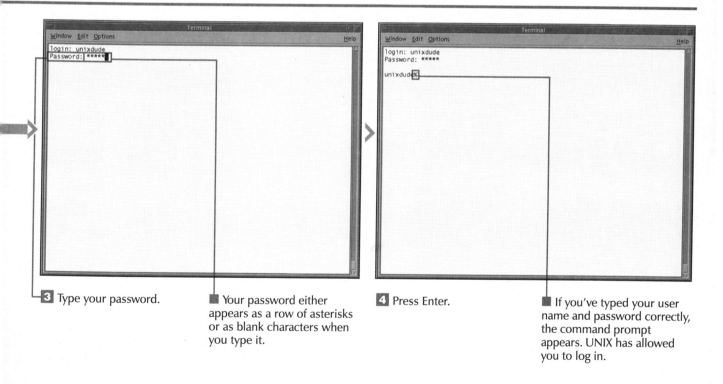

3 Type your password.

■ Your password either appears as a row of asterisks or as blank characters when you type it.

4 Press Enter.

■ If you've typed your user name and password correctly, the command prompt appears. UNIX has allowed you to log in.

LOG IN AS THE ROOT ACCOUNT

You can log into the UNIX system as the root account whenever you want to perform an administrative task. The *root* user account is the administrative account that is granted privileges over all the other accounts and files on the UNIX system. For this reason, the root account is known as the *superuser* account. As root, you can edit any file, change any permissions, even read everyone's mail.

On any UNIX system, there is only one root account — but other accounts can have the same privileges as root. These users are also known as *superusers*. However, for security purposes, root privileges should be granted sparingly, if at all.

There are several ways to enter the root account. These range from the typical login to performing the su command. Unlike many commands, su can be nested or run multiple times during one UNIX session.

LOG IN AS THE ROOT ACCOUNT

```
Terminal                                    Help
Window  Edit  Options

login: root
Password:
```

```
Terminal                                    Help
Window  Edit  Options

login: root
Password: *****

#
```

■1 At the login screen, or the login prompt, type **root**.

■2 Press Enter.

■ The Password prompt appears.

■3 Type the password for the root account.

■ This may be represented with asterisks, or by no text at all.

■ If the password is accepted, you are logged in as root.

Extra

Changing from user account to the root account without the root password

The root password is an absolute requirement to becoming the root account. If you're a regular UNIX user and not an administrator, don't try to become the root account in any case. Root privileges should be reserved for the people who maintain or installed the UNIX system.

Installing UNIX and choosing the password

When you install UNIX, it asks you to set the root password before rebooting. If you administer a system where you didn't perform the install, you must receive the password from the person who did or another administrator.

Uh-oh, I don't know the password for the root account

Unfortunately, you may need to reinstall UNIX to reset the password.

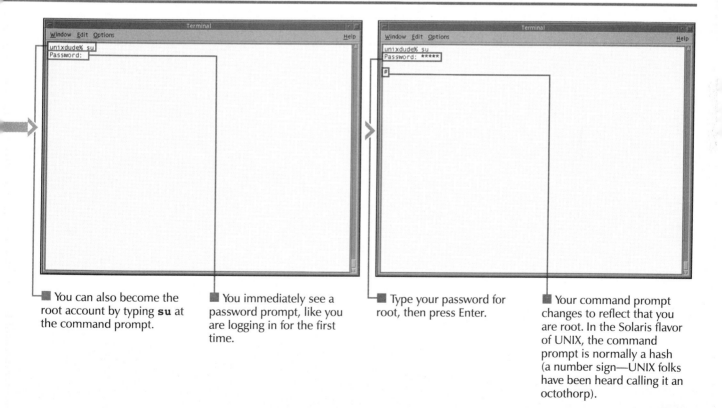

■ You can also become the root account by typing **su** at the command prompt.

■ You immediately see a password prompt, like you are logging in for the first time.

■ Type your password for root, then press Enter.

■ Your command prompt changes to reflect that you are root. In the Solaris flavor of UNIX, the command prompt is normally a hash (a number sign—UNIX folks have been heard calling it an octothorp).

LOG OUT OF UNIX

When you're finished with your UNIX session, you should always *log out*. Logging out of UNIX serves two purposes:

• Logging out of UNIX effectively closes all of the sessions where you can do work — preventing others from using your account to change or damage the system.

• Leaving the UNIX environment frees resources for the remaining users on the system.

You should always keep in mind that logging out of UNIX is not the same as shutting the system down. When you log out of UNIX, the operating system is still active — only you aren't logged onto the system, so you can't make edits, changes, or create files.

You can log out of UNIX in two ways. First, you can click the Exit button on the main desktop toolbar. Alternatively, you can select Logout from the pop-up menu that is displayed when you right-click your mouse.

LOG OUT OF UNIX

LOG OUT FROM THE TOOLBAR

1 Move the mouse pointer to the button marked Exit and click it.

■ UNIX displays the Logout Confirmation screen.

2 If you're sure that you want to continue the logout process, click OK.

Logout Confirmation

Exiting the desktop session...

Application updates you have not saved may be lost.

Your current session will be saved and returned to upon your next login. For more detail, select Help.

Continue Logout?

OK   Cancel   Help

Extra

Leaving sessions open

UNIX doesn't automatically log you out, so you don't have to take action. However, leaving sessions open and unattended is strongly discouraged. Aside from taking system resources, this is a major security risk, especially if you are logged in as the root administrator account.

Recovering from a power outage

Turn off all the UNIX machines on your network. Since you can't perform a standard shutdown with the loss of power, simply press the power switch on each machine. This is important, since it prevents power spiking when the electricity is restored, which can blow a fuse. When the power is restored, start your UNIX machines one at a time to gently bring power usage to what it was before.

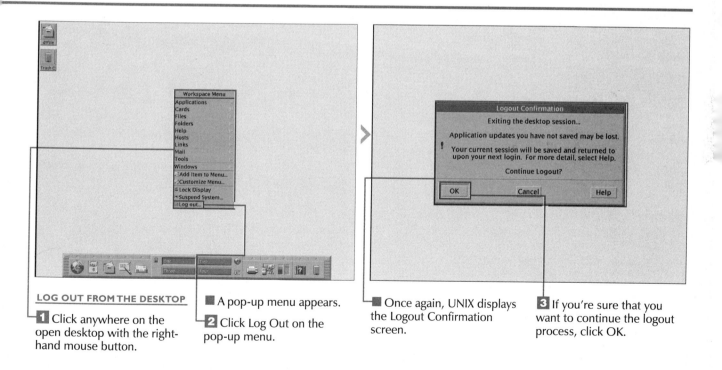

LOG OUT FROM THE DESKTOP

◀1 Click anywhere on the open desktop with the right-hand mouse button.

■ A pop-up menu appears.

◀2 Click Log Out on the pop-up menu.

■ Once again, UNIX displays the Logout Confirmation screen.

◀3 If you're sure that you want to continue the logout process, click OK.

LOCK THE SCREEN

You can lock your computer's screen if you're called away from your desk and you don't plan to return to your computer for a while. Locking the screen is not the same as shutting the machine down, since the machine's power supply isn't affected. It's also not the same as logging out of the system, since once you unlock your computer, you can continue to use system resources and edit files.

By selecting the button with the icon of the padlock, the computer displays a blank screen to hide the desktop. This screen also prevents anyone from viewing your work or entering commands until you unlock it. You unlock the computer by typing in your user account password. The desktop reappears, and you can continue working where you left off.

LOCK THE SCREEN

1 Move your mouse pointer over the padlock icon on the desktop toolbar, then click it.

■ The lockout screen appears. This screen either displays a miniature login screen or a simple login prompt, as in this example.

2 Type your password.

3 Press Enter.

SHUT DOWN UNIX

Whenever you're finished with the day's work and you don't plan to return to your computer for a while, you can shut it down to save power. Shutting the system down has the same effect as turning the power off on your machine. While this saves some electricity, it also forces you to reenter UNIX through the Start Up process where UNIX has to perform the same system checks before it allows you to log in.

Keep in mind that if you run UNIX on a computer where multiple people access it over

a network, you should shut down UNIX only to perform system maintenance, prevent an electrical outage, or upgrade hardware. Most upgrades or system maintenance are scheduled outages, meaning that you should plan to shut UNIX down ahead of time to do these tasks.

Be sure that you notify other people that use the machine well in advance that the UNIX server will shut down and may affect their work.

SHUT DOWN UNIX

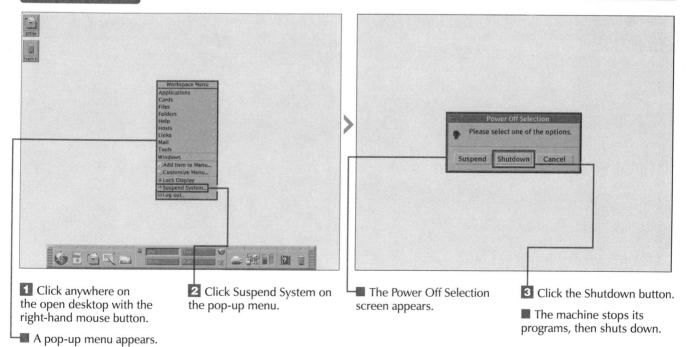

1 Click anywhere on the open desktop with the right-hand mouse button.

■ A pop-up menu appears.

2 Click Suspend System on the pop-up menu.

■ The Power Off Selection screen appears.

3 Click the Shutdown button.

■ The machine stops its programs, then shuts down.

SHUT DOWN UNIX OUTSIDE OF THE GUI

You can also shut down your UNIX machine without relying on tools in the GUI-based Common Desktop Environment. If you're working in the UNIX terminal, there are a number of different commands that you can use to shut the machine down without having to go back to the desktop and the mouse buttons.

The most common commands used to shut a UNIX machine down are variations on the *shutdown* command. Shutdown allows you to specify a certain amount of time, in seconds, from when you issue the shutdown command

to when the shutdown actually takes place. You can use this option to delay the machine's actual shutdown while you finish a task or close windows on the desktop. It is especially useful if there are multiple users logged into the machine.

Even if your version of UNIX comes with a GUI, consider using this method to shut down your system when you're performing maintenance on a multiple-user network. This allows you to operate more efficiently if you're busy working outside of the desktop or if the desktop is having difficulties.

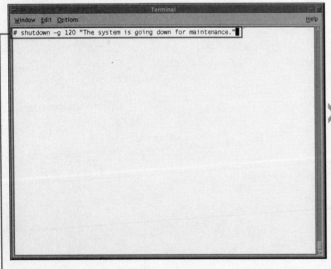

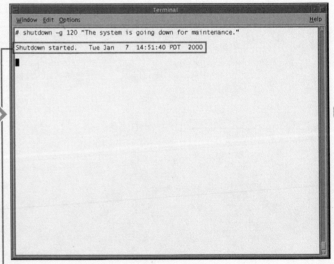

1 To shut the system down for system maintenance, type **shutdown -g** at the command line, then type the number of seconds (here, 120) to wait for shutdown, then type a message that explains the shutdown.

2 Press Enter.

■ The shutdown command acknowledges that the system will shut down.

Extra

Notifying system users when the system shuts down

The shutdown command's notification feature is useful, but it should not be the only way you notify other people working on the system that you're shutting the computer down. Ideally, you should send an e-mail a day or so in advance of your work, so users aren't surprised when they receive your shutdown message.

Choosing a time delay for the system shutdown

By default, the time interval in UNIX is 60 seconds. Whenever you specify the delay time, the default interval is seconds. Therefore, if you want a five-minute delay, you enter the period as 300 seconds (shutdown -g 300).

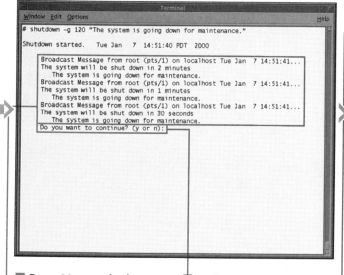

■ Every 30 seconds, the **shutdown** command broadcasts the messages listed below to every user of the system. This notifies the users on the system that they should log off immediately.

■ At the 30-second mark, **shutdown** asks you a final time whether you really want to shut the system down.

3 Press **y** for yes, **n** for no.

■ To shut down immediately without any warning messages or final confirmation, type **shutdown -g 0** at the command prompt, then press Enter. The shutdown commences without any waiting.

STOP UNIX WITH HALT

You can also stop the UNIX machine with the *halt* command. Halt, as its name implies, stops the machine more quickly, without regard to the programs or applications that may be running on the machine at the time it is shut down.

Halt is a very useful command in certain situations. For example, if the machine is *hung*, meaning that it refuses to respond to any commands at all, then halt may succeed in shutting your machine down where the shutdown command may fail.

On the flip side, halt is not as desirable a method of shutting a machine down as the shutdown command. This is because shutdown automatically makes sure that programs or applications that are running have time to exit, thereby preventing data corruption. Unless specified, halt doesn't do this, which increases the chance that you may damage or corrupt a program that is running at the time halt is initiated.

STOP UNIX WITH HALT

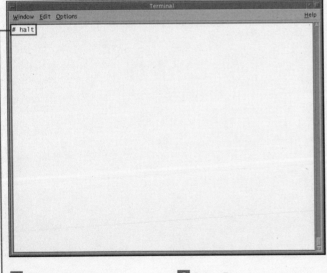

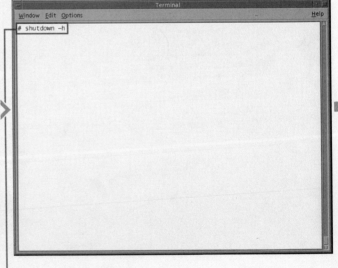

1 To run the `halt` command, type **halt** at the command prompt.

2 Press Enter.

■ The system shuts down.

■ An alternative to `halt` is to specify that the `shutdown` command uses `halt` when it shuts programs down. Type **shutdown -h** at the command line, then press Enter. This is useful if programs don't respond to the `shutdown` command.

Extra

Timing shutdown with the halt command

Unlike the shutdown command, halt doesn't allow you the flexibility of waiting 30 or 60 seconds before it begins to shut the machine down. This is because halt is normally used when there is something wrong on the system, so waiting is not a preferable option.

Unlike shutdown, there is no delay. Once you type halt and press Enter, the system is immediately shut down.

Using the sync command before halt

This isn't absolutely necessary, but typing in the sync command twice gives you an extra measure of protection, or at least makes you more secure that your data won't be corrupted when you halt the machine.

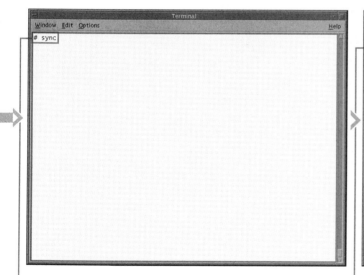

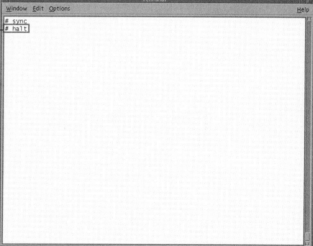

■ A third option is to make sure that the halt command doesn't cause damage to the system. Type the **sync** command at the command line, then pressing Enter. The sync command synchronizes system data, thereby preventing data corruption.

■ After running sync, type **halt**, then press Enter. The system shuts down.

RESTART UNIX

You can specify that the UNIX system reboot when you shut the machine down by any method except halt or pressing the power switch. There are a number of commands that you can use to restart the system that perform the same task. Which method you use depends solely upon your personal preference.

Restarting the UNIX machine more closely resembles a shutdown procedure than a logout procedure. With any form of restart in UNIX, you are first logged out, then the system acts as if you pressed the power button to switch it off.

The operating system is then booted as if you had first switched the machine on. This is helpful to you if you are experiencing problems with the operating system, since it allows UNIX to scan the system as part of its boot process and fix any problems with the disk or with the software that it finds.

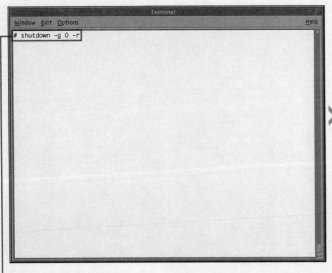

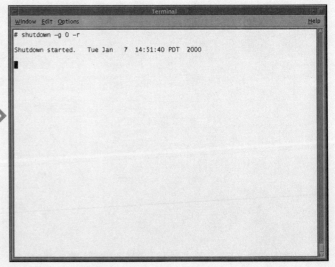

RESTART USING THE SHUTDOWN COMMAND

1 Type **shutdown -g 0 -r** at the command prompt.

2 Press Enter.

■ The system shuts down completely, then reboots automatically.

■ The system notifies you that it is shutting the system down and rebooting. You eventually return to the login screen, where you can log back into the system.

Extra

Using the shutdown, init 6, or reboot commands when rebooting

Both shutdown and init 6 do the exact same tasks when it comes to allowing your machine to reboot. However, using shutdown gives you time between typing the command and initiating it, if you want to shut down programs manually. It also notifies any other users on the system of the impending shutdown reboot.

Init 6 and reboot are more similar to the halt command in that they don't send notification to other users, and they aren't as careful to ensure that running programs are shut down without the possibility of corruption. Consider using sync with these commands.

Other keyboard shortcuts to reboot the system

On Solaris machines, you can press the Stop and the A keys simultaneously to stop the machine. On other forms of UNIX, press Ctrl+Alt+Del to reboot the system.

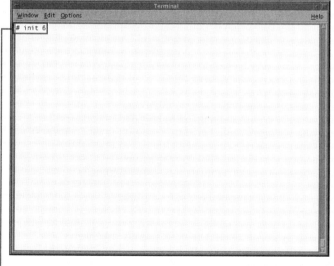

RESTART USING THE INIT 6 COMMAND

1 Type **init 6** at the command line.

2 Press Enter.

■ The init command changes the state of your system to condition 6, reboot. The system shuts down, then reboots, reverting to a login screen.

RESTART USING THE REBOOT COMMAND

1 Type **reboot** at the command line.

2 Press Enter.

■ The machine reboots in 60 seconds, then displays a login screen.

OPEN A NEW TERMINAL

If you're running a UNIX system with a graphic desktop like CDE, the Common Desktop Environment, UNIX is directly accessible by opening a special window on the desktop called a *terminal*. You open UNIX terminals on the desktop to access the UNIX operating system directly. When you work in the terminal, you're *outside* the GUI (Graphical User Interface) so you don't find any icons or directories to click.

UNIX terminals are technically *windows* (marked areas of the screen to perform certain tasks within their boundaries). However, these windows are called terminals to avoid confusion.

Terminals bypass the desktop when tasks can be performed only from the UNIX command prompt. The command prompt, which is usually marked with a #, %, or $ character, is where you type commands for UNIX to run. If you're familiar with the world of Microsoft Windows, the UNIX terminal is like the MS-DOS Prompt window.

OPEN A NEW TERMINAL

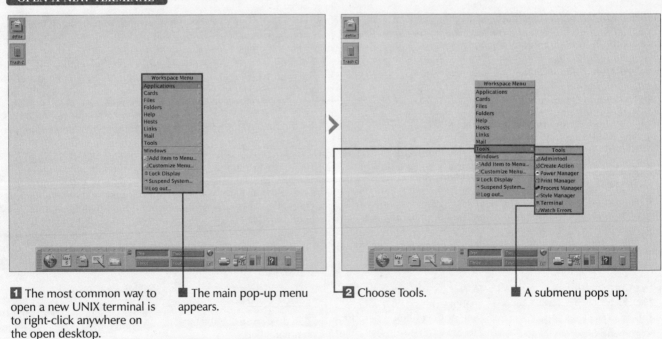

■1 The most common way to open a new UNIX terminal is to right-click anywhere on the open desktop.

■ The main pop-up menu appears.

■2 Choose Tools.

■ A submenu pops up.

Extra

Identifying whether a menu leads to another submenu

When you activate any menu (such as the pop-up menu that appears when you right-click the desktop), any selection with a submenu has a small right-pointing arrow at the right of the menu entry. Moving your mouse pointer over any menu entry with this little arrow reveals the submenu.

Opening a new terminal window from the desktop toolbar

If you click the arrow above the Hosts button on the toolbar, a console is accessible from the panel that slides out. Make this selection by clicking Console when the panel appears.

Using a console instead of a terminal

A console handles the commands you enter like a terminal. Both windows interact directly with the UNIX operating system.

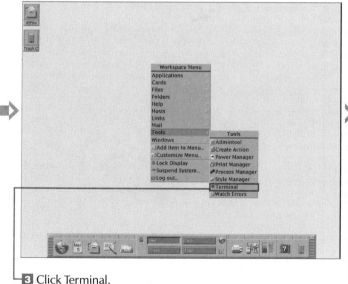

3 Click Terminal.

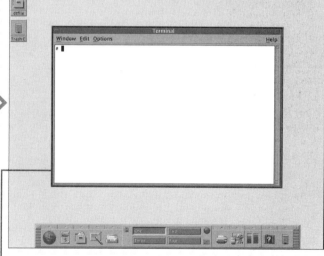

4 The pop-up menu disappears and a new Terminal window appears on the desktop.

START A UNIX APPLICATION FROM THE DESKTOP

S everal kinds of UNIX applications start from the desktop. Because the desktop in the GUI (Graphical User Interface) is part of the operating system, you can start any graphics-based program on the UNIX desktop.

For example, in the UNIX desktop environment, you activate such programs as the Netscape Web browser, a calendar schematic, or a text editor similar to Microsoft Word. However, a graphics-based text editor

doesn't operate with the terminal, because the UNIX operating system itself can't handle graphics (though you can run a graphics-based text editor in a separate window from the terminal just fine).

In the terminal, you use terminal-specific applications that don't use graphics. In the case of the text editor, you use one of the native UNIX text editors, vi. (Chapter 7 covers vi.)

START A UNIX APPLICATION FROM THE DESKTOP

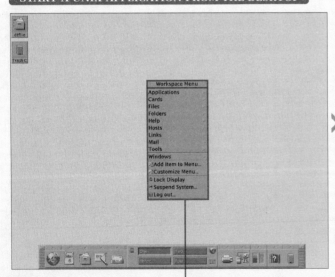

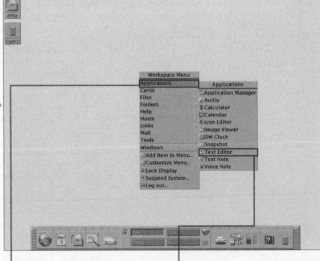

■1 You can start a UNIX program by right-clicking an open spot on the desktop.

■ A pop-up menu lists your options.

■2 Choose Applications.

■ A submenu appears.

■3 Click on the application you want to start.

■ The program appears.

Extra

Distinguishing between a UNIX application and a UNIX utility

There's a lot of debate over which is which. However, as a general rule, a UNIX *application* is a program that runs on UNIX for the general user. This includes text editors and Web browsers.

A UNIX *utility,* on the other hand, is a program that administers or repairs the UNIX system itself. Programs that monitor performance or are used to automate tasks are UNIX utilities.

Starting a GUI-based UNIX application in the terminal

You can't, usually. There are a few exceptions to the rule. For example, typing Netscape in the terminal and pressing Enter usually starts the Netscape Web browser on the desktop.

Starting a non-GUI-based application in the UNIX terminal

Simply type the name of the application at the command prompt inside the terminal and press Enter.

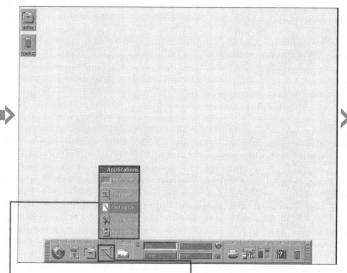

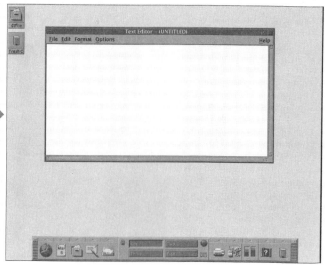

■ Alternatively, you can click the upward-facing arrow above the Applications button on the desktop toolbar. The Applications panel slides out.

■ The Applications button on the toolbar is the fourth button from the right; it has the picture of a penciled note on it.

■ Click on the desired application in the Applications panel. The panel slides back down and the application screen appears.

MOVE A WINDOW ACROSS THE DESKTOP

When you're working with more than one window on the desktop, it's important to move windows so they don't overlap each other. It's also helpful to switch between windows to jump between tasks on the desktop.

A key concept to grasp when you're dealing with more than one window is that only one window is *active* at any given time. An active

window accepts input and commands from you. An active window is easy to spot on the desktop because its upper border is a darker color (normally purple or blue on a color monitor) than the other windows.

A window that's *inactive* isn't the same as a window that's *closed*. Windows that aren't active still have their programs running or their command prompts available.

MOVE A WINDOW ACROSS THE DESKTOP

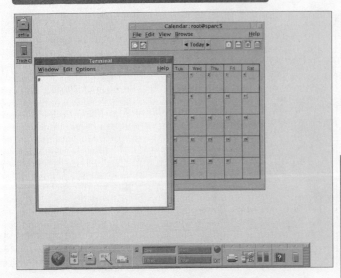

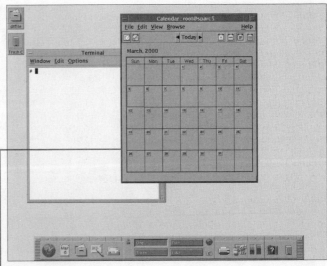

■ On a screen with more than one open window, only one window is active at any time. Of the two windows here, only the top one, a UNIX terminal, is active.

■ An active window is always in the *foreground*, which means the window is displayed on top of other objects, such as another window.

1 Click on a window to make it active.

■ In this example, clicking on the open Calendar application window makes it active.

■ Activating a window brings it to the foreground. It covers inactive windows on its part of the screen. Here, making the Calendar active covers the UNIX terminal.

Extra

Other ways to prevent overlapping windows on a desktop with limited space

The next section on resizing and closing windows gives you additional methods of preventing overlapping.

Completely losing a window behind another larger window

Make the larger window active, then minimize it. This lets you click and drag the previously hidden window to an area of the desktop where it isn't blocked by the larger window. To see how to do this, read "Maximize and Minimize a Window" in this chapter.

Limiting windows open on the desktop

There is no minimum or maximum number of windows to have open, though having many open at the same time slows older machines. Unless you're cutting and pasting information between windows, it's simplest to have one window open and leave other ones closed or minimized.

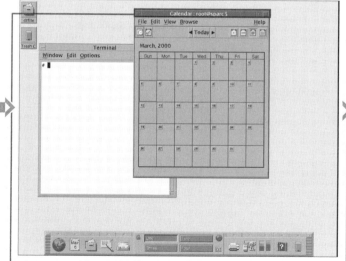

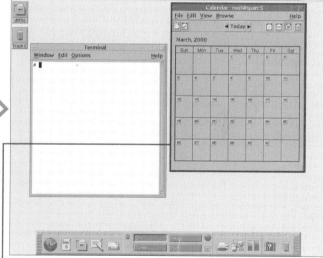

2 To move a window, place the mouse pointer over the window's title bar.

■ In this example, the title bar is labeled `Calendar: root@sparc5`.

3 Click the title bar and hold down the mouse button.

■ The top border appears slightly recessed, as if you're pressing it.

4 Drag the window where you want it and release the mouse button.

RESIZE A WINDOW

You can resize or close windows on your desktop for any number of reasons. For example, you can make a window smaller to reach a part of the desktop or toolbar that's hidden behind the window.

More commonly, you may find that you have multiple windows open to work with several applications at once. If you have multiple windows open on your desktop, you may need to adjust the size of each window.

You can enlarge a window to see more of its contents. Of course, if you have 50 items in a given window, you may not be able to expand the window enough to see all of the items. In this case, the desktop GUI automatically provides a scroll bar that you click and drag to see the entire list of items.

RESIZE A WINDOW

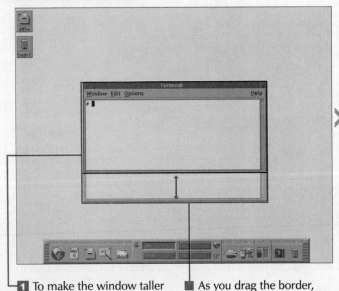

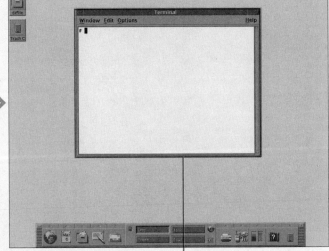

1 To make the window taller or shorter, click and drag the upper or lower border of the window.

■ To make the window wider or narrower, click and drag the left or right border of the window.

■ As you drag the border, you see an outline of where the window's new border will be.

2 Release the mouse button.

■ The window changes size.

Extra

Preventing windows from overlapping when I resize them

Watch the black outline when you're dragging the window borders. The outline shows exactly where the window fits when you release the mouse button.

Adjusting when the edge of the window is off screen

Moving the entire window is your best bet. This is covered in the "Move a Window across the Desktop" section of this chapter.

Seeing files or file systems in a window when you can't see everything

Use the scroll bars inside each window frame. Scroll bars automatically appear when more files or file systems are off screen. Click and drag the bar to scroll the files in the window.

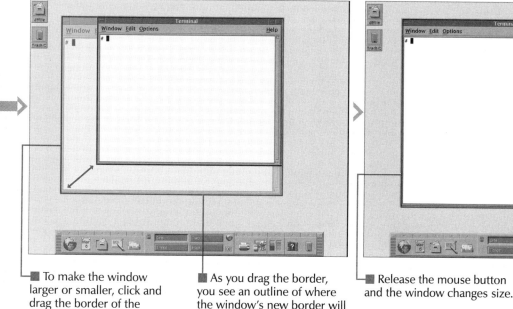

■ To make the window larger or smaller, click and drag the border of the window in any corner.

■ As you drag the border, you see an outline of where the window's new border will be.

■ Release the mouse button and the window changes size.

MAXIMIZE AND MINIMIZE A WINDOW

Y ou maximize or minimize the windows in your desktop environment by using the default controls on every window in the environment. Whether you're working with a desktop window, a program window, or a UNIX terminal, two buttons always have the same purposes. These buttons are located at the upper-right corner of each window and let you maximize or minimize the window or terminal.

You can maximize a window to see as much of the window's contents as possible. On the other hand, if you need more space on the desktop, minimizing a window hides it without stopping the program or closing the terminal. In either case, maximizing or minimizing a window is often more efficient than resizing by clicking and dragging; maximizing and minimizing require only one click of the mouse.

MAXIMIZE AND MINIMIZE A WINDOW

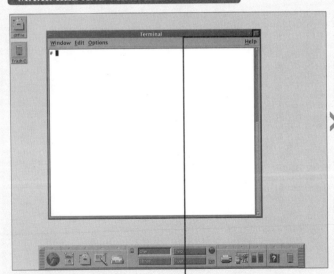

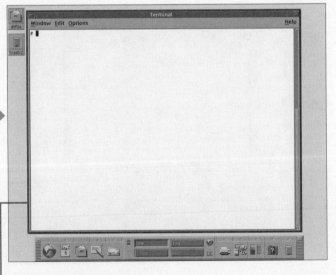

MAXIMIZE A WINDOW

1 Move your mouse pointer over the Maximize button.

■ On any window, the Maximize button is in the upper-right corner and has a square on it.

2 Click the Maximize button.

■ The window expands to its maximum size. A maximized window usually fills the entire screen. The pictures and words stay the same size.

Extra

Restoring a window to its former size

If you maximized the window, click the Maximize button again to return it to its previous size. If you minimized the window, an icon is on the desktop. Double-click that icon to restore the window. (If you closed the window entirely, you need to open a new window.)

Restoring a window and then resizing it

After you restore a window, simply resize it. Follow the directions in Resizing Windows part of this chapter.

Other ways to maximize or minimize a window

Clicking the button located at the upper left-hand corner of any window gives you a pop-up menu. In these options, you choose Minimize or Maximize from the menu.

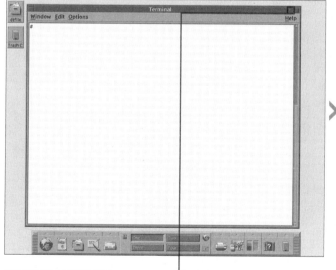
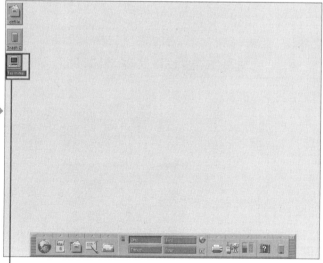

MINIMIZE A WINDOW

1 Move your mouse pointer over the Minimize button.

■ The Minimize button is to the left of the Maximize button and has a single dot on it.

2 Click the Minimize button.

■ The window disappears. An icon on the left side of the screen represents it.

CLOSE A WINDOW

You close a window to get to a section of the desktop or to retrieve a smaller window that is hidden behind a larger one. Remember, closing a window isn't the same as minimizing a window. Minimizing or maximizing a window is simply a shorthand way of resizing the window or moving it out of the way. It doesn't affect the window or the window's contents in any way; it only alters the shape or dimensions of the window.

On the other hand, closing a window effectively removes it from your desktop. It can also stop or shut down any UNIX program you run from inside the window. For this reason, always be sure that you really want to close a window before you close it.

CLOSE A WINDOW

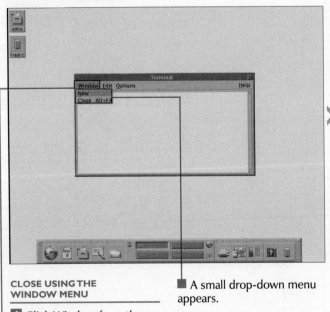

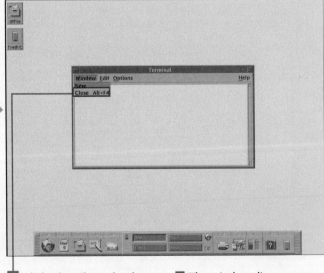

CLOSE USING THE WINDOW MENU

1 Click Window from the left side of the toolbar.

■ A small drop-down menu appears.

2 Click Close from the drop-down menu.

■ The window disappears.

Extra

Closing an application window, such as a text editor, that doesn't have a Windows selection in its toolbar

If an application doesn't have a Windows selection in its toolbar, it usually has a File selection. Choose File to get the application's drop-down menu. Exit or Close options usually are available.

Closing a window without a Close option in the File menu

In this case, click the button with a dash on it in the upper left-hand corner. This button exists in all windows by default. The drop-down menu always includes a Close option.

Closing a window when it's an icon on the desktop

Right-click the icon. A pop-up menu appears that lets you choose Close.

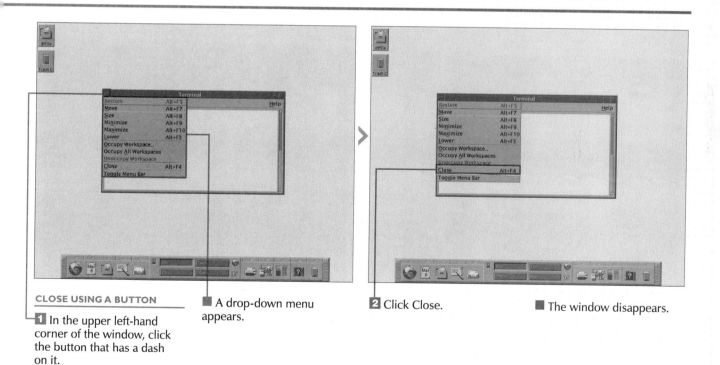

CLOSE USING A BUTTON

1 In the upper left-hand corner of the window, click the button that has a dash on it.

■ A drop-down menu appears.

2 Click Close.

■ The window disappears.

MOVE BETWEEN WINDOWS

You can use the UNIX desktop
environment to move text or binary files
into different areas. Often, instead of
copying a file to multiple locations, you can
use the UNIX network system and simply
move a file to a common directory that all
users access.

You can do this with one open window, but it's
usually easier with two windows open. This
lets you select files from one area and place

them into another area without having to
browse through different directories to get
where you want to put the file.

In this example, you see how to move a file
called `testfile` from the /export directory to
the root directory. This example begins
with two open windows; move one into the
root home directory and the second into the
/export directory.

MOVE BETWEEN WINDOWS

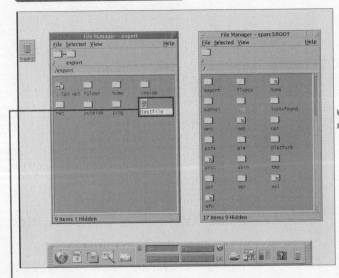

1 Click the file's icon once
to select it.

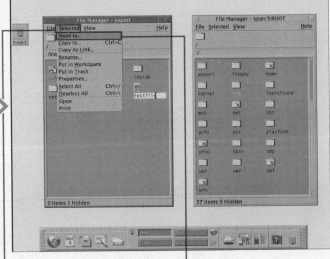

2 Choose the Selected menu
on the toolbar.

3 Choose the Move to...
option.

Extra

Other ways to move files between windows

You click and drag the file between the windows. This method works just as well for small files, or for multiple files. It's also faster and requires less in the way of typing skills. This method is slower for moving extremely large files, such as text files containing large tables or reports.

Moving files between windows with the UNIX terminal

No, because the terminal isn't a graphical environment. You move files between two directories in the terminal by using the move, or mv, command (see Chapter 3).

Moving a file in the UNIX terminal to a window on the desktop

You do this by closing the terminal and opening a regular window on the desktop that shows the contents of the directory that you were working in. The file that you were working on appears as an icon in the window, which you then move by using the instructions in this section.

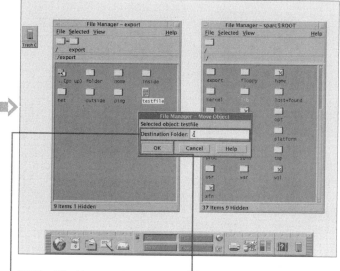

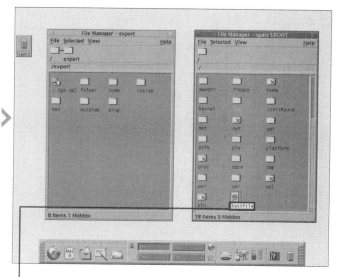

■ The File Manager Move Object window appears.

4 Type the destination folder's name in the text field.

■ The symbol for the root directory is a single slash, /.

5 Click OK.

■ This process removes the testfile icon from the /export directory window on the left and places it in the root directory window on the right.

COPY FILES BETWEEN WINDOWS

You use the UNIX desktop environment when copying text or binary files into different directories or folders. To make backup copies of a file in multiple locations, use the desktop's easy method of copying files. This lets you place a file in a different directory. You can fall back to the copy if the original changes or corrupts for any reason.

Although you can do this with only one open window, it's usually easier if you open two.

This lets you select files from one area and place them into another without having to browse through different directories to get where you want to put the file.

In this example, you see how to copy the file named `testfile` from the root directory to the `/export` directory. This example begins with two open windows; copy one into the root home directory and the other into the `/export` directory.

COPY FILES BETWEEN WINDOWS

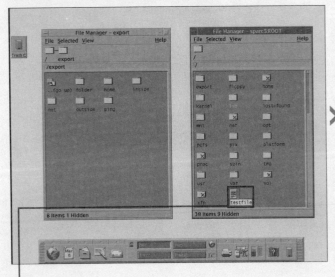

1 Click the file's icon in the root directory.

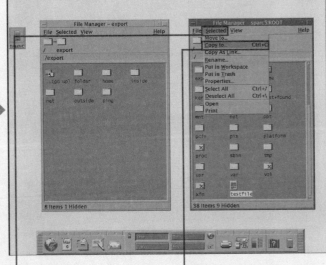

2 Click the Selected menu on the toolbar.

■ A pop-up menu appears.

3 Click the Copy to... option.

Apply It

Choosing to move a file instead of making a copy of the file

This depends on what you want to do with the file and the condition of your system. If your goal is to keep a backup of a file that you can edit later, you should use the `copy` commands. If you just want to make a file more accessible, you should simply move it from one location to another.

Also, you should move files instead of copying them when you're running short of space. Making multiple copies eats storage space and can fill your entire system if you're not careful.

Copying files as the root account

You can't copy files unless you either own the file or have permission to do so. Permissioning and root access are covered in Chapter 4.

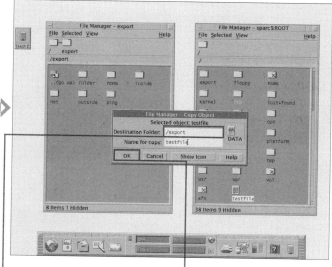

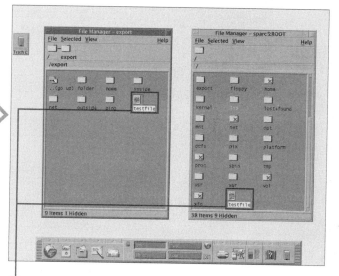

■ The File Manager Copy Object window appears.

■ Type the destination folder's name into the Destination Folder text box.

■ To copy to the /export directory, you simply type **/export**.

5 Click OK.

■ The file's icon appears in the /export directory window on the left as well as in the root directory window on the right.

START UNIX DESKTOP ENVIRONMENT HELP

You have several options when it comes to documentation on UNIX or GUI configuration on the desktop. The tools in the toolbar on your desktop point to stored documentation and automatically start a Help Manager to sort through the multitude of help entries.

The Help selections also include a guided tour through the desktop environment for new users. More importantly, if you have an Internet connection set up for your UNIX machine, you see documentation directly online by clicking `SunSolve Online`, which automatically starts a Web browser and connects to the Web site for you.

Of all the tools, the Help Manager is especially useful because it covers both desktop-specific and UNIX-specific topics. Whether you need to find out how to change the color of your desktop background or find out the syntax for a command in the UNIX terminal, the Help Manager usually has what you need.

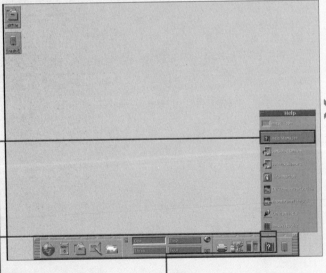

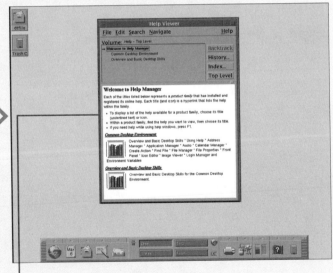

■1 To open the Help Manager, click the upward-facing arrow above the Help Index button.

■ This button is the second from the left and has a picture of a row of books on it.

■ The Help panel slides out.

■2 Click Help Manager to open the utility.

■ The Help Manager appears as a Help Viewer window.

Extra

Getting help with the Help Index

The menu at the right-hand side of the toolbar is the Help menu for the Help Viewer. This menu explains some of the obscure steps of operating the Help Index.

Returning to an area of the Help Index

If you know you will revisit an area, click the Backtrack button on the Help Viewer window. If the area is several pages back, click the History button for a list of your prior stops. This will usually be quicker than if you have to click the Backtrack button six or seven times.

Other online resources

Remember, the Help Viewer is only part of the Help documentation in UNIX. The tools under the Help button on the desktop toolbar take you to the SunSolve Web site, where you browse more technical documents on UNIX.

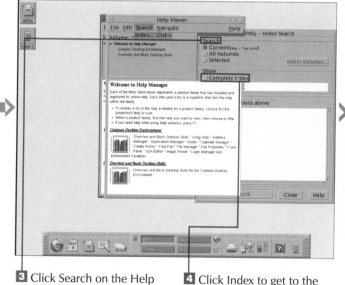

3 Click Search on the Help Viewer menu.

4 Click Index to get to the Search tool.

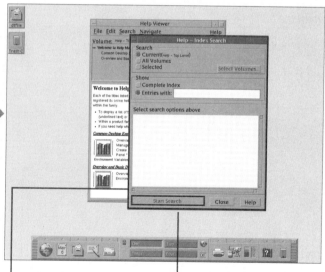

■ The Help Index Search window appears.

5 To start a search, type the subject you want to search on into the Entries With text box and click the Start Search button.

CUSTOMIZE THE DESKTOP BACKGROUND

Part of the fun of working with a GUI-based desktop system is decorating your work area. Besides allowing you to express your creative side, changing the appearance of your desktop can help you avoid eyestrain.

The main change to make to the desktop is a different backdrop for your icons and windows. Sun's brand of UNIX comes with several backgrounds for your desktop. Because

the process isn't unlike pasting patterns on your walls at home, it's called changing your desktop *wallpaper*.

Select your wallpaper based on your personal taste and the quality of your lighting and monitor. A light gray background may be bland, but it's a lot less stressful on the eyes when you're in an area with too little light, or if you have a blurry monitor.

CUSTOMIZE THE DESKTOP BACKGROUND

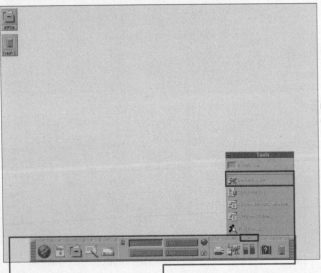

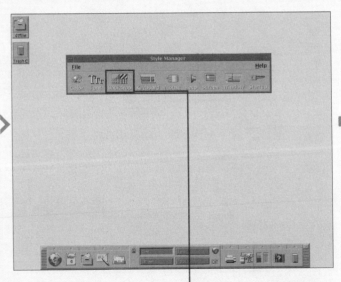

1 Start by clicking the arrow above the Tools button, which has a palette and font sample on it, on the desktop toolbar.

■ The Tools selections panel slides out.

2 Click Desktop Style.

■ The Style Manager toolbar appears.

3 Click Backdrop to change your desktop's background pattern.

Extra

Adjusting the desktop wallpaper on a monochrome (black-and-white) screen

On a monochrome screen, you select a background to adjust the scale and brightness of the pattern on the screen. The light gray and dark gray patterns work very well in monochrome.

Choosing background wallpaper

Besides your personal preference, you should choose your wallpaper to avoid unnecessary eyestrain. If you're working on a monitor that isn't that bright or sharp, pick simple, bright backgrounds like light gray.

Saving pictures off the Internet and using them as a desktop background

When you're in Netscape or Internet Explorer, choose the File drop-down menu and choose Save As. Make sure to save the image to a floppy disk or directly on your UNIX machine. The image is automatically saved as the type of file it is, whether a .gif, .bmp, or .tif file.

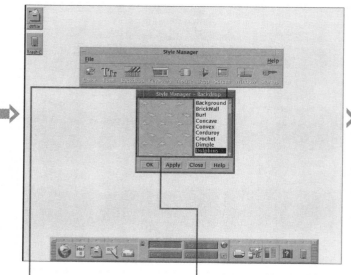

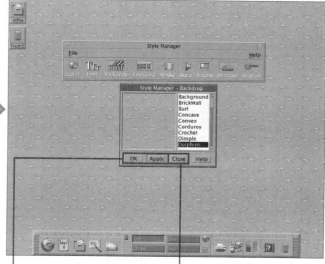

4 In the Style Manager Backdrop window, choose a backdrop style from the list.

■ In this example, Dolphins is selected.

■ A small frame at the left automatically shows what your changes will look like before you apply them.

5 Click OK or Apply to place the new pattern on your desktop.

6 After you finish, click Close and then close the Style Manager window.

CUSTOMIZE YOUR SCREEN SAVER

Screen savers are programs that automatically start after your computer is left inactive for a set amount of time. These programs serve several purposes, depending on how you configure them.

The main purpose of a screen server is to prevent screen burn-in. The image on a computer screen is composed of phosphor dots that glow when struck by electrons. If the image doesn't change for a long time, that

image can literally get *burned* into the screen, blurring any new image that appears. A constantly changing pattern on the screen prevents burn-in.

Screen savers also reduce the amount of power expended by a computer because the processes take less energy to run and the screen is, on the average, darker than when in use. Finally, you find out how screen savers can act as a security measure if set properly.

CUSTOMIZE YOUR SCREEN SAVER

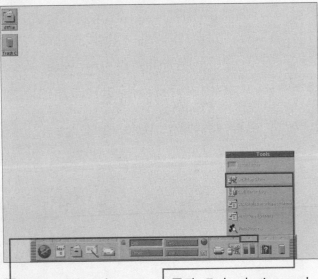

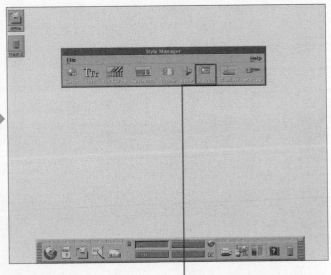

1 Start by clicking the arrow above the Tools button, which has a palette and font sample on it, on the desktop toolbar.

■ The Tools selection panel slides out.

2 Click Desktop Style.

■ The Style Manager toolbar appears.

3 Click Screen to change your screen saver.

Extra

Eliminating screen savers

You do this by selecting the Blank Screen setting in the Style Manager–Screen dialog box, in the list of screen savers that come with your UNIX installation.

Having the computer lock the screen when unattended

First, click the Off button to the right of the Screen Saver selection, near the top of the Style Manager–Screen dialog box. Next, click the On button to the right of the Screen Lock selection near the bottom of the Style Manager–Screen dialog box.

Deciding to use a screen saver

Ideally, you should always use a screen saver. Screen *burn-in* isn't caused by a bright screen or a lightly colored screen. Instead, it's caused by the projection of one image on the screen for extended periods of time, no matter how the screen is lit or colored.

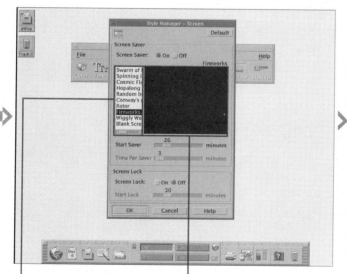
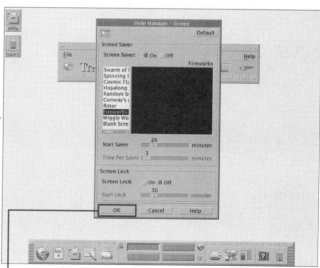

■4 In the Style Manager— Screen dialog box, choose a screen saver style from the list at the left.

■ In this example, Fireworks is selected.

■ A small frame on the right automatically displays what your changes will look like before you apply them.

■5 Click OK to accept your changes and then close the Style Manager toolbar.

CUSTOMIZE YOUR MOUSE

You want to get full functionality out of your UNIX system, including how well you use the mouse to open, close, and activate items on your desktop. In addition, you should also want to set up your mouse according to your desires and reflexes. Setting up your mouse to move swiftly across the desktop or to repeat clicks as needed can save you a lot of frustration later.

For example, if you plan to use the mouse in the UNIX environment primarily for clicking

icons and opening folders, you probably want your mouse to accelerate as quickly as possible. On the other hand, if you're doing a lot of fine work, such as drawing or repositioning windows, you can slow down the speed of your mouse.

Luckily, in UNIX you customize the speed that the mouse pointer moves across the screen, and you can even set the all-important mouse as left-handed instead of right-handed.

CUSTOMIZE YOUR MOUSE

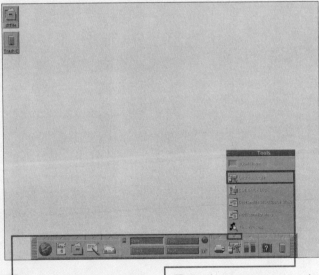

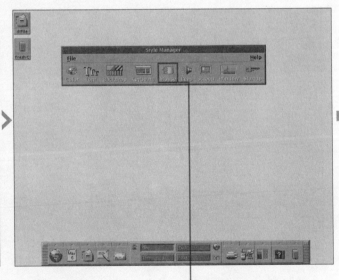

1 Start by clicking the arrow above the Tools button, which has a palette and font sample on it, on the desktop toolbar.

■ The Tools Selection panel slides out.

2 Click Desktop Style.

■ The Style Manager toolbar appears.

3 Click Mouse to change your mouse settings.

Apply It

Making the my mouse right- or left-handed

Click the Right or Left button to the right of the Handedness selection in the Style Manager–Mouse window.

Choosing the Button 2 setting in the Style Manager–Mouse screen

Buttons on the mouse are labeled 1, 2, and 3 for the buttons from left to right. If you're using a two-button mouse, then you don't have a number 2 button. You only have a number 1 button on the left and a number 3 button on the right.

Applying the two Button 2 settings, Transfer and Adjust

If you choose Adjust, then Button 2 is used for Adjustment tasks, such as copying highlighted text from one window to another. Choosing Transfer restricts Button 2 to Transfer tasks, such as clicking and dragging.

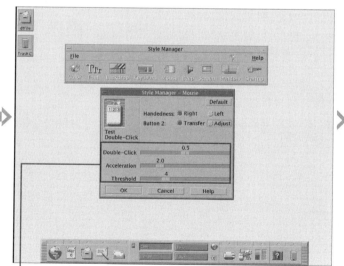

4 In the Style Manager-Mouse window, choose a mouse speed, double-click interval, and threshold from the list at the left by dragging the slide bars at the right.

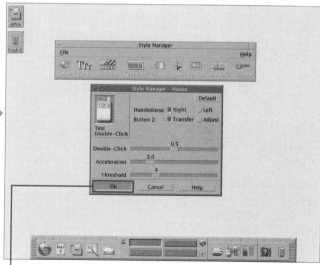

5 Click OK to apply your changes.

6 After you finish, you can close the Style Manager window to return to the desktop.

CUSTOMIZE DESKTOP SOUND

You can customize the volume, tone, and duration of the default sound in your UNIX desktop environment. While UNIX isn't designed as a high-fidelity sound system, it is easily configured to give you a distinctive sound for alerts and notices. This is particularly useful when you're working on a UNIX network with a large number of similar machines in the same general area. Giving your machine a distinct sound serves to distinguish it from other background noises while you're working.

UNIX normally doesn't come with a sound player to work other sounds into your desktop. However, you may find utilities on the Web that let you do this. Downloading and installing a sound-player utility expands the range of sounds that play on your UNIX machine so that it is similar to a regular IBM-based PC or Macintosh.

CUSTOMIZE DESKTOP SOUND

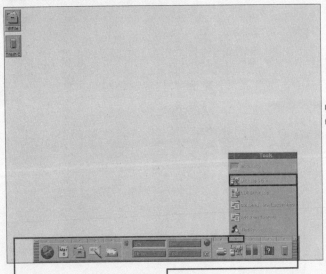

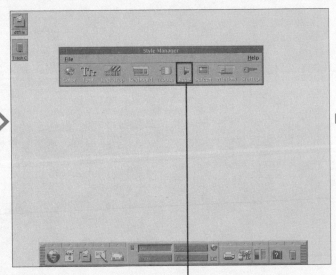

1 Start by clicking the arrow above the Tools button, which has a palette and font sample on it, on the desktop toolbar.

■ The Tools Selection panel slides out.

2 Click Desktop Style.

■ The Style Manager toolbar appears.

3 Click Beep from the toolbar.

Extra

Playing MP3 files on UNIX

There are free utilities available for download to play MP3 files. Check out www.opensound.com or any MP3 site that has UNIX programs for MP3. If it works on one version of UNIX, there's a good chance that it will work on other UNIX systems.

However, MP3s are a still-evolving system; you may run into trouble with odd or off-market combinations of hardware To maximize the chance of success, stick to mainstream sound cards and consult information on MP3 manuals or Web sites to see which hardware works best for playing back these sound files.

Using sounds when UNIX doesn't recognize a sound card

If you're not using a sound card from a major manufacturer, you may need different drivers for a nonstandard sound card. Check out www.sunsolve.com for a list of available solutions and go from there.

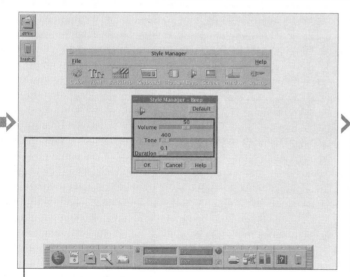

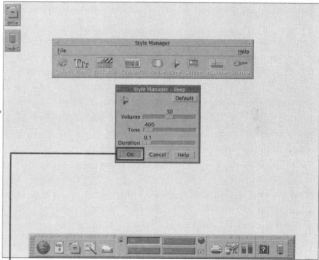

4 In the Style Manager-Beep dialog box, choose the sound volume, tone, and duration from the list at the left by dragging the slide bars at the right.

5 Click OK to accept this change.

6 After you finish, close the Style Manager toolbar.

LIST FILES

Files are listed in several ways within the UNIX Terminal. The basic ls, or *list,* command provides the most basic listing of files in your current directory. However, you can use the list command to give you more detailed information about your files.

The key is to know the different command options you can use with the list command in UNIX. A *command option*, sometimes just called an *option* or a *flag,* is a letter or letters you append to most UNIX commands. Usually, a space and a dash separate the command and the option. For example, the ls command,

typed with the appropriate command option to list detailed file information, is listed at the command prompt as follows:

ls -l

Most UNIX command options have a logic to the letter used. Here, the -l is for detailed information; think of the l as *long listing.*

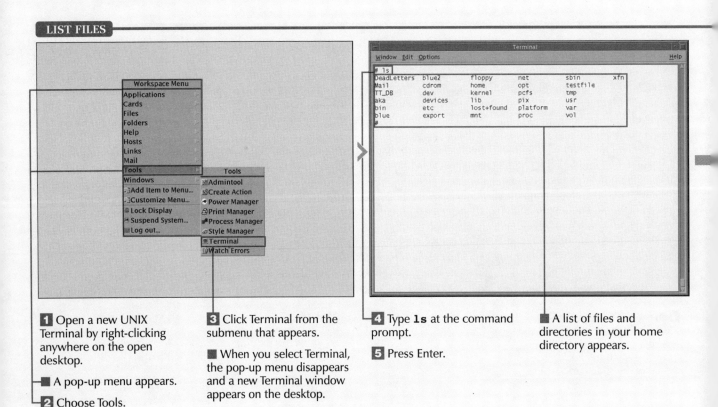

1 Open a new UNIX Terminal by right-clicking anywhere on the open desktop.

■ A pop-up menu appears.

2 Choose Tools.

3 Click Terminal from the submenu that appears.

■ When you select Terminal, the pop-up menu disappears and a new Terminal window appears on the desktop.

4 Type **ls** at the command prompt.

5 Press Enter.

■ A list of files and directories in your home directory appears.

Apply It

Remote Directory Listings

You can list the contents of other directories without having to change your location. To do this, type `ls` at the command prompt, then type the directory name, then press Enter.

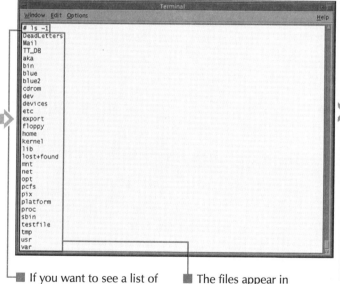

```
# ls -1
DeadLetters
Mail
TT_DB
aka
bin
blue
blue2
cdrom
dev
devices
etc
export
floppy
home
kernel
lib
lost+found
mnt
net
opt
pcfs
pix
platform
proc
sbin
testfile
tmp
usr
var
```

```
# ls -l
total 119
drwx------    2 root     other         512 Mar  3 17:11 DeadLetters
drwx------    2 root     other         512 Mar  3 17:11 Mail
drwxr-xr-x    2 root     root          512 Feb 29 10:34 TT_DB
lrwxrwxrwx    1 root     other          10 Mar  8 23:43 aka -> /etc/alias
lrwxrwxrwx    1 root     root            9 Feb 28 15:57 bin -> ./usr/bin
drwxr-xr-x    2 root     other        1536 Mar 10 23:18 blue
drwxr-xr-x   10 root     other         512 Mar  8 23:29 blue2
drwxr-xr-x    3 root     nobody        512 Feb 29 10:26 cdrom
drwxrwxr-x   18 root     sys          3584 Mar  6 00:51 dev
drwxr-xr-x    5 root     sys           512 Feb 28 17:08 devices
drwxr-xr-x   33 root     sys          3072 Mar  8 23:42 etc
drwxr-xr-x    8 root     sys           512 Mar  6 19:14 export
drwxr-xr-x    2 root     nobody        512 Mar  6 21:28 floppy
dr-xr-xr-x    1 root     root            1 Mar  6 00:51 home
drwxr-xr-x    9 root     sys           512 Feb 28 15:57 kernel
lrwxrwxrwx    1 root     root            9 Feb 28 15:57 lib -> ./usr/lib
drwx------    2 root     root         8192 Feb 28 15:49 lost+found
drwxrwxr-x    2 root     sys           512 Feb 28 15:57 mnt
dr-xr-xr-x    1 root     root            1 Mar  6 00:51 net
drwxr-xr-x    7 root     sys           512 Feb 28 16:55 opt
drwxr-xr-x    2 root     other         512 Feb 29 14:34 pcfs
drwxr-xr-x    2 root     other        1024 Mar  3 19:46 pix
drwxr-xr-x    4 root     sys          1024 Feb 28 15:59 platform
dr-xr-xr-x   50 root     root        16064 Mar 10 23:18 proc
drwxrwxr-x    2 root     sys           512 Feb 28 16:06 sbin
-rw-r--r--    1 root     other          15 Mar  6 18:58 testfile
drwxrwxrwt    7 sys      sys           457 Mar 10 23:18 tmp
drwxrwxr-x   31 root     sys          1024 Feb 28 16:53 usr
```

■ If you want to see a list of your files in a single column, type **ls -1** and press Enter.

■ The files appear in alphabetical order in a single column.

■ To see a more detailed listing of your files, type **ls -l** and press Enter.

■ Your files appear in column format, along with file permissions, ownership, and date of creation.

FIND FILES IN THE UNIX TERMINAL

Y ou can use the *find* command to locate files. Whether you misplace a file, copy it to an area that you shouldn't, or simply can't remember where something is, *find* searches an area of the system for the missing file.

Luckily, *find* is automatically *recursive*, meaning that it searches all the subdirectories under a given search point. For example, if you specify /var as the starting point for the search, *find* searches /var, /var/subdirectory, /var/sub/subdirectory, and so on.

It's important to know where you begin your search. Searching from a directory that's more than three subdirectories away means you'll spend too much time waiting for UNIX to go through a massive number of files. On the other hand, you can't find the file you want if you search under /var when the file is in the /etc directory tree.

The find command uses the format: find <search point> <command option> <file name>.

FIND FILES IN THE UNIX TERMINAL

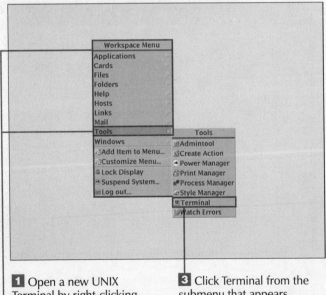

1 Open a new UNIX Terminal by right-clicking anywhere on the open desktop.

■ A pop-up menu appears.

2 Choose Tools.

3 Click Terminal from the submenu that appears.

■ When you select Terminal, the pop-up menu disappears and a new Terminal window appears on the desktop.

4 Type **find .** at the command prompt.

■ The period tells UNIX to search only the directory you're currently in.

Extra

Using *find* to search a remote machine

You must be logged into the machine. Again, you don't have to be physically present, but you can log in remotely (see Chapter 12 for *login* and *telnet* on how to do this).

Limitations to using *find*

Find is an exceptionally powerful tool, and because it lacks limits on its range (unless you set them), you can really slow things down. For example, be careful when using *find* to search under /. The / directory is the root directory under which *all* directories are subdirectories.

Searching under / when the system is busy during the day is a bad idea, as *find* takes a lot of CPU cycles to search every subdirectory. That slows the system for everyone.

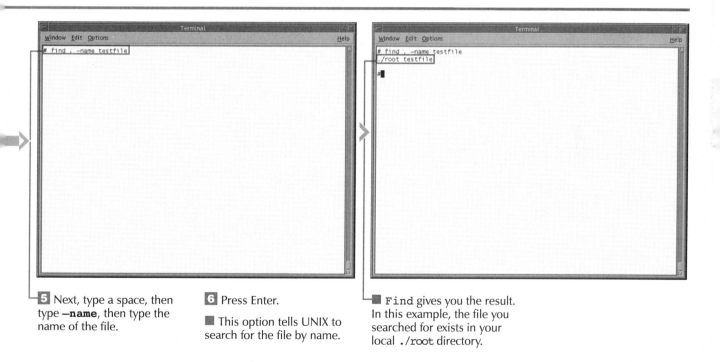

5 Next, type a space, then type **–name**, then type the name of the file.

6 Press Enter.

■ This option tells UNIX to search for the file by name.

■ Find gives you the result. In this example, the file you searched for exists in your local **./root** directory.

CHANGE DIRECTORIES WITH CD

You can change directories in the UNIX Terminal with the cd, or *change directories,* command. Getting around the UNIX file structure is just as important when you're in the Terminal window as in the graphically based desktop. If you're used to a GUI-based operating system, practice moving around in the Terminal without the visual cues of an icon, folder, or other pictures.

It's especially worthwhile to learn this if you plan to work in several different locations on the UNIX machine, or if you're an administrator. In either case, you perform this task several times every day.

When you first log in, your 'starting point' will always be your home directory, normally called /home/<your username>. From your home directory, you can use the cd command to get to more distant file systems and return to your home directory again.

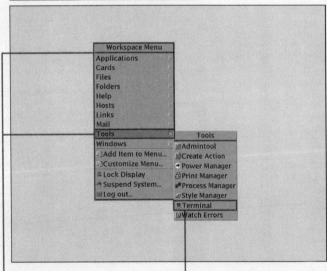

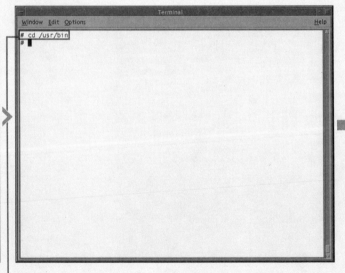

1 Open a new UNIX Terminal by right-clicking anywhere on the open desktop.

■ A pop-up menu appears.

2 Choose Tools.

3 Click Terminal from the submenu that appears.

■ When you select Terminal, the pop-up menu disappears and a new Terminal window appears on the desktop.

4 To change your location, type **cd** at the command prompt, then type the path of the directory you want.

■ The full directory location, which lists the directories that exist above your destination directory, is also known as the *filepath.*

5 Press Enter.

Apply It

Changing Directories to the Root Directory

The highest level directory on your system is called the root directory. This is because the rest of the UNIX system exists on subdirectories that branch out from the root directory in what's called a tree structure. In UNIX, the symbol for the root directory is a slash sign, so to cd to the root directory, type the following at the command sign, then press Enter.

```
cd /
```

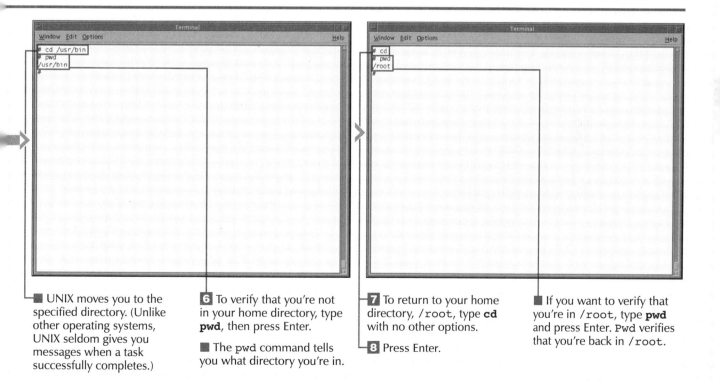

■ UNIX moves you to the specified directory. (Unlike other operating systems, UNIX seldom gives you messages when a task successfully completes.)

6 To verify that you're not in your home directory, type **pwd**, then press Enter.

■ The pwd command tells you what directory you're in.

7 To return to your home directory, /root, type **cd** with no other options.

8 Press Enter.

■ If you want to verify that you're in /root, type **pwd** and press Enter. Pwd verifies that you're back in /root.

CREATE NEW FILES

You can easily create new files in the UNIX Terminal. A new file can be the product of a utility, an application, an automated cron job, or a regular file you create on the fly. Of course, you have complete flexibility to create new text, graphics, or binary files in UNIX, depending on the program you're using.

Usually, you create files in the UNIX Terminal with the key UNIX utility, the vi text editor (the vi editor is covered in Chapter 5). However, for the purposes of this example, you use one of the oldest UNIX utilities, specifically designed to create files with a single command. The command, touch, creates an *open* ASCII text file. This means that you're going to be creating a file that has no data inside of it, but that you can edit with any of the UNIX system's text editing utilities like the vi editor.

CREATE NEW FILES

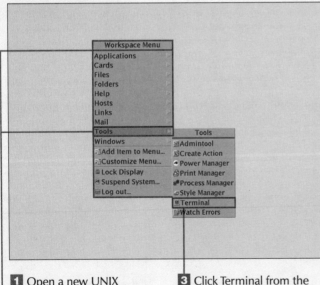

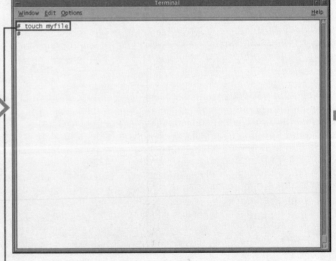

1 Open a new UNIX Terminal by right-clicking anywhere on the open desktop.

■ A pop-up menu appears.

2 Choose Tools.

3 Click Terminal from the submenu that appears.

■ When you select Terminal, the pop-up menu disappears and a new Terminal window appears on the desktop.

4 To create a file, type **touch**, then type the name you want for the file.

5 Press Enter.

User access on the system to `touch`

Touch is one of the most basic UNIX commands, created back when UNIX itself was a new operating system.

Creating files with `touch` in restricted areas

If you're not root, you're not allowed to edit some directories by adding new files to them. If you are root, then you may have permissioned the directory so that nobody can write a new file into it — of course as root you can change this, so it's not 100 percent invulnerable.

Using new files if there's nothing inside of them

Sometimes, creating a new empty file can serve as a placeholder or a reminder to put data in a specific file. For example, if later in your busy, hectic day you plan to save a mail file to a log, you can create the blank file in advance, calling it `mail-log`, and then add to it when you're ready.

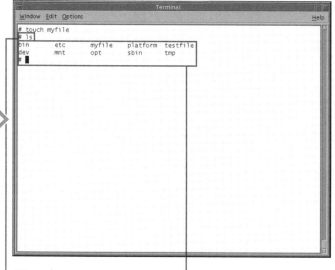

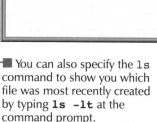

6 Because UNIX doesn't tell you that the task is complete if it is successful, type **ls** at the command line and press Enter to see the new file.

■ The `ls` command shows your new file added to the list of files in your home directory.

■ You can also specify the `ls` command to show you which file was most recently created by typing **ls -lt** at the command prompt.

■ Press Enter. `ls -lt` shows the detailed listing of files in the order they were created.

■ Your new file, `myfile`, is the most recently created, and because you didn't enter anything into it, its size is zero.

CREATE NEW DIRECTORIES

You can create new directories in UNIX if you want to keep your environment organized. In your home directory, for example, you can create two separate directories, one for work and one for home. As a general rule, it's easier to keep files organized if your directories are created and named by some category or function.

To create a new directory, use the mkdir, or *make directory*, command. At the command prompt, type in the mkdir command, followed by the name you wish to give the directory.

When creating directories in the UNIX Terminal, it's improper to use the term *folder*. While essentially the same, a *folder* is a directory represented by an icon. To avoid confusion when using icon terms in an environment where no icons exist, you should refer to /etc as the etc directory.

CREATE NEW DIRECTORIES

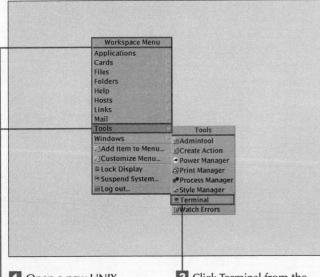

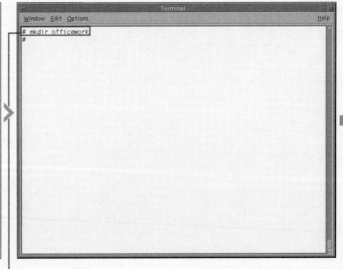

■1 Open a new UNIX Terminal by right-clicking anywhere on the open desktop.

■ A pop-up menu appears.

■2 Choose Tools.

■3 Click Terminal from the submenu that appears.

■ When you select Terminal, the pop-up menu disappears and a new Terminal window appears on the desktop.

■4 Create a new directory by typing **mkdir** at the command prompt, then type the name of the new directory.

■5 Press Enter.

Extra

Reading file error messages when creating directories

This is an old terminology issue. The short answer is that the UNIX operating system treats *everything* — text files, binaries, symbolic links, and more — as a file. Therefore, the correct error message is `File exists`.

Restrictions on directory names

UNIX won't allow directory names with slashes, because slashes confuse the operating system. You also can't name directories `//`, `/`, or `..` because these symbols already have meaning within the UNIX operating system.

Names you shouldn't use

Ideally you never want to use names that already exist, particularly if they're a system directory name. If you're in your home directory, you can easily create a directory called `/etc`, but you run the risk of confusing yourself if you're trying to locate programs that belong in the *real* `/etc` area.

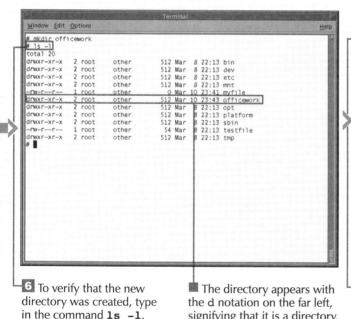

6 To verify that the new directory was created, type in the command **ls -1**.

7 Press Enter.

■ The directory appears with the **d** notation on the far left, signifying that it is a directory.

■ You can also specify the `ls` command to show your most recently created directory by typing **ls -lt** at the command prompt.

■ Press Enter. **ls -lt** shows the detailed listing of files in the order that you created them.

■ Your new directory is the newest in the list.

COPY FILES AND DIRECTORIES

You can copy files and entire directories in UNIX with the cp, or *copy,* command. When you copy a file, you can create an exact duplicate of the file with a new name. You also can create a duplicate of the file with the same name, but only if you save the file to a different location.

The UNIX operating system treats everything as a file, including directories. However, you use the -R command option when you copy entire directories. The -R stands for *recursive.*

When you *recursively* copy a directory, you copy the directory and all of the files inside it. If you're just *renaming* a directory, the path of the files and subfolders in the directory are automatically altered to reflect the change. You don't need to specify a recursive change.

COPY FILES AND DIRECTORIES

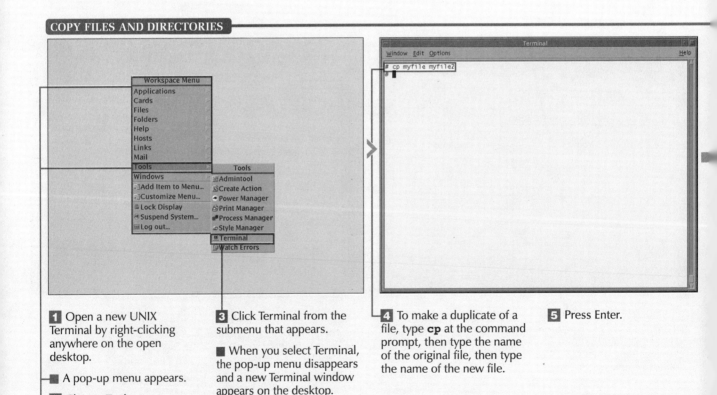

1 Open a new UNIX Terminal by right-clicking anywhere on the open desktop.

■ A pop-up menu appears.

2 Choose Tools.

3 Click Terminal from the submenu that appears.

■ When you select Terminal, the pop-up menu disappears and a new Terminal window appears on the desktop.

4 To make a duplicate of a file, type **cp** at the command prompt, then type the name of the original file, then type the name of the new file.

5 Press Enter.

Apply It

Copying a file to a different location

Of course, you don't have to make a copy of a file in the same location. If you want to copy a file to a different directory than the one you are currently in, do so by using typing in the following at the command prompt, then press Enter.

```
cp <filename> <directory
location><new filename>
```

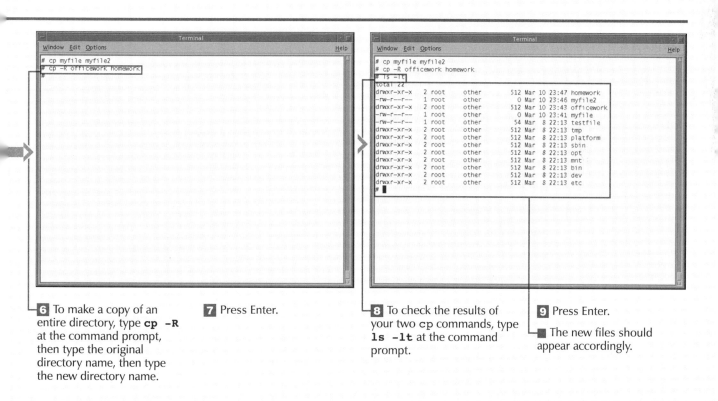

6 To make a copy of an entire directory, type **cp -R** at the command prompt, then type the original directory name, then type the new directory name.

7 Press Enter.

8 To check the results of your two **cp** commands, type **ls -lt** at the command prompt.

9 Press Enter.

■ The new files should appear accordingly.

RENAME FILES AND DIRECTORIES

You can rename any kind of file or directory in the UNIX Terminal with the mv command. You can more effectively organize the contents of your home directory — any system directory — with a few strategically placed naming conventions. The key to doing this is simply being consistent.

The mv command is actually the *move* command in UNIX, but it's primarily used for renaming files and directories because it's so convenient. Of course you can also use mv for moving files and directories. The advantage is that it's automatically *recursive*; that is, it

applies to the selected item and all items that exist beneath the item you change. Just make sure that you understand that you're not making a *copy* — you're moving the actual file or directory to a different location. To rename a file, use the syntax mv <filename> <new filename>.

UNIX automatically warns you if you're naming a file or directory identically to another one. However, UNIX only issues the warning if the identically named file is in the same directory, so it's best to just give everything a unique name.

RENAME FILES AND DIRECTORIES

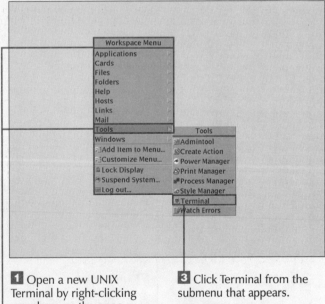

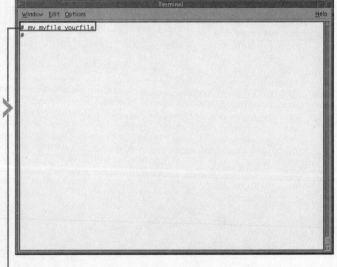

1 Open a new UNIX Terminal by right-clicking anywhere on the open desktop.

■ A pop-up menu appears.

2 Choose Tools.

3 Click Terminal from the submenu that appears.

■ When you select Terminal, the pop-up menu disappears and a new Terminal window appears on the desktop.

4 To rename a file, type **mv** at the command prompt, then type the original name of the file, then type the new name of the file.

5 Press Enter.

Extra

Naming files or directories with spaces, hyphens, colons, or slashes

This isn't recommended. Naming files with slashes or colons can cause confusion when you work with files, especially in the UNIX Terminal window. It's best if you don't name files with any of these symbols.

Renaming directories won't affect the files stored inside of them

Renaming directories does not change files inside the directories, so if you want to change the name of a directory — and all of its contents — to the name `ditto.txt`, it simply won't work.

Changing the extensions on a file

You can change the file extensions, with the mv command as follows: `mv bubbles.bmp bubbles.txt`. However, the file probably will become unusable, so it's best not to do this.

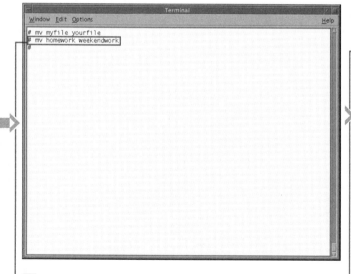

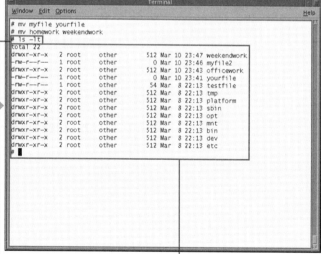

6 Similarly, if you want to rename a directory, type **mv** at the command prompt, then type the original directory name, then type the new name of the directory, then press Enter.

7 To see the results, type **ls -lt**.

8 Press Enter to see the newly renamed files.

DELETE FILES AND DIRECTORIES

You can delete files and directories in the UNIX Terminal with the rm, or *remove file*, command. This command is one of the most powerful, and potentially the most dangerous. When you delete a file or directory, UNIX asks you if you're sure you want to delete it. Make sure you pay attention here, because after you answer yes, there is no turning back or restoring the file, unless you made a backup copy.

You can also delete entire directories in UNIX by using the -R command option with the rm command. This is where using the rm command can get you into a lot of trouble if you're not careful. When you delete an entire directory, you delete all of the files inside the directory as well. If you want to keep any files that are still inside the directory, move or copy them elsewhere.

Workspace Menu
Applications
Cards
Files
Folders
Help
Hosts
Links
Mail
Tools
Windows
Add Item to Menu...
Customize Menu...
Lock Display
Suspend System...
Log out...

Tools
Admintool
Create Action
Power Manager
Print Manager
Process Manager
Style Manager
Terminal
Watch Errors

```
Terminal
Window  Edit  Options                              Help
# rm myfile2
#
```

1 Open a new UNIX Terminal by right-clicking anywhere on the open desktop.

■ A pop-up menu appears.

2 Choose Tools.

3 Click Terminal from the submenu that appears.

■ When you select Terminal, the pop-up menu disappears and a new Terminal window appears on the desktop.

4 To delete a file, type **rm** at the command prompt, then type the file name.

5 Press Enter.

■ The file is deleted.

Extra

Stopping a delete in progress

If you're deleting a truly gigantic file which takes UNIX several minutes to get rid of, you can try to kill the delete process, but you can save only what the delete function didn't delete.

Deleting multiple files at once

Use the asterisk (*) as a wildcard (for example, rm *ing deletes all files that end in *ing*). But don't do this. The potential for catastrophe by deleting something that is system critical is too high.

Deleting files while logged in as another user

When you're logged in as the *root* account, you have complete administrative privileges over any file. When you're logged in as a regular user, you can only delete files for which you have permission, such as your own text or graphics files in your home directory.

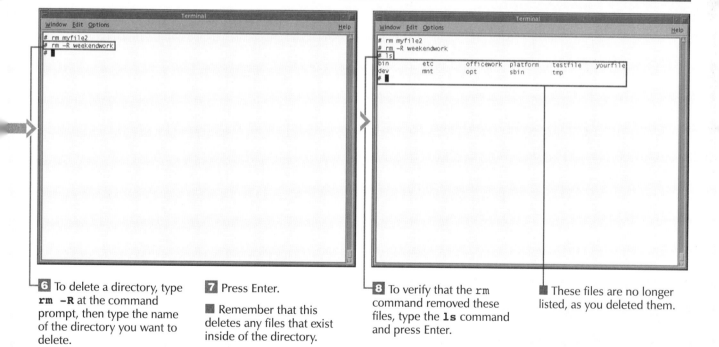

6 To delete a directory, type **rm -R** at the command prompt, then type the name of the directory you want to delete.

7 Press Enter.

■ Remember that this deletes any files that exist inside of the directory.

8 To verify that the rm command removed these files, type the **ls** command and press Enter.

■ These files are no longer listed, as you deleted them.

CREATE SYMBOLIC LINKS

Symbolic links are *bridges* to files and directories that you use on a frequent basis. For example, a link is useful to access a file in a location that takes some typing to reach, such as /etc/sound/ events. If you're familiar with Microsoft Windows, think of a symbolic link as the equivalent of creating a *Shortcut* icon on the Windows desktop.

In UNIX, links come in two varieties, *hard* and *soft*. *Soft links,* which you should prefer, are less *persistent* than hard links. If a soft link doesn't work, UNIX stops trying to use it. If a hard link doesn't work, your entire computer can stop.

To create a link, use the ln or *link* command. The – option makes the link soft, or *symbolic*. The format for this command is ln – <location/name of file> <name of link>

CREATE SYMBOLIC LINKS

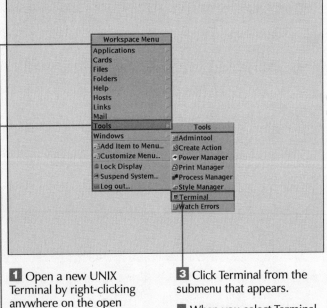

1 Open a new UNIX Terminal by right-clicking anywhere on the open desktop.

■ A pop-up menu appears.

2 Choose Tools.

3 Click Terminal from the submenu that appears.

■ When you select Terminal, the pop-up menu disappears and a new Terminal window appears on the desktop.

4 To create a link to a directory, type **ln -s** at the command prompt, then type the name of the directory, then type the name of the link.

5 Press Enter.

Extra

Linking strategies

You should use links sparingly. If you have too many, you forget where everything really is!

Making a link to a link

You can create a symbolic link to another second link, but this isn't recommended practice either. Again, you're likely to lose track of where files are kept in actuality. And each link you create is a potential *break point* on your system. So when you link to a file or directory, only use one link.

Giving links the same names as the linked files

You shouldn't give links the same name as linked files. If you want to do this to help you remember, use the format <filename_link> to differentiate the link from the original file.

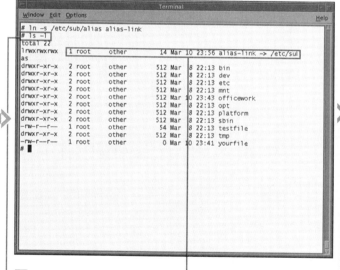

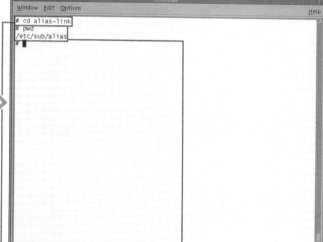

■6 Verify the link's creation by typing **ls -l** at the command prompt, then press Enter.

■ The new link's name appears with an l in the leftmost column. This identifies it as a link. Also, the link is listed with an arrow pointing to its destination directory.

■7 To test the link, type **cd** at the command prompt, then type the name of the link.

■8 Press Enter.

■9 Type **pwd**, then press Enter. Pwd verifies that you're already in the directory, thanks to the timesaving symbolic link.

CHANGE FILE PERMISSIONS

You can change a file's permissions in UNIX in order to grant or restrict access of other people to the contents of your file. If you change the permissions to a directory, you can grant or restrict access to entire groups of files at one time. You can change a file's permissions in the UNIX operating system to one of three settings. Your options are r for *readable*, w for *writable*, and x for *executable*. If a file is readable, then the contents can be viewed with the vi editor, but not changed. By contrast, a file that is writable *can* be altered or renamed. Finally, a file that is executable can be run as a script or program.

UNIX divides permissions into three areas: file permissions for the *user*, for the *group*, and *other*. User is, of course, the user account who owns the file, and group is the user group that the user belongs to. Other is everyone else on the system.

UNIX permissions are viewed in groups of three symbols: r's, w's, and x's. For example, the user's permissions on a file may be set to readable and writable, which equals rw-. Depending on how you change the permissions, the letters signifying the accessibility of the file are added or deleted.

CHANGE FILE PERMISSIONS

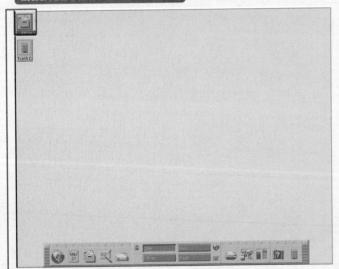

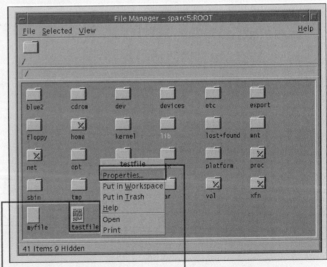

1 To see a file in your home directory, double-click on the home directory icon, usually labeled dtfile.

■ The directory opens so that you can see the files inside.

2 To see permissions for a file, right-click on the file's icon.

■ A pop-up menu appears.

3 Click on Properties.

Extra

Changing a file's permissions

If you want to use the Terminal, you can use the chmod command. You can look up the syntax of the chmod command by opening a Terminal, type man chmod and then press Enter. With chmod, you can use the r-w-x letters to change permissions, or you can use numbers based on the hex system: for example, chmod 664 <filename>. If you really want to try chmod with this system, look up the different hex codes in a UNIX reference book.

Setting a file that should be kept out for public reference

The best is rw-r--r-- because that would allow anyone to read the file, but prevent anyone but the owner from making changes.

Setting for privacy

Your best bet is rw-------. Only you can read or write to the file, and nobody else can even see the contents, let alone change them!

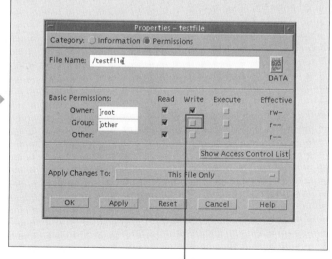

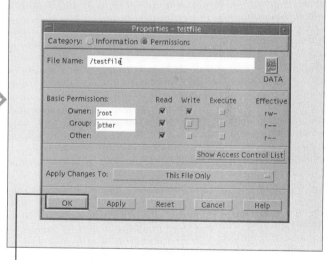

■ The Properties screen appears.

4 Select or deselect the check boxes in the middle of the screen to set the file's permissions.

■ To make the file writable for the user group, you need to select the Write check box.

5 Save your changes by clicking OK.

EDIT DIRECTORY PERMISSIONS

You edit a directory's permissions in the same way you edit a regular file in the UNIX operating system. This is because UNIX treats all objects — including directories, symbolic links, scripts, and applications — as files.

You may see directories listed in the GUI desktop as *folders*. Folders and directories are the same — they exist to organize your files into order, much like your file cabinet holds manila folders to separate your documents on taxes, reports, and office memos. The term *directory* is more common in UNIX, and it is more appropriate to use the term directory

when you're working in the terminal. However, *folders* is appropriate whenever you're working in the GUI, because you click on an icon that represents your file cabinet's manila folder.

The key concept with permissioning directories is *recursiveness*. If you change a directory's permissions, by default the result is not recursive. In other words, the change does not affect the files and subfolders in the directory. However, in UNIX you can specify that your change applies to all the files underneath the directory you're editing.

EDIT DIRECTORY PERMISIIONS

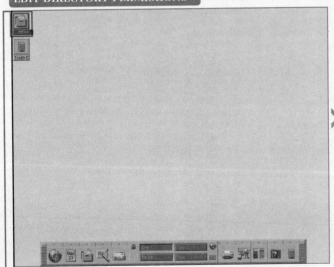

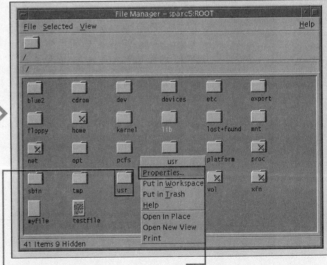

1 To see a file in your home directory, double-click on the home directory icon, usually labeled dtfile.

■ The directory opens so that you can see the files inside.

2 To see permissions for a file, right-click on the file's icon.

■ A pop-up menu appears.

3 Click on Properties.

Extra

Setting a directory's permissions

That depends on what the contents of the directory are. (Always ensure that you can open a directory by making the directory *executable*.) Beyond that, you decide whether you want users to be able to read or edit the files within the directory.

Applying changes to all the files underneath a directory except one

Your best bet is to simply apply your changes to This Folder and its subfolders and then go change the remaining file to the way you want.

Changing permissions for directories and files in the Terminal

It's worth repeating that to UNIX, directories and files are exactly the same. If you want to use the Terminal, use the `chmod` command. With `chmod`, you can use the `r-w-x` letters to change permissions, or you can use numbers based on the hex system.

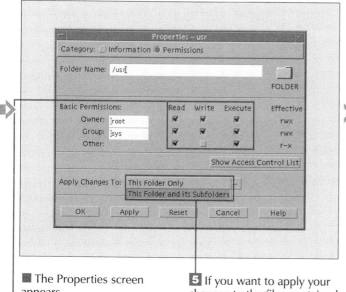

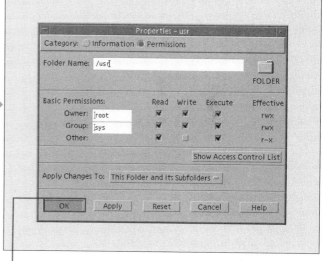

■ The Properties screen appears.

4 You can select and deselect check boxes in the middle of the screen to change the folder's permissions.

5 If you want to apply your changes to the files contained in this folder, click the bar next to Apply Changes To and choose This Folder and its Subfolders from the pop-up menu that appears.

6 Save your changes by clicking OK.

CHANGE FILE OWNERSHIP

You can change the ownership of a file in UNIX as another way of increasing or decreasing the level of access to a file. For example, you can change the ownership of a file to the root administrative account if you want to restrict access without changing the file permissions. Alternatively, you can change the ownership of a file to Other to make it more public and easier to access.

Users can also change a file's ownership if they want to transfer ownership of a file to a different user or even to the root account. Of course, users who make a change of ownership to a file should know that it is very hard to *take back* ownership of a file after it is given away. The root account can restore file privileges if ownership has been accidentally given away.

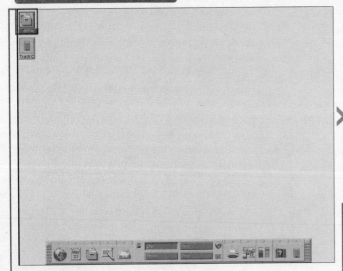

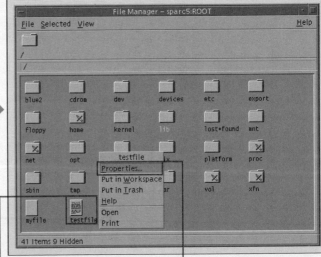

1 To see a file in your home directory, double-click the home directory icon, usually labeled dtfile.

■ The directory opens so that you can see the files inside.

2 To see the permissions for a file, right-click the file's icon.

3 Choose Properties from the pop-up menu that appears.

Extra

Changing a file's ownership to a nonexistent user account

UNIX checks against the user accounts you have listed. If the user doesn't exist, you can't change ownership.

Oddly, you can change the owner to Nobody, because Nobody is a UNIX default account. Don't do this unless you have no other alternative because Nobody is a *dummy account* that the UNIX system uses for maintenance tasks.

Logging in as the root administrative account and editing a user's files

There is no need to do this. Remember, when you are logged in as the root administrative account, you have what are called 'root privileges.' One of the privileges that root has is the ability to edit any file on the system at any time, without having to own the file or to change the file's permissions to be able to read, write, or execute it.

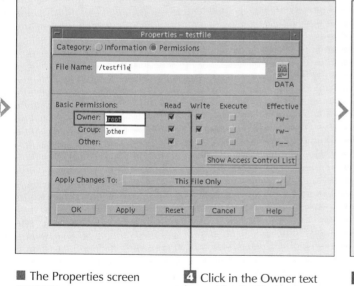

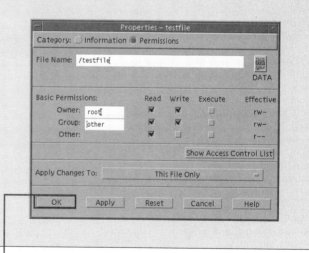

■ The Properties screen appears.

4 Click in the Owner text box under the Basic Permissions section.

5 Type in the new owner's name.

6 Save your changes by clicking OK.

ALTER DIRECTORY OWNERSHIP

You can make changes to the ownership of whole directories in UNIX if you want to increase or decrease the level of access to an entire set of files. For example, you can change the ownership of a directory to the root administrative account if you want to restrict access to a whole set of administrative or sensitive files. On the other hand, you can change a directory's ownership to a new group to make the files inside more accessible to a different user group.

Once again, with ownership as well as permissioning, the key concept when editing directories is *recursiveness*. If you change a directory's ownership, by default the result is not recursive, so the change won't affect the files and subfolders in the directory. However, you can specify that your change applies to all the files underneath the directory you're editing by selecting the appropriate option from the Apply Changes To area of the Property window.

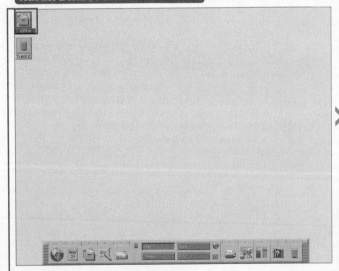

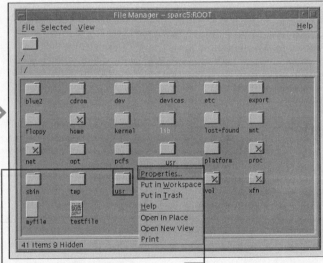

1 To see a file in your home directory, double-click on the home directory icon, usually labeled dtfile.

■ The directory opens to show you the files inside.

2 To see the permissions for a folder, right-click the folder's icon.

3 Choose Properties from the pop-up menu that appears.

Extra

Other ways of changing a directory's ownership

You can change the ownership of a directory in UNIX by using the chown, or *change ownership* command. The format for chown is: chown <new owner> <filename>.

Recursive changes with chown

By default, a change to the directory's ownership is not recursive. It only becomes recursive when you add the command option -R.

Changing the directory's ownership to a user that does not exist

UNIX won't let you complete this task. When you change a directory's ownership, UNIX compares your request against the users listed in the /etc/passwd file, which stores all of the existing user names. If the name is not on the list, the original ownership remains the same. If you're the root account, create a new user first, then change the directory's ownership to that newly created user.

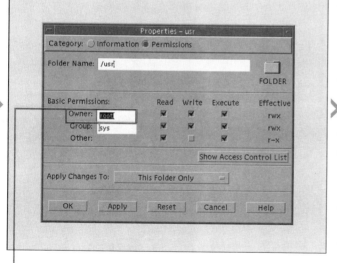

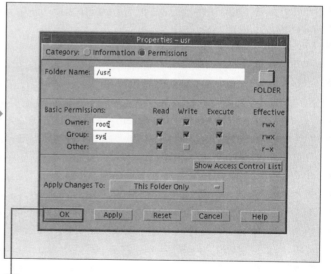

■ The Properties screen appears.

4 Click in the Owner text box under the Basic Permissions section.

5 Type in the new owner's name.

6 Save your changes by clicking OK.

CONFIGURE GROUP OWNERSHIP

You can also change the group ownership of a UNIX file in the file's Properties window. This is much like changing the file's ownership, which directly impacts the user. By changing the group ownership of a file, you can either restrict access or make the file more publicly available. This is most commonly done in an organization or company that has made a significant reorganization by departments. UNIX lists group ownership in the same screen, below the User Ownership text field.

Changes to group ownership affect the readability, writability, and execution of a file, depending on the file's permissioning. If a file is listed as writable by a user and the user's group, then changing a file's group can help grant access to a file if the user wants his or her group to be able to use it. However, this setting still restricts access for everyone else on the system.

CONFIGURE GROUP OWNERSHIP

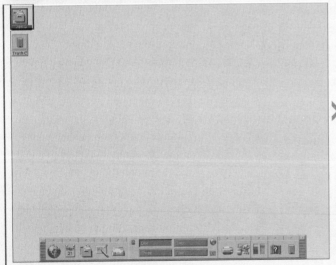

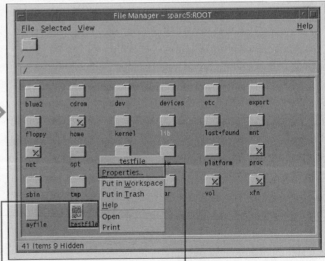

■1 To see a file in your home directory, double-click the home directory icon, usually labeled `dtfile`.

■ The directory opens to show you the files inside.

■2 To see the permissions for a file, right-click the file's icon.

■3 Choose Properties from the pop-up menu that appears.

Extra

Changing a file's ownership to a nonexistent group	Performing the same kind of permissioning with the `chown` command
UNIX won't let you complete this task. When you change a directory's ownership, UNIX compares your request against the groups listed in the `/etc/groups` file, which stores all of the existing group names. If the name is not on the list, the original ownership remains the same. If you're the root account, create a new group first, then change the directory's ownership to that newly created group.	You can use the `chmod g+` or `g-` options to grant or restrict permissions as you wish. However, there are times that programs in UNIX access files and check the file's ownership and group ownership, not their permissions, so this is a worthwhile command to learn.

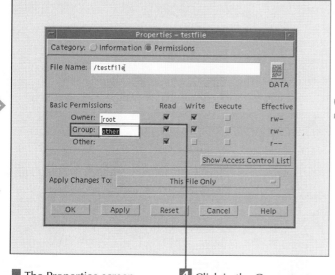

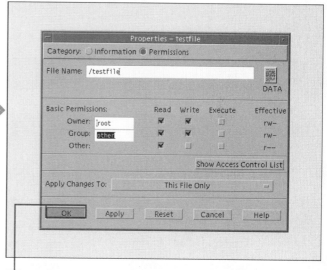

■ The Properties screen appears.

4 Click in the Group text box marked under the Basic Permissions section.

5 Type in the new owner's name.

6 Save your work by clicking OK.

MAKE A FILE EXECUTABLE

You can edit a file's properties to make the file *executable*. This means that you can run the file as a program. This is handiest to convert a file into a script or disable a program so that it can't run by accident.

If you're used to Microsoft Windows, you may be a little confused at the terminology *to make a file executable*. After all, in the Microsoft world, a program either has an `.exe` attachment or it does not.

In the UNIX world, everything is a file, whether it is a document or a program. Making a text file executable doesn't make it a program. But if you construct your own program with UNIX commands (also known as *shell scripting*), then this is the last step to make your file into a UNIX system script.

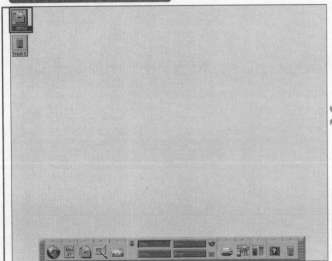

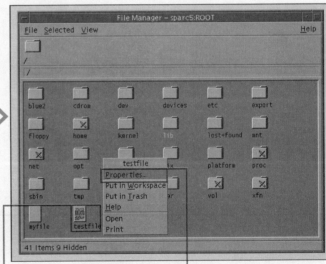

1 To see a file in your home directory, double-click the home directory icon, usually labeled `dtfile`.

■ The directory opens to show you the files inside.

2 To see the permissions for a file, right-click the file's icon.

3 Choose Properties from the pop-up menu that appears.

Apply It

What if a file is marked as not executable to the user group, but is executable by everyone else

If a file is marked in this manner, everyone, including the user group, can execute the file. The user group is just a subgroup of the total number of UNIX users represented by the Other setting in the UNIX scheme of permissioning.

Reading and editing a file after making it executable

Making a file executable only gives you another option to use — it doesn't block out or restrict your option to read or write to a file at all. This lets you make changes to a file if you plan to run it as a script.

Running an executable program

In most cases, you just type the name of the file and press Enter.

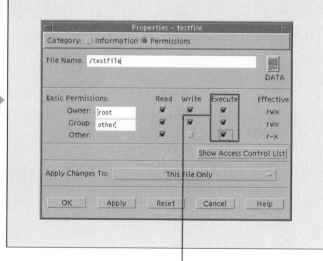

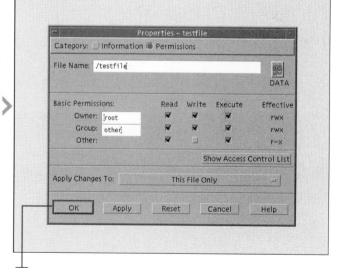

■ The Properties screen appears.

4 Select or deselect the check boxes in the Execute column.

5 Save your changes by clicking OK.

START THE VI EDITOR

You can use the vi editor as a text-editing utility. However, you also can use the vi editor for everything from creating entire documents to writing scripts, editing files, and searching through log files with more detail than other UNIX commands. For many UNIX users, vi is the main utility in the UNIX world that you should be familiar with.

Other text editors exist in UNIX, such as Emacs, Ex, and the GNOME-based

WordPerfect or WordStar programs. However, only vi automatically comes with all UNIX installations and is universally popular with both beginning users and administrators.

Because vi is not graphics-based like today's word processors, it can seem more challenging and esoteric than most text-processing programs. However, for this book, you learn the most simple yet important and useful commands that you're likely to use every day.

START THE VI EDITOR

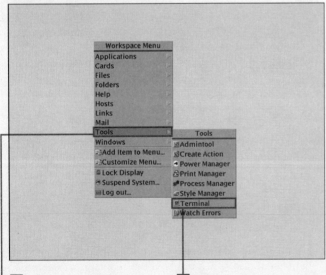

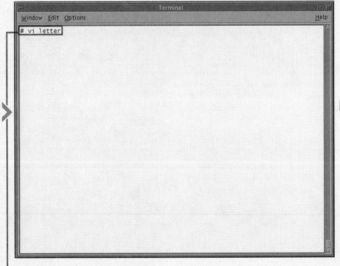

1 Open a new UNIX Terminal by right-clicking anywhere on the open desktop.

■ A pop-up menu appears.

2 Choose Tools.

3 Click Terminal.

■ After you choose Terminal, the pop-up menu disappears and a new Terminal window appears on the desktop.

4 To open a file, type **vi** at the prompt, then type the name of the file.

5 Press Enter.

Extra

Choosing the vi editor

The vi editor is used because compared to other graphics-based editors, vi doesn't perform such tasks as formatting and font changes. Such formats make a printed document look good, but make a log file or script confusing to read.

The vi editor is one of the oldest utilities, dating back to the original creation of UNIX itself. Vi was developed at a time when UNIX machines didn't even use monitors — they used teletype machines. To save paper, the vi editor — and by extension, all of UNIX itself — is very light on any graphics and long-winded messages.

Limitations on naming a file on vi

Because vi creates such files as `touch` and `mkdir`, the same restrictions apply — don't name your file ., .., or /. It's a good idea to make the name unique and not use any slashes in your file name.

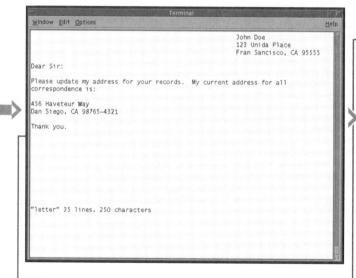

■ The vi editor opens. You are *inside* the file's text.

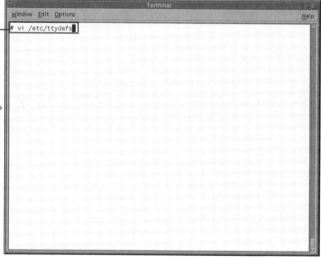

■ Alternatively, you can open files in other directories. Type the file's name and location (path), then press Enter.

MOVE AROUND IN VI

You can move around your document line by line, word by word, or even character by character. Vi, not being GUI-based, has no scroll bar to skip back and forth between sentences or paragraphs. Vi is *pattern and line-oriented,* rather than *scroll bar–oriented,* so using vi may get you where you want to be in your document faster than in a GUI-based editor.

You can move through small documents character by character with the *arrow* keys. However, you can use other commands to move more quickly around any document. You can practice moving around in any UNIX text file in the same way you see this demonstrated in the file we opened in the preceding task, "Start the vi Editor."

MOVE AROUND IN VI

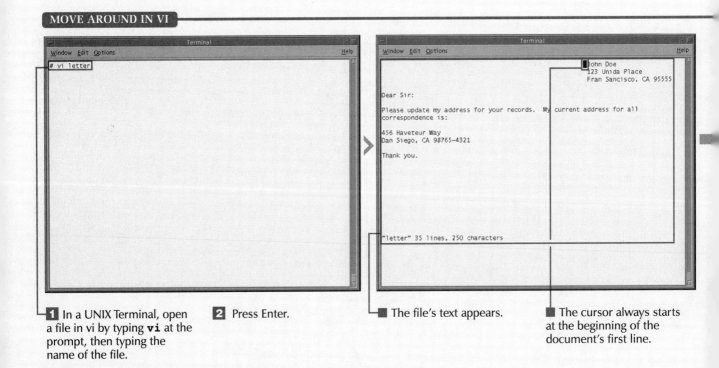

1 In a UNIX Terminal, open a file in vi by typing **vi** at the prompt, then typing the name of the file.

2 Press Enter.

■ The file's text appears.

■ The cursor always starts at the beginning of the document's first line.

Extra

Moving screen by screen

For longer documents, you move by screen lengths because you don't have a scroll bar in vi. To move down one screen, press Ctrl-F To move up one screen, press Ctrl-B.

Moving the cursor to the middle of the screen in one step

Use the command capital M to jump directly to the center of your screen. This doesn't move you to the center of your entire *document*, unless your document fits in one screen.

Moving paragraph by paragraph

You can move to the beginning of the following paragraph by typing { (the curly *French brace* that points left). To move to the start of the preceding paragraph, type } (the curly French brace that points right).

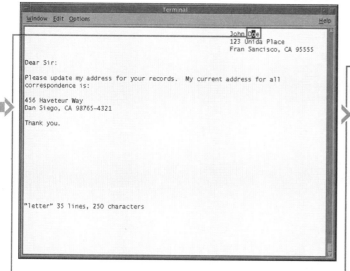

■ In order to move to the middle of the next word, "Doe," press the right-arrow key six times. The cursor moves over the *o* in *Doe*.

■ In order to move forward from word to word, press the *w* key. If you press the *w* key ten times, the cursor moves to the tenth word in the document. To move backwards word by word, use the *b* key.

COMMAND AND INSERT MODE

You can only be in one of two modes in the vi editor. You switch between two *modes* depending on what you wish to do in the document. In *Command mode,* you move within the document, change formatting, delete text, quit, or save the document. In Command mode, you can't add text.

In *Insert mode,* you can add text, but you can't perform any fancier functions.

Every time you start vi, you start in Command mode. There are several ways to get into Insert mode. To get back into Command mode, there is only one option — pressing the Esc key, also known as the Escape key. On most keyboards, this key is in the upper left-hand corner.

COMMAND AND INSERT MODE

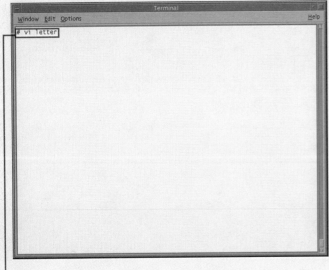

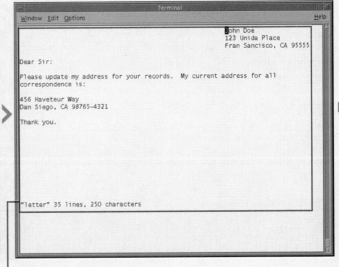

1 In a UNIX Terminal, open a file by typing **vi** at the prompt, then typing the file name.

2 Press Enter.

■ The file's text appears. The cursor always starts at the beginning of the document's first line.

Extra

Going from Insert mode to Command mode

The Escape key is your only option to switch from Insert to Command mode.

Other ways of going from Command mode into Insert mode

The most common way is using the commands to insert a new (blank) line of text, or to paste text. I discuss this task in "Copy and Paste Text," in this chapter.

Identifying the selected mode

Always assume you're in Insert mode. Press the Escape key to ensure that you're in Command mode before you try to move the cursor. On most UNIX systems, pressing Escape repeatedly rewards you with a beep.

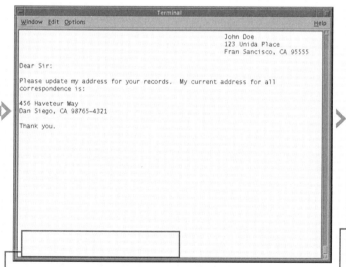

■ By default, you are in Command Mode. In order to switch to Insert mode, press either **a** or **i**, as if you were going to insert text. The file's name and statistics at the base of the screen disappear when you change modes. You can't move the cursor with the arrow keys.

■ To return to Command mode, press the Esc key. Although there is no visible change in the file, you can confirm your return to Command mode by pressing an arrow key so the cursor moves.

INSERT TEXT

You can add text in the vi editor by switching from Command mode into Insert mode. Depending on the way you enter Insert mode, you can enter text at the position of the cursor on the vi screen, or immediately after the cursor.

The methods shown here are to add text at the most basic level, which is simply typing it letter by letter. If you want to add text by copying or pasting, see "Copy and Paste Text," later on in this chapter.

As a rule, vi is much less complicated than current text processors. Because vi is designed to code programs in UNIX and the C programming language, it avoids confusing the operating system and C compilers with fancy text formatting, such as text styling and templates.

INSERT TEXT

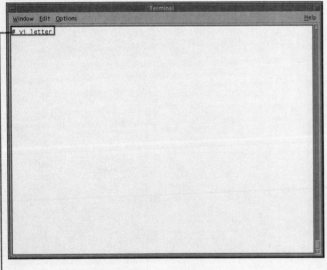

1 In a UNIX Terminal, open a file by typing **vi** at the prompt, then typing the file name.

2 Press Enter.

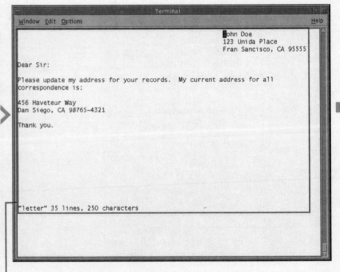

■ The file's text appears. The cursor always starts at the beginning of the document's first line.

Extra

Printing a document created in vi

You send the document to your printer in the exact same manner you send any document that you create in a graphics-based text editor. I cover this process in Chapter 11.

Changing the font size of the text in vi

Changing the font size or style is confusing to the operating system and C compilers, so this effect isn't included. You can change the size of the characters in your Terminal window, but this doesn't change how the text looks when you print the document.

Writing with fancy fonts

You need to use a GUI-based UNIX text editor, such as WordPerfect, WordStar, or Gnotepad.

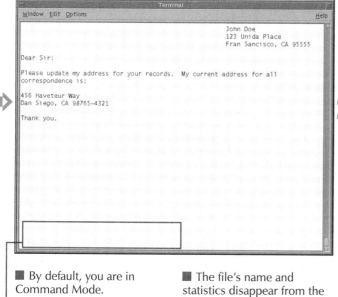

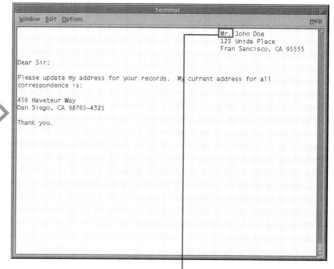

■ By default, you are in Command Mode.

3 In order to enter Insert mode, press either **i** or **a** to insert text at the command prompt.

■ The file's name and statistics disappear from the base of the screen when you change modes.

4 Type in your new text.

■ For example, type **Mr.** at the prompt to make the first line read "Mr. John Doe."

DELETE TEXT

You can delete text from your vi document in several ways. You can delete single characters, an entire line of text, or even the entire line in the paragraph itself (in other words, deleting the text and the carriage return). You can even simultaneously delete and replace characters.

Knowing which method to use when editing text in the vi editor saves you a lot of extra keystrokes. If you're new to the vi editor, you should use the x command, as it's the simplest way to delete text.

Remember, you can only delete text when you're in the Command mode. As a habit, you can press the Esc key to ensure that you're in Command mode before trying to delete text.

DELETE TEXT

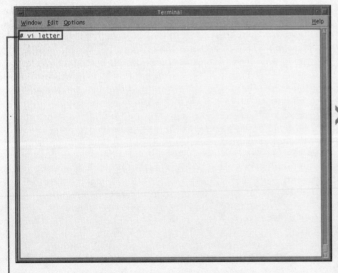

1 In a UNIX Terminal, open a file by typing **vi** at the prompt, then typing the file name.

2 Press Enter.

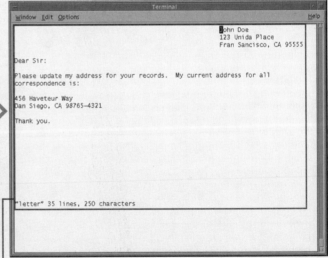

■ The file's text appears. The cursor always starts at the beginning of the document's first line.

Extra

Recovering an accidentally deleted character

Try to undo your last command. First, press the Esc key to ensure that you're in Command mode, then type **u**.

Undoing an action

You can undo a command to delete an entire line, regardless of whether you used dd or s. Press the Escape key to ensure you're in Command mode and type **u**. (If you deleted a character, then did another action, you can't restore your deletion.)

Multiple-step undo functions are a fairly recent addition to text editors, but this is an option that hasn't been ported to vi yet. If this is a serious error, you can exit vi without saving, then reopen your document and start again. However, be careful — if you exit vi without saving, you also lose all of the changes you've made to this document since the last time you saved it, possibly causing you to redo a lot of work.

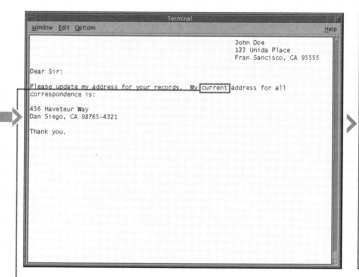

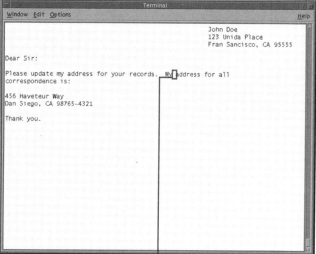

3 Use the arrow keys to move the cursor to the start of the word to be deleted.

4 Press the x key once for each letter and space to be deleted.

■ For example, press the x key eight times to delete the seven-letter example word and the space at the end of it. The sentence now reads: "My address for all correspondence is:"

FIND WORDS IN VI

You can find text patterns in vi. A *search* is actually a more flexible task than it appears, because you're looking for a *pattern* of text in a document, not just a *word*. For example, searching for *day* finds the word, plus every word that contains *day*, such as *daylight* and *Saturday*. This is particularly useful if you're working with long documents or pages of complex coding, because it would take you much longer to read through a 500-page document in search of specific text patterns.

If you're working with a particularly long document, you may also take advantage of the different directions of search possible with vi. For example, if you're in the middle of a 300-page document and you're sure that the pattern you want is in the first half, you can specify that vi should search all text above versus below the cursor.

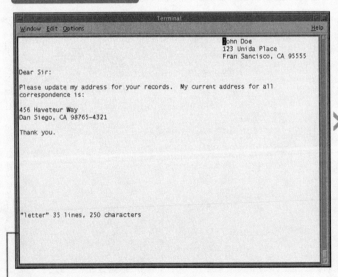

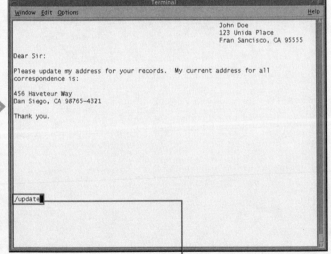

1 In a UNIX Terminal, open a file by typing **vi** at the prompt, then typing the file name.

2 Press Enter.

■ The file's text appears. The cursor always starts at the beginning of the document's first line.

3 To search for a text pattern, press the Esc key to ensure you're in Command mode, then type a slash, **/**, and the pattern, such as the word "update."

■ The slash and the search pattern appear at the base of the screen.

4 Press Enter to execute the search.

Extra

Limiting a search to a single line of a document

You can do this by using the lowercase f to search forward of your cursor's position, and a capital F to search backwards from your cursor position.

Switching the direction of a search while in the middle of a search command

If you're searching for "termcap" with the slash (searching forward in the document), you can type a capital N to repeat the search, going in the opposite direction (backward in the document).

Case-sensitive searches

By default, all searches in vi are case-sensitive. This is because vi is not designed to simply search for letters, it's designed to search for text patterns. To vi, the text patterns "This," "this," and "tHiS" are completely different.

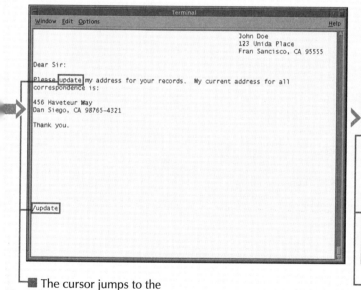

■ The cursor jumps to the first occurrence of the pattern.

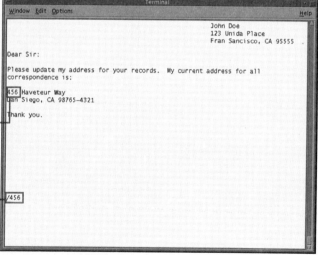

■ You can search for numerical patterns by typing a slash, followed by the numerals. When you press Enter, the cursor jumps to the first occurrence.

REPLACE TEXT

You can replace text in your vi document by using a number of different commands to substitute one character for another. Substituting text allows you delete and simultaneously replace text with the new characters that you wish. This can save you both time and keystrokes when editing a file by not requiring you to delete text and then go back to type your corrections. Also, it automatically puts you into the all-important Insert mode.

Because you're automatically placed into Insert mode when you use the Replace command, be sure to press the Escape key when you need to return to Command mode. For example, to move the cursor to make further changes to your document, switch between Insert and Command mode to complete the changes you want to make to different locations within the file.

REPLACE TEXT

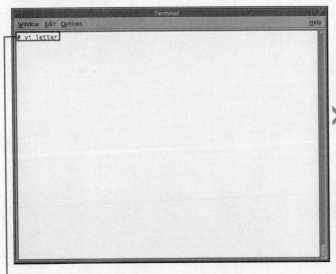

1 In a UNIX Terminal, open a file by typing **vi** at the prompt, then typing the file name.

2 Press Enter.

■ The file's text appears. The cursor always starts at the beginning of the document's first line.

Extra

Undoing substitution or replacement commands

Press the Escape key to ensure you're in Command mode, then type **u**. The Undo command works equally well with any replacement, insertion, deletion, or substitution command. If the error is extremely serious, you can exit vi without saving, then reopen your document and begin again.

Deleting text while I'm in Insert mode

You can delete characters, but you can't perform deletion functions by the word or line. When you're in Insert mode, the Delete and Backspace keys work like any other word processor.

Differences between Replace, Substitution, and Insert

There is no difference. It's a term that vi uses to distinguish one form of text manipulation over another.

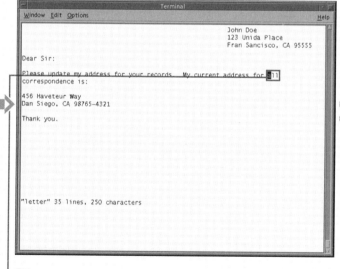

3 Move the cursor to the beginning of the word to be replaced.

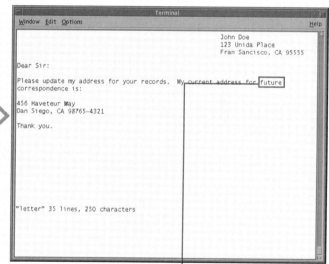

4 Type **R** and then type the replacement word.

■ If you're used to other text editors, R is similar to Insert in that it writes over old text without adding new spaces.

COPY AND PASTE TEXT

You can cut and paste words, paragraphs, and even whole pages of text in vi with the `cut` command, then paste them into a different part of your document. When you cut text in the UNIX CDE environment, it doesn't disappear as if it has been deleted, nor does it appear in a separate screen.

In fact, the text is placed into what's called a *text buffer,* which is not visible on screen. If you're familiar with Microsoft Windows editors, this buffer is also called the Clipboard.

(Unlike the Windows Clipboard, however, UNIX won't ask you if you want to do anything with text in the buffer when you exit vi.)

When you paste your cut text back into the document, note that the location of the paste is dependent on the location of your cursor. Be sure to move your cursor exactly where you want to place the text. After you paste the text back into the document, the buffer is then free to perform a second cut-and-paste job.

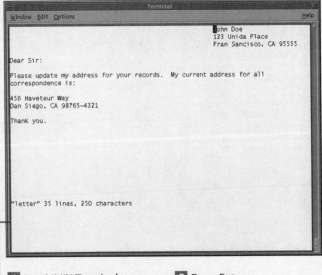

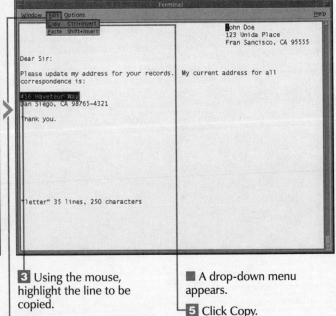

1 In a UNIX Terminal, open a file by typing **vi** at the prompt, then typing the file name.

2 Press Enter.

■ The file's text appears. The cursor always starts at the beginning of the document's first line.

3 Using the mouse, highlight the line to be copied.

4 Next, click Edit from the top of the Terminal window.

■ A drop-down menu appears.

5 Click Copy.

Extra

Cutting and pasting with the mouse

Another option is to remotely log into your UNIX machine from a Microsoft Windows machine. UNIX operates in a DOS prompt window on your screen, which has the Edit drop-down menu.

Copying and pasting with the CDE (Common Desktop Environment) as my desktop GUI

You can do this. However, different desktop environments, such as KDE, Motif, and GNOME (if you're using Linux), may have slightly different menus and commands.

Copying and pasting without a GUI-type interface, such as CDE (Common Desktop Environment)

Type **man yank** at the command prompt and press Enter. This gives you information on the yank command, which is the only way you can copy and paste on the command line without a GUI window.

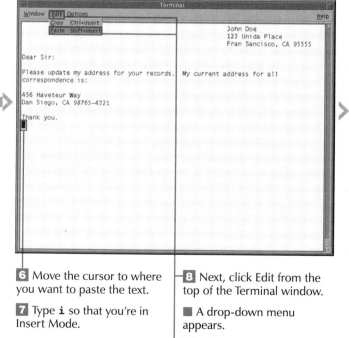

6 Move the cursor to where you want to paste the text.

7 Type **i** so that you're in Insert Mode.

8 Next, click Edit from the top of the Terminal window.

■ A drop-down menu appears.

9 Choose Paste.

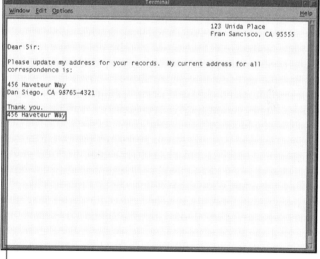

■ The vi editor pastes the text in the new location.

SAVE FILES

You can save your document in vi to work on later. When you finish in vi, you will be inside the open document. You use a different command to quit. You can't exit a document and still remain in a blank vi text document. This is unlike Microsoft Word, where you can exit from a document while remaining in the Word program.

As a general rule, you should save a document at regular intervals to prevent loss of data should there be a loss of power or another accident. Unlike Microsoft Word, for example, the vi editor does not have an Auto Save feature.

Also, vi won't ask you if you want to save changes before you quit. Instead, vi will not let you quit if you've edited a file at all. To bypass this, you must either save or perform a *force quit* (which is covered in "Force Quit and Save" later in this chapter).

SAVE FILES

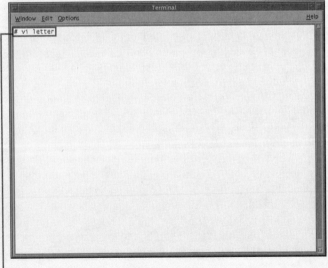

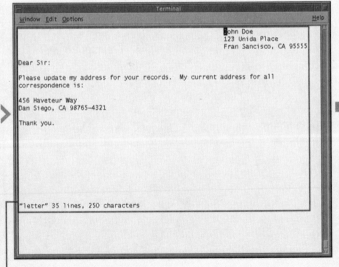

1 In a UNIX Terminal, open a file by typing **vi** at the prompt, then typing the file name.

2 Press Enter.

■ The file's text appears. The cursor always starts at the beginning of the document's first line.

Apply It

Saving a File with a Different File Name

If you're working on a file that already has a file name, you can save it under a different file name in vi from the :w command. Press Escape to enter Command mode, then type the following:

:w <new filename>

Note, however, that you can't save a file with multiple names from the :w command. For example, if you try to save the file under two separate names at the same time, with the following command:

:w <new filename1> <new filename2>

vi will refuse to complete this command, and instead return:

Only one filename allowed.

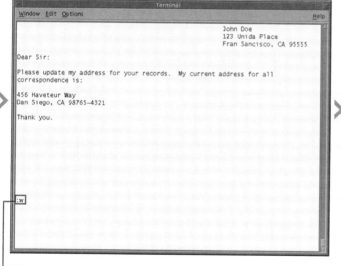

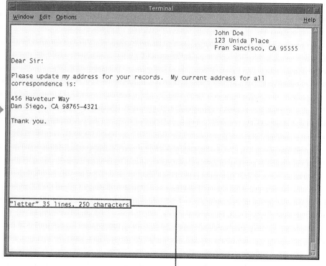

3 Press the Esc key to make sure you're in Command mode, then type **:w**.

4 Press Enter to save the file.

■ Note that the file's statistics are updated and displayed at the base of the screen.

EXIT VI

When you've finished working in vi, you should exit the vi editor without closing the terminal window. The following figures illustrate the proper method of entering the Command mode and using the : q command.

By contrast, there are several ways you shouldn't exit the vi editor. For example, if you are working with vi inside of a Terminal window on the CDE desktop or other environment, you shouldn't simply close the Terminal window. Neither should you shut down or turn off the UNIX machine until you have exited from the vi editor properly. Failing to exit vi in the correct manner and opting for one of the other methods may result in the corruption of your file or data.

Note that if you make a change to the file and try to simply quit, vi warns you that you haven't saved since you made your last changes. To bypass this, see "Quit and Save" in the following section.

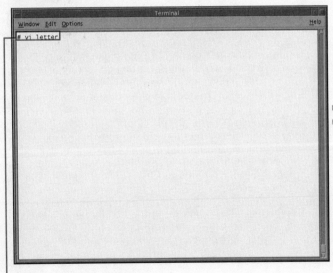

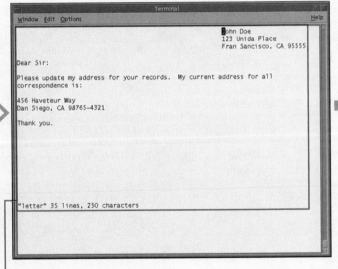

1 In a UNIX Terminal, open a file by typing **vi** at the prompt, then typing the file name.

2 Press Enter.

■ The file's text appears. The cursor always starts at the beginning of the document's first line.

Apply It

Additional Ways of Exiting vi

You can also exit vi without closing the terminal window by pressing Esc to ensure that you're in Command Mode, then typing either of the following and pressing Enter:

`:exit`

`:quit`

The reason these methods aren't as useful as typing `:q` is that you can't use the `w` command together with `exit` or `quit` to Save and Quit together.

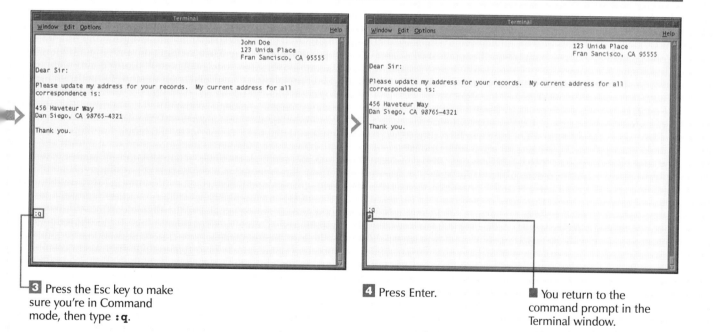

3 Press the Esc key to make sure you're in Command mode, then type **:q**.

4 Press Enter.

■ You return to the command prompt in the Terminal window.

QUIT AND SAVE

You can quit and save a document at the exact same time in the vi editor. This is a handy technique to use when you've made significant changes to a document, and you're ready to exit vi to return to the Terminal command prompt.

Quitting and saving take place in vi's Command mode. If you've just finished making a large number of changes to a document, and you're unable to quit and save,

first check to see if you are actually in Command mode. After spending a great deal of time in Insert mode, it's easy to forget that you must switch back to Command mode to save what you've done.

It's also worth checking a document one last time before you quit and save. This is because the undo command doesn't work on the save function and if it did, it's doubtful you could use the undo command after you exit vi.

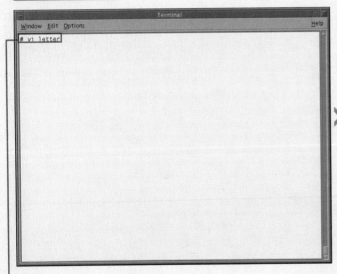

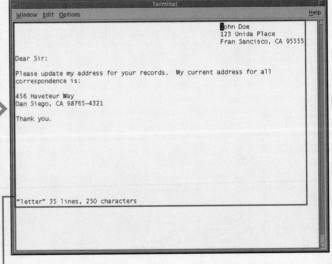

1 In a UNIX Terminal, open a file by typing **vi** at the prompt, then typing the file name.

2 Press Enter.

■ The file's text appears. The cursor always starts at the beginning of the document's first line.

Apply It

Using :qw instead of :wq

Although the w (write) and q (quit) commands are often used together, they can't be used out of order. This is because vi recognizes both the w and q as separate commands. Therefore, the program understands writing (saving), then exiting. It makes no sense to exit and then try to save a document, so if you press the Escape key to get into Command mode, then type the following and press Enter:

:wq

vi complains:

```
Not an editor command
```

You remain in Command mode, but you neither save nor quit the program.

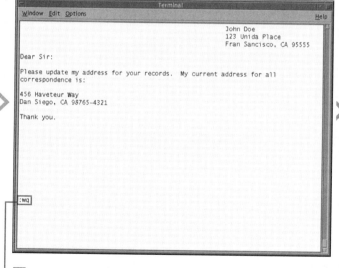

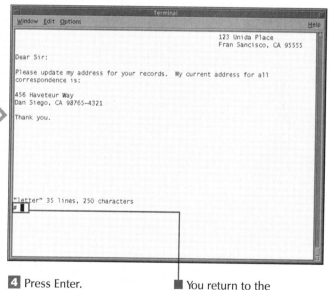

3 Press the Esc key to make sure you're in Command mode, then type :**wq**.

4 Press Enter.

■ You return to the command prompt in the Terminal window.

FORCE QUIT AND SAVE

Y ou can *force* the vi editor to quit, save, or
do a combination of both commands.
This is a very useful tool to have at your
fingertips, because it both lets you impose
your will on a reluctant editor and also helps
prevent you from making mistakes.

Although the first concept may come to mind
from the `force` command, the second doesn't
seem as straightforward. However, the force
option is most commonly used when trying to
avoid an error.

For example, if you just want to read through a
file and you accidentally end up inserting some
characters into it, how can you quit vi without
having to save the changes? Instead of
laboriously deleting the extra, unwanted
characters, you can *force* vi to ignore the
warning that you haven't saved since your last
changes, and then exit.

FORCE QUIT AND SAVE

1 In a UNIX Terminal, open
a file by typing **vi** at the
prompt, then typing the file
name.

2 Press Enter.

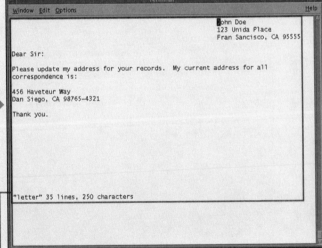

■ The file's text appears. The
cursor always starts at the
beginning of the document's
first line.

Extra

When a forced write doesn't work on certain text documents

There are two possibilities. First, even a forced write won't work on a file with no write permissions, as described in Chapter 4. Second, you may not be the owner of this file. As I discuss in Chapter 4, you are barred from *writing* to documents that you do not own.

Using a *force write and quit* on certain files, even when I am logged in as the root administrator account

Some systems require this as an extra safeguard against accidental editing. Because adding in extra characters in a major file, such

as /etc/password, can disable the system, this essentially makes you look a second time at the file to make absolutely sure that you want to save your latest changes.

Calling the exclamation point a *bang*

The short answer is that it's traditional. Also, it's easier to say and avoids confusion.

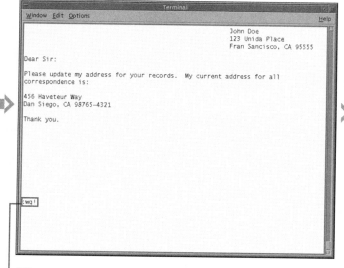

3 Press the Esc key to make sure you're in Command mode and type **:wq!**.

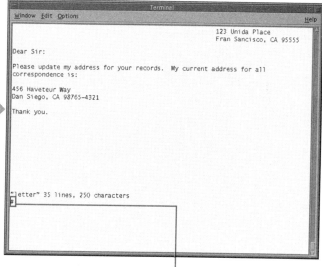

4 Press Enter.

■ You return to the command prompt in the Terminal window.

DISPLAYING THE TEXT FILE WITH cat

Y ou see the entire contents of a file without editing it or entering the vi editor by using the `cat` command. `Cat` is short for the term *concatenate*, which is itself a fancy way of saying that the information in the file is joined to the display for your easy viewing. The syntax for cat is simply `cat <file name>`. By default, cat sends the information in a file directly to the screen. In UNIX, this is also called *standard output*.

Cat is useful for taking a quick glance at short text files or other small UNIX files. Cat is also useful when you want to send the information in a file to a second UNIX command for further processing.

Finally, cat also shows you how long a file is. When cat is used with the `@ndn` option, each line in the file is labeled with a number. The number on the last line tells you how many lines the file has in total.

DISPLAYING THE TEXT FILE WITH CAT

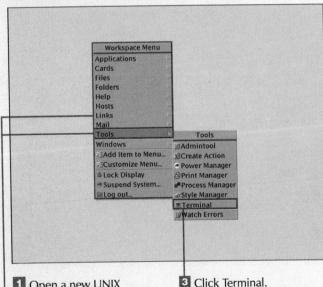

1 Open a new UNIX terminal by right-clicking anywhere on the open desktop.

■ A pop-up menu appears.

2 Choose Tools.

3 Click Terminal.

■ After you select Terminal, the pop-up menu disappears and a new Terminal window appears on the desktop.

4 To see the contents of the file, type **cat** and the name of the file (here, `quote`) at the command prompt.

5 Press Enter.

Extra

Counting the number of lines in the file when there are a lot of blank lines mixed in the file

Add the command option @ndb to the command when you enter it in. The complete command string looks like cat @ndb <filename>.

How cat moves text to other commands

Cat's main purpose is to send the contents of a file to an area. The default area is your screen, which is also known as *standard output*. However, cat can send information to other commands such as *pipe* and *grep*, which I discuss in Chapter 7.

If your file is very long, consider viewing only a part of it. You do this by using the head or tail commands, which I discuss later in this chapter.

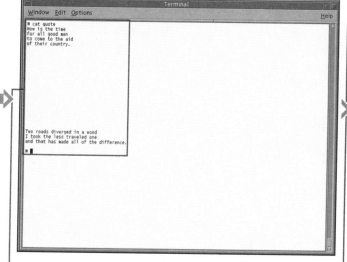

■ The entire contents of the file display.

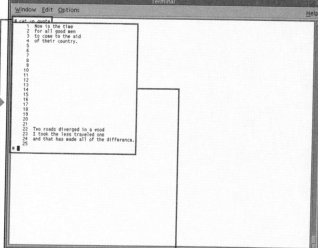

■ Alternatively, if you want to see the file with line numbers, type cat -n and the name of the file, then press Enter. To see the quote file with line numbers, you would type cat -dn quote.

■ The quote file results appear as follows: File quote has a total of 25 lines.

VIEWING THE START OF A FILE

Y ou're able to see the beginning lines of any file with the *head* command. Head, short for *header*, displays the first ten lines of a given file by default. The command syntax for using the head command is simply head <file name>. You also specify how many lines from the top of the file appear for access to more data from the file. To do this, use the @ndn command option.

Head is useful in a way similar to the cat command for a quick glance at short text files or other small UNIX files. Head is especially helpful when there are a large number of files in a directory and the file names aren't easy to remember.

VIEWING THE START OF A FILE

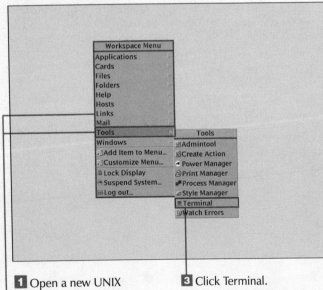

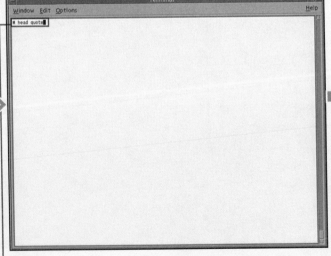

■ Open a new UNIX terminal by right-clicking anywhere on the open desktop.

■ A pop-up menu appears.

■ Choose Tools.

■ Click Terminal.

■ After you select Terminal, the pop-up menu disappears and a new Terminal window appears on the desktop.

■ To see the first 10 lines of a file, type **head** and the name of the file at the command prompt.

■ For example, to see the first 10 lines of a file called quote, type head quote at the command prompt.

■ Press Enter.

Apply It

Using head -v

When head is used with the -v option, the command executes in *verbose* mode. The verbose, or *more detailed* mode for head will print out the name of the file at the start of the display, followed by the first 10 lines of the file.

```
==> <file> <==
Text line 1
Text line 2
Text line 3
Text line 4...
```

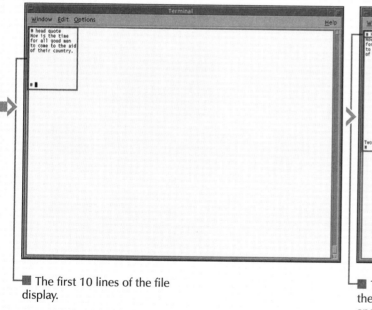

■ The first 10 lines of the file display.

■ To see the first 22 lines in the file, type **head -n 22** and the name of the file, then press Enter.

■ The results appear on the screen below the command line.

VIEWING THE END OF A FILE

You see the ending lines of any file with the *tail* command. `Tail` is short for *tailing* because one relatively sophisticated variation of the tail command allows a UNIX network administrator to continuously track a file that logs UNIX activity.

As with the `head` command, the last ten lines of any given file appear by default. The command syntax for using the head command is simply `tail <file name>`. You also

specify how many lines from the bottom of the file appear for access to more data from the file. To do this, use the +n command option.

`Tail` is most useful when you want to take a quick glance at the latest entry in a file or a list. For example, if you're viewing a file that gets added to every day, you may be interested only in the latest addition, which is normally placed at the end of a file.

VIEWING THE END OF A FILE

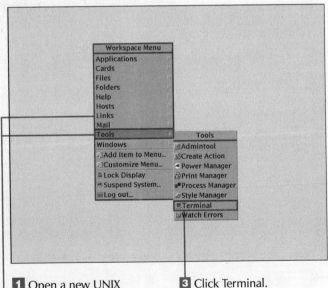

1 Open a new UNIX terminal by right-clicking anywhere on the open desktop.

■ A pop-up menu appears.

2 Choose Tools.

3 Click Terminal.

■ After you select Terminal, the pop-up menu disappears and a new Terminal window appears on the desktop.

4 To see the last 10 lines of a file, type **tail** and the name of the file at the command prompt.

■ For example, to see the first 10 lines of a file called `quote`, type `tail quote` at the command prompt.

5 Press Enter.

Apply It

Using tail -v

When tail is used with the -v option, the command executes in verbose mode. The verbose, more detailed mode for tail will print out the name of the file at the start of the display, followed by the last 10 lines of the file.

```
tail -v <file>
==> <file> <==
Text line 97
Text line 98
Text line 99
Text line 100...
```

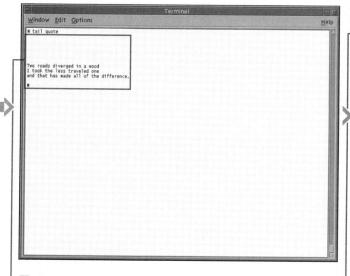

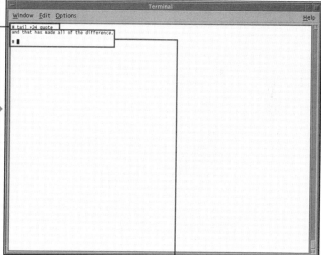

■ The last 10 lines of the file display.

■ To see the last two lines in a 25-line file, type **tail +n 24** and the name of the file, then press Enter.

■ The results appear on the screen below the command line.

COMPARING TEXT FILES WITH cmp

You compare the contents of two text files, no matter how similar they are, by using the cmp command. cmp, which is short for *compare*, lets you determine where one file differs in content from another. The syntax for the cmp command is as follows: cmp <file1> <file2>.

When the cmp command finds a discrepancy between two files, it gives the location of the difference in terms of number of characters from the start of the file, and the line number

the difference occurs on. So, if the first character on the first line in a document is the location of a difference, cmp reports that the location is char 1 (first character), line 1.

If you're dealing with slightly larger files, you may not be sure where line 56 out of 100 really is. In these cases, it's helpful to use the cat command to display the file, complete with line numbers, to see the differences between the files' contents.

COMPARING TEXT FILES WITH CMP

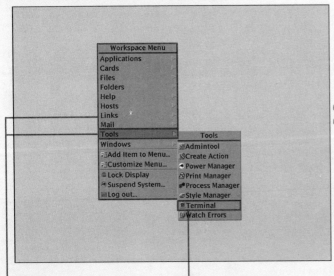

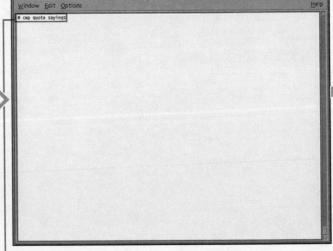

1 Open a new UNIX terminal by right-clicking anywhere on the open desktop.

■ A pop-up menu appears.

2 Choose Tools.

3 Click Terminal.

■ After you select Terminal, the pop-up menu disappears and a new Terminal window appears on the desktop.

4 Type **cmp** followed by the names of the two files you want to compare at the command prompt.

■ For example, to compare the contents of files quote and sayings, type cmp quote sayings.

5 Press Enter.

Extra

Counting characters with cmp

cmp always starts at 1. Therefore, the second character in a line is number 2, the third number 3, and so on.

cmp counts spaces as characters

A space, although nothing is printed on screen, is a keyboard stroke, which UNIX reads as a form of input. Seven spaces on a line, followed by one letter, causes cmp to count the letter as the eighth character.

When two files are absolutely identical in every way

cmp has no differences to report back to you. In true UNIX fashion, cmp doesn't give you back a message saying These files are the same. Instead, the cmp command is silent, and returns you back to the command prompt for further input.

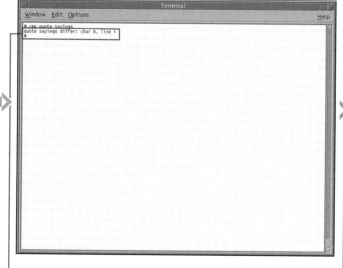

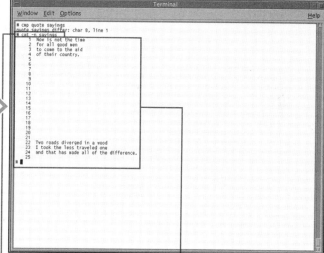

■ The results appear on the screen below the command line.

■ You can see the sayings file by typing cat -n sayings and pressing Enter.

■ You can see that the 8th character in line 1 is different, because the word "not" is used, where in quote it is not.

LOCATE PROCESSES

Yes ou locate processes that are currently running on your system with the process search command, ps . The syntax for process searching is ps <command options>.

A useful command option that works with ps to get a snapshot of what's running on the system is ps -e. The -e option enables ps to find and display every process currently running on the machine. From left to right, the -e option shows you the PID (Process ID Number, which you use to terminate a process); the TTY, or location where the

process was started; the TIME the process was started; and the CMD, or actual command name of the process.

The most popular command option is -ef, which gives more information than -e alone. The extra information that is useful is the UID, or User Identification, which tells you which user account started a given process, and the STIME, which gives the date that the process was started.

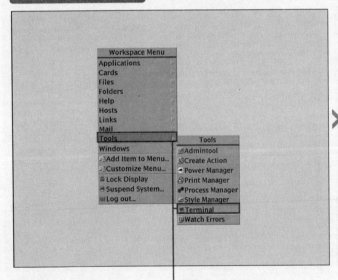

1 Open a new UNIX Terminal by right-clicking anywhere on the open desktop.

■ A pop-up menu appears.

2 Choose Tools.

3 Click Terminal.

■ A new Terminal window appears on the desktop.

4 At the command prompt, type **ps -e**.

5 Press Enter.

Apply It

Using the -1 option

When the ps command is used with the -1 option, the command lists the processes found in *long* mode. This mode will print out complete information on each process, which usually results in the information scrolling off the screen to be printed on the next line. For this reason, it is rarely used. To use this option, type the following at the command line and press Enter.

```
ps -elf
```

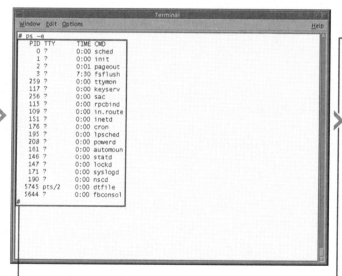

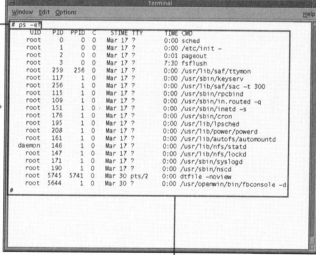

6 Every process currently running on the machine appears.

Note: The TIME for these processes is 0:00. This is because most of these are system processes that started when you first powered up the machine.

7 For more detailed information, type **ps -ef** at the command prompt,

8 Press Enter.

■ Every process currently running on the system appears.

Note: The UID for most of these processes is root. This is because all system processes are owned by the root administrator account.

USE THE PIPE SYMBOL

You transfer the output of one UNIX command to another with the help of a UNIX shell utility called *pipe*. For example, pipe is normally used to send the output of the `ls` or `cat` command into a new text file.

Pipe actually isn't a UNIX command, so you don't find it in a listing of UNIX commands. Instead, pipe is a utility that automatically comes with the UNIX shell, or the operating environment you enter into when you use the UNIX Terminal.

As a consequence, you don't type `pipe` to use the utility. Instead, you type the pipe symbol directly from the keyboard. The pipe symbol looks like this: | You normally find the symbol on the backslash key, located above the Enter key.

To type this symbol, make sure that you hold down the Shift key while you press the backslash key. Note that simply using the Caps Lock function will not let you type a pipe — you must create it by pressing Shift+\ to create the symbol.

USE THE PIPE SYMBOL

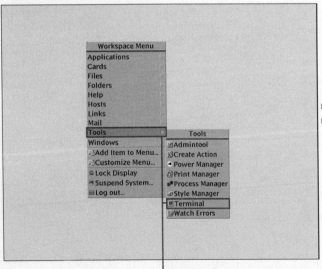

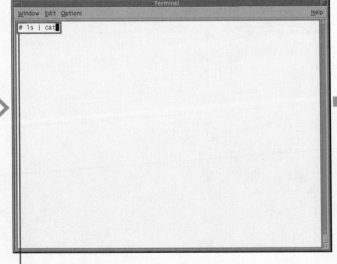

1 Open a new UNIX Terminal by right-clicking anywhere on the open desktop.

■ A pop-up menu appears.

2 Choose Tools.

3 Click Terminal.

■ A new Terminal window appears on the desktop.

4 Type **ls | cat** at the command prompt.

5 Press Enter.

Extra

Output through broken pipes

A misused pipe is sometimes called a "broken" pipe by UNIX wonks. This is a good visual image, but it's misleading. When a pipe symbol is misused, no data is lost because no data is sent anywhere.

Fixing a broken pipe

First, make sure that you're not accidentally trying to connect a command and a file. If you're using two commands, make sure that one isn't a text-creating command like vi. Barring those difficulties, make sure that both commands are functioning properly.

Placing spaces around the pipe symbol

Type either `ls | listings` or `ls|listings`. Both work. But `ls | listings` is easier to read.

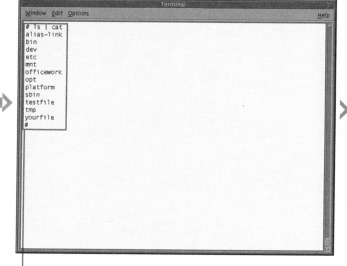

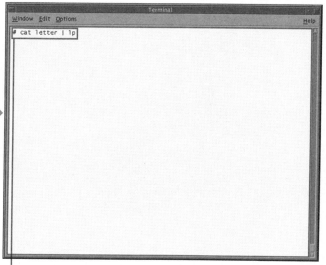

■ In the result, note that while `ls` by itself lists in rows, pipe funneled the information from `ls` to `cat`, allowing the information to be printed in column form.

6 Alternatively, you can send the output of `cat letter` directly to the `lp`, or print command by typing **cat letter | lp** at the command prompt.

7 Press Enter.

SEARCH WITH THE grep COMMAND

You can find information, text, numbers, or expressions within a file in UNIX. This is done with the grep command and its command options. Grep stands for *get regular expression*, which is a very descriptive way of saying what this command really does.

The command format for grep is: grep <searched-for pattern> <file to be searched>. For instance, if you want to find the pattern "the" in a text file called

thx1138, you use the command grep the thx1138. Similarly, you can find the numeric pattern "123" in the file, or even a combination of text and numbers, such as "abc123."

Grepping for patterns or words is the easiest, most convenient way to locate a phrase or character pattern from a long text file. For this example, I use grep on the quote file from Chapter 5.

SEARCH WITH THE GREP COMMAND

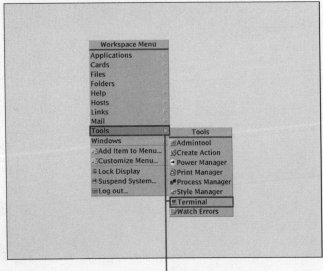
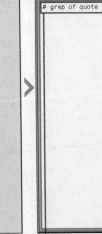

■1 Right-click anywhere on the open desktop.

■ A pop-up menu appears.

■2 Choose Tools.

■3 Click Terminal.

■ A new Terminal window appears on the desktop.

■4 To search for the occurrences of the test pattern "of" in the file quote, type **grep of quote** at the command prompt.

■5 Press Enter.

Extra

Searching for upper- and lower-case characters

`grep` searches for the exact matching text pattern. Searching for "The" finds "Their" or "Themselves" but not "their" or "therein." To ignore case sensitivity, use `grep -i <searched-for pattern>`.

Counting how many times a pattern appears in a file

You use the `-c` option with `grep`. With the preceding example, if you want to count the lines that don't use "A," you type `grep -vc A <filename>`.

Finding lines that don't match

This is a common use of `grep`. If you have a document that has 10,000 lines, and all but five start with "A," you find what you want by using the **-v** option, which inserts the search.

`grep -v A <filename>` gives you all the lines that don't start with "A."

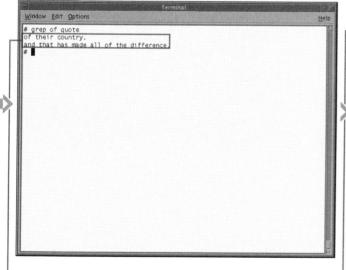

■ The two lines in the file that contain "of" appear.

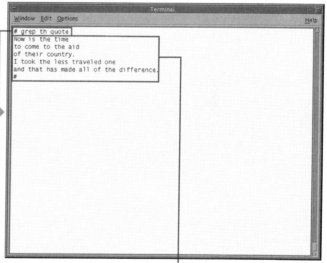

6 Similarly to search for the text pattern "th", type **grep th quote** at the command prompt.

7 Press Enter.

Note: `grep` *returns not only the "th" in "the", but also in "their" and "that." This is because* `grep` *is searching for all instances of the pattern "th".*

POWER SEARCHES

Y ou find specific UNIX processes that are currently running on your system by combining the ps and grep commands together with the pipe symbol. This triple combo of UNIX commands and symbols is one of the most powerful and useful in this operating system. That's because you can find processes by command name, process identification number, or — most commonly — by user name.

The command syntax for this combination always follows the same pattern: ps -ef | grep <search pattern>. Because the

grep command searches for either numeric or alphabetical patterns, you specify the pattern to be a user's name, the digit of the process identification number, or the command name.

Grep's ability to find patterns within longer text or number strings is a wonderful asset for you. For example, if you're searching for a process but you're not sure if it's called "telm," "telnet," or "telwm," tell grep to find "tel," and all three commands are found.

POWER SEARCHES

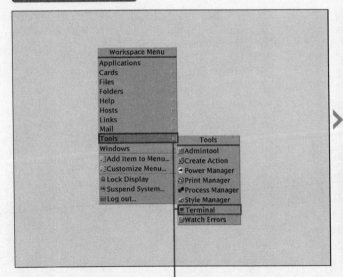

1 Open a new UNIX Terminal by right-clicking anywhere on the open desktop.

■ A pop-up menu appears.

2 Choose Tools.

3 Click Terminal.

■ A new Terminal window appears on the desktop.

4 Type the search command syntax and search pattern.

5 Press Enter.

Note: This example will search for all processes that were started by the user "james."

Extra

Variations between flavors of UNIX

The way the `ps` command works depends on the flavor or brand of UNIX you're using. Remember that the version of UNIX you're using can be Solaris, SunOS, HP-UX, Xenix, or Irix. In some of these different types of UNIX, the command options may be different. Some machines use `ps -aef` while others use `ps -aux` to get results.

Identifying whether `grep` is running

Usually, you see the `grep` process as part of a `ps` readout. That's because `ps` is taking a snapshot of what you're running as it works. If the `grep` command happens to finish before `ps` finishes, you don't see it in the list. Either way, it doesn't affect your process search.

■ UNIX returns the matches for the search. In this case, UNIX returns.

Note: The one process currently running that user account james has started.

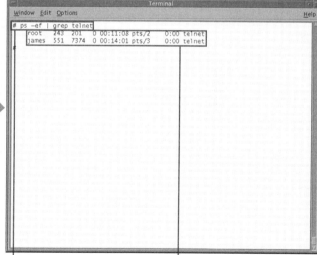

6 Similarly, to search for all the currently running processes called "telnet," type **ps -def | grep telnet**, then press Enter.

■ UNIX returns two telnet processes, one run by james, the other by the root account.

VIEW RUNNING PROCESSES WITH PROCESS MANAGER

You see all of the currently running processes on your UNIX system in the CDE (Common Desktop Environment) desktop if you stick to a graphics interface. One utility that fills the same function as the ps command on the CDE desktop is the Process Manager tool.

The Process Manager is a sort of one-stop shop for administering your UNIX processes. It lets you see, find, display, and stop currently running processes. However, it isn't available on all UNIX systems, so it's still worthwhile to learn how to perform the same functions as Process Manager in the UNIX Terminal window at the command prompt.

Remember, you can start the Process Manager by right-clicking on the desktop and choosing Tools, then Process Manager, or you can open the utility as I describe in the following steps.

VIEW RUNNING PROCESSES WITH PROCESS

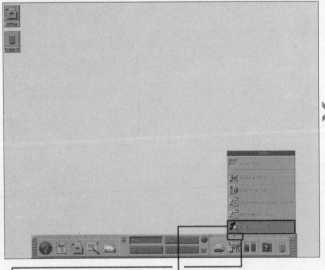
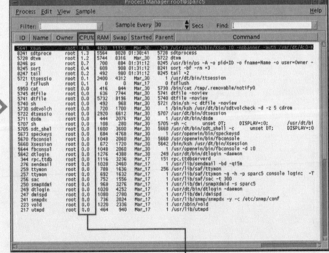

1 Click the arrow above the Tools button on the Main Toolbar.

Note: For a quick review of the Toolbar buttons, see Chapter 1.

2 Choose Find Process from the pop-up menu.

■ The Process Manager window appears.

■ By default, processes are listed in order of CPU percentage (the higher the percentage, the harder the computer is working on this process).

Extra

Clicking on the ID button to list processes by process ID number

This is a quirk of the creators of the Process Manager tool. ID is really the same thing as the PID, but it's labeled differently.

Listing a process owned by a particular user as in the ps -ef | grep command string

Click the Owner button, which is third from the left in the line of the Process Manager buttons.

Setting the Process Manager to check the number of processes running every minute

By default, if you leave the Process Manager running by itself, it updates its findings every 30 seconds. By clicking on the up or down arrows next to the Sample Every field, you either increase or decrease the number of seconds the update occurs.

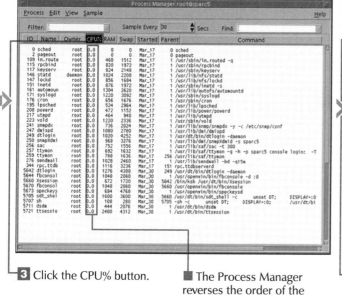

3 Click the CPU% button.

■ The Process Manager reverses the order of the listed processes so that the process taking up the smallest CPU percentage appears first.

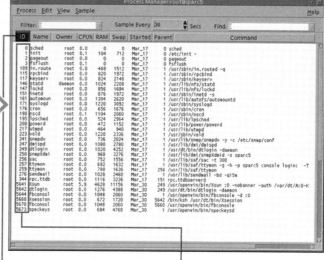

4 Click the ID button.

■ The processes list by Process ID Number.

SEARCH FOR SPECIFIC PROCESSES

The Process Manager is an extremely useful tool to have on your computer when you're trying to determine whether a particular process is dead, running, or spawning out of control.

Normally, UNIX has a large number of background or *system* processes that run more or less continuously. These processes are absolutely vital to keep your UNIX operating system functioning properly. Of course, when you're trying to find one process, this becomes troublesome when the sheer number of processes makes it difficult to find the one you need.

In fact, if you have several different users on the same system running different processes, the task becomes the equivalent of finding the needle in the haystack. Luckily, the Process Manager can help you get around this, much as using the `ps` and `grep` commands together did.

SEARCH FOR SPECIFIC PROCESSES

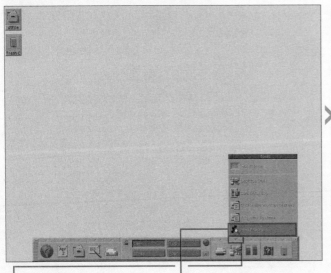

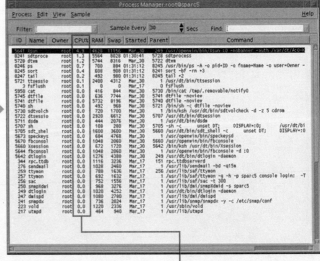

1 Click the arrow above the Tools button on the Main Toolbar.

2 Choose Find Process from the pop-up menu.

■ The Process Manager window appears.

■ By default, processes are listed in order of CPU percentage (the higher the percentage, the harder the computer is working on this process).

Apply It

Using the Filter field

When using the Filter field to find a particular process, you can also use the UNIX wildcard character * to find a range of processes. For example, to find all processes that begin with *tail*, you type the following in the Filter text field on the upper left of the screen.

```
tail*
```

This will give you processes named "tail," "tailed," or "tailor" (assuming processes with these names are running).

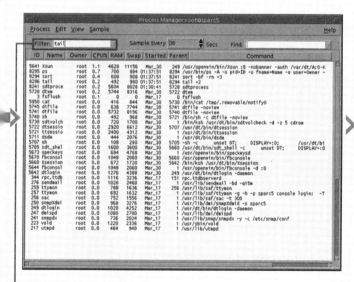

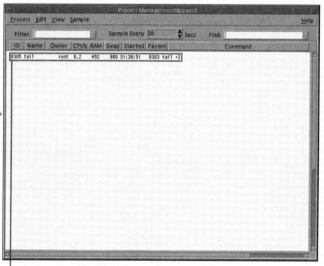

■3 To search for a particular process, such as the `tail` process, type **tail** in the Filter text field on the upper left of the screen.

■4 Press Enter.

■ The `tail` processes are listed in the Process Manager window. (Here, there is only one.)

STORE PROCESS MANAGER OUTPUT

You store the output of the Process Manager utility by directing the program to send its snapshots of the activity on your system to a log file. A log file is a generic term in UNIX to describe any file that is used to store output from a given command or program.

Often, the data stored in the log file is literally in the form of a "log." That is, the data contains entries from a program's output that list both the activity of the program and the

time or date the action took place. This is a crucial tool for an administrator who is trying to determine the cause of a particular problem — he or she can see a log file and see what activity at what time corresponds with the problem.

The disadvantage of a log file is that log files take up space. Furthermore, log files that are left unchecked can continue growing as more and more data are stored inside of them, eventually filling up the disk partition they reside on.

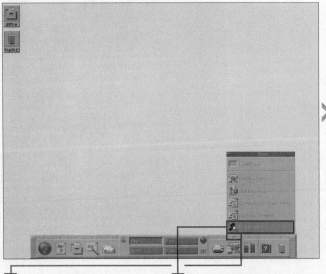

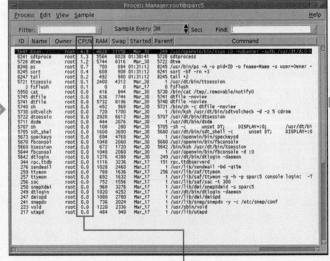

1 Click the arrow above the Tools button on the Main Toolbar.

2 Choose Find Process from the pop-up menu.

■ The Process Manager window appears.

■ By default, processes are listed in order of CPU percentage (the higher the percentage, the harder the computer is working on this process).

Extra

The best location for storing log files

Although you can store log files at any location on your UNIX system, such as your home directory, the root directory, or the /etc directory, you're best off saving log files to the /tmp, or *temporary* directory. This helps prevent problems caused if your disk partition runs out of space because the log file has grown too large.

Using the /tmp directory

The /tmp directory can fill up, but there are two advantages. First, the /tmp directory is usually on its own partition, so problems isolated on that part of the disk cause fewer difficulties elsewhere. Second, the /tmp directory is automatically emptied every time the system is rebooted, helping to prevent buildup.

Preventing a disk partition from filling up and causing problems

You should delete the log file from time to time unless you're trying to spot problems. Also, change the Sample Every setting from 30 seconds to 60 seconds.

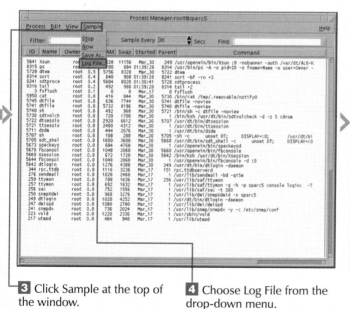

3 Click Sample at the top of the window.

4 Choose Log File from the drop-down menu.

■ The Process Manager–Log File window appears.

5 Type a name for your log file, such as **systemlogs**, in the Enter File Name text field.

6 Press Enter.

■ From here on, the output of the Process Manager is stored in the **systemlogs** file.

119

UNIX

RUN A PROCESS IN THE BACKGROUND

You can run a process in the background from the UNIX command prompt by adding an ampersand, or "&," after the process name. Often, when a process is run right off of the command prompt, it needs to continue running for the duration of the task. If this is the case, then until the task finishes or you stop the process, you don't return to the command prompt. That means you can't run any other commands in the Terminal window.

For example, if you start the Netscape Web browser from the command prompt, you can't run any other commands until you quit Netscape. This is because until Netscape stops, the Terminal doesn't display a command prompt to enter commands. By specifying that a command needs to run in the background, you essentially free up the command line while the process is still running.

RUN A PROCESS IN THE BACKGROUND

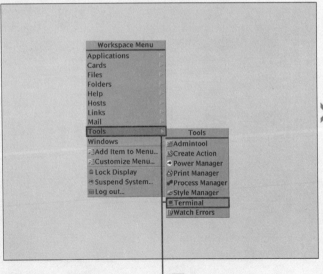

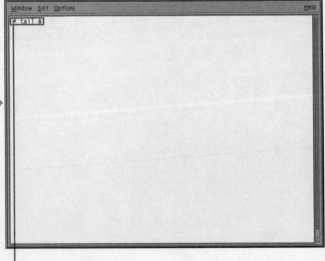

■1 Open a new UNIX Terminal by right-clicking anywhere on the open desktop.

■ A pop-up menu appears.

■2 Choose Tools.

■3 Click Terminal.

■ A new Terminal window appears on the desktop.

■4 If you want to run a command called tail in the background, type **tail &** at the command prompt.

■5 Press Enter.

Extra

Processes running in the background at one time

Theoretically, there is no limit to the number of processes that run at any one time. However, the practical matter of slowing your UNIX system if you end up running two or three dozen processes at the same time limits this.

Stopping processes that are running in the background

If you have the process ID number of the process from the Process Manager or the `ps` command in the Terminal window, you can stop the process with the `kill` command, which I describe later in this chapter.

Processes that can't run in the background

Certain commands, such as `cat`, print out the contents of the file right to the screen. Backgrounding any command that puts its output directly to the screen will not work.

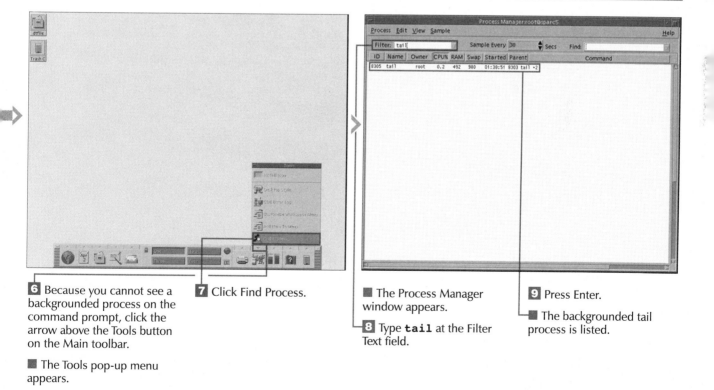

6 Because you cannot see a backgrounded process on the command prompt, click the arrow above the Tools button on the Main toolbar.

■ The Tools pop-up menu appears.

7 Click Find Process.

■ The Process Manager window appears.

8 Type **tail** at the Filter Text field.

9 Press Enter.

■ The backgrounded tail process is listed.

REDIRECT OUTPUT

You redirect the output of a program, binary, or script in the UNIX operating system by using the arrow keys, < and >. These are also known as the *lesser than* and *greater than* signs. Redirection is superior to using the pipe shell utility, |, because it directs output from a program into a text file, while the pipe only lets you transfer information from one process into another.

The ability to direct output into a file gives you tremendous flexibility. This lets you isolate and read output from a program, such as a log file, at your leisure. If you're short on space in a particular area of your system, you shunt the data off to a remote location where space isn't in as high demand.

The format for redirection is normally `<program> <redirection sign> <output file>`.

REDIRECT OUTPUT

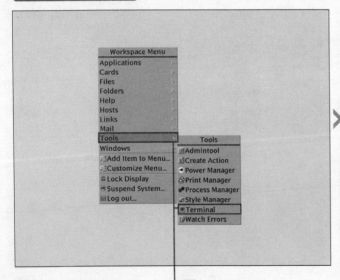

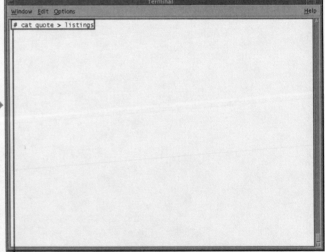

1 Open a new UNIX Terminal by right-clicking anywhere on the open desktop.

■ A pop-up menu appears.

2 Choose Tools.

3 Click Terminal.

■ A new Terminal window appears on the desktop.

4 To add the contents of the file quote, which was used in Chapter 5, to a new file, listings, type **cat quote > listings** at the command prompt.

5 Press Enter.

Apply It

Redirection of output to files in different locations

You also redirect the output of a command to a file in a different directory than the location where you're running the command. For example, to redirect the output of the file quote to a file in another area, you can use any of the following commands:

```
cat quote > /tmp/<filename>

cat quote > /var/tmp/<filename>

cat quote > /usr/bin/tmp/
testfile/<filename>
```

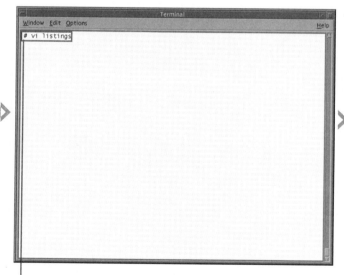

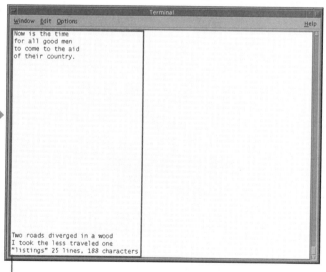

6 To check the results of this command string, view the contents of the file by typing **vi listings** at the command prompt.

7 Press Enter.

■ The contents of the file listings are shown in the vi editor to be identical to the contents of the file quote.

APPEND OUTPUT

You append the output of a program, binary, or script in the UNIX operating system by using the arrow keys to form the symbols, << and >>. Appending output into a file prevents you from accidentally erasing the former contents of a given file when you redirect data into the file.

Appending data into a file lets you isolate and read output from a program, such as a log file, at your leisure like a redirect command. The

difference is that the data that already exists at the destination file isn't overwritten.

Remember this if you're short on space in a particular area of your system: Appending, unlike redirecting, causes files to grow in size, which causes problems if the disk partition fills up.

The format for appending is normally `<program> <append sign> <output file>`.

APPEND OUTPUT

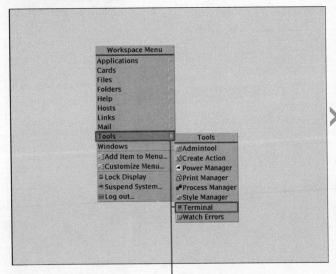

1 Open a new UNIX Terminal by right-clicking anywhere on the open desktop.

■ A pop-up menu appears.

2 Choose Tools.

3 Click Terminal.

■ A new Terminal window appears on the desktop.

4 Append the results of the `ls` (list) command to the file `listings` by typing **ls >> listings** at the command prompt.

5 Press Enter.

Extra

How much an append command enlarges a file

That depends entirely on the amount of output you're adding. The append command itself doesn't enlarge a file but adding 20 text pages to a file does.

Using redirection with ps command instead of a pipe

You can certainly redirect the output of the ps command to a file and then read the file, but it's cumbersome. You can't use redirect to send the output of ps directly through a grep command. Instead, you must use a separate grep command on the file where you directed the output.

Using redirection instead of a pipe with ps

In situations where you use a redirect, you're transferring data from a file to a command, or vice versa. Pipes are designed to separate information between separate commands.

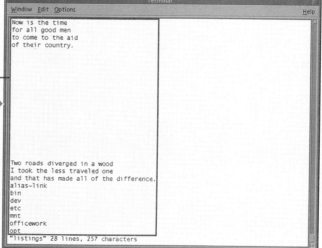

6 In order to check on the results of this command string, view the contents of the file by typing **vi listings** at the command prompt.

7 Press Enter.

■ The contents of the file listings are shown in the vi editor to contain the elements of the quote file, followed by the results of the ls command.

STOP PROGRAMS WITH `kill`

You can stop all programs in UNIX with the `kill` command. `kill` is really a signal that is sent to the operating system to terminate a given program that is operating. Although it sounds harsh, `kill` actually by default sends out a signal that tells the program to end only after it completes its standard exit procedure.

To kill a process, use the `ps` command or the Process Manager utility to get the PID, or

Process ID number. The correct syntax for the `kill` command is `kill <PID>`.

`kill` should be used only when a program *hangs*, or refuses to exit. A program is said to hang in UNIX if it malfunctions or is waiting for information relayed from a pipe or a secondary process. Hung processes just sit on the system without terminating, making them appropriate targets for the `kill` command.

STOP PROGRAMS WITH KILL

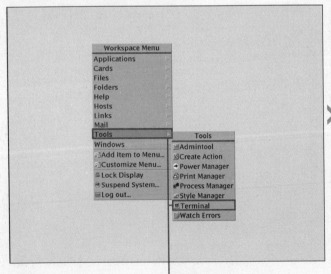

1 Open a new UNIX Terminal by right-clicking anywhere on the open desktop.

■ A pop-up menu appears.

2 Choose Tools.

3 Click Terminal.

■ A new Terminal window appears on the desktop.

4 For example, to kill a telnet command that user james is running, find the process by typing **ps —ef | grep james**.

5 Press Enter.

Extra

Using PIDs

`kill` is written specifically to use PIDs only. If it were otherwise, there would be serious problems on the UNIX system if you killed the job vi and all vi processes run by all other people were also killed.

Accidentally stopping the Unix session

By default, UNIX runs several background processes in its operating system. If you kill everything run by your name and you are logged in as root, for example, you terminate your UNIX session by accident.

Applying `kill` within a program

No problem. Because your kill command aims at a specific PID, if the program with that PID isn't running, the signal isn't received by anyone.

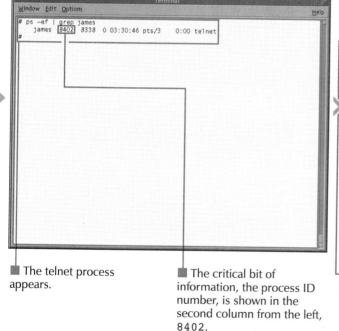

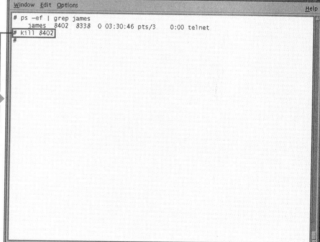

■ The telnet process appears.

■ The critical bit of information, the process ID number, is shown in the second column from the left, 8402.

◢ **6** To kill this process, type **kill 8402** at the command prompt.

7 Press Enter.

Note: You can check whether the process has been killed by running the ps *command a second time.*

STOP PERSISTENT PROGRAMS

You can stop programs that fail to respond to the initial `kill` command. In a small percentage of cases, a program doesn't respond to the `kill` command properly. It tends to happen more on a busy machine with dozens of different processes running. It can very well mean that the process is so busy and CPU time so limited that the process can't complete its exit cycle.

In this case, you still need the `kill` command, but with a special command option, `-9`. The `kill -9` command is the equal of the Force Quit in the Microsoft Windows world. No matter where the program is, in mid-command or near the end, the program terminates immediately. This may produce a core file, which you must delete.

STOP PERSISTENT PROGRAMS

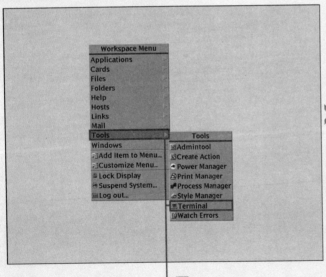

1 Open a new UNIX Terminal by right-clicking anywhere on the open desktop.

■ A pop-up menu appears.

2 Choose Tools.

3 Click Terminal.

■ A new Terminal window appears on the desktop.

4 For example, the `telnet` command that user james is running did not respond to the `kill` command, so find the process again by typing `ps -ef | grep james`.

5 Press Enter.

Extra

Choosing to use kill -9

`kill -9` should be used only in emergencies. When used on a program that is vital to your system, such as a print job, this can cause other programs to crash, such as the daemons that run the UNIX print queue.

Other side effects you encounter when you use kill -9 too often

Most likely, you run into problems running the process or program that you've given the kill -9 signal more than once. This is because without allowing the procedure to shut down properly, the utility or program may have become corrupted.

Inside the core file

A core file is a dump of all the half-processed data that the killed program handled when it crashed. Core files are usually incredibly large, so you must clean up as quickly as possible or run the risk of running out of space on your disk drive.

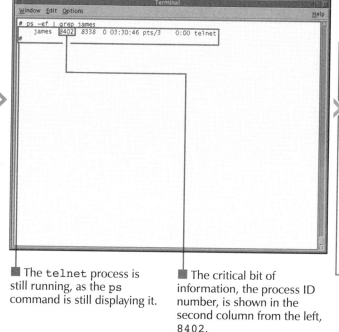

■ The `telnet` process is still running, as the `ps` command is still displaying it.

■ The critical bit of information, the process ID number, is shown in the second column from the left, 8402.

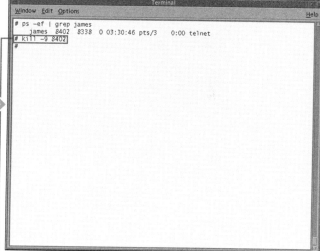

6 To kill this process for good, type **kill -9 8402** at the command prompt.

7 Press Enter.

Note: You can check whether the process has been killed by running the ps *command a second time.*

DETERMINING THE SHELL

You determine which shell you're using in UNIX by using the `echo` command to display your `$SHELL` system variable. The *shell* is the program that translates the commands you enter at the command prompt (or in the desktop) into instructions that the computer can comprehend. Because of this function, a shell is also sometimes called a *command interpreter*.

`Echo` displays your shell, because it simply plays back (*echoes*) what you ask it to show. By placing the $ symbol in front of `SHELL`, you're telling it to print out your preassigned shell setting, or system variable (more on this later on in this chapter).

For your purposes, the shell you use doesn't make too much of a difference, because the commands are standard fare. There are different shells in UNIX, such as the Bourne shell, C-Shell, and Korn shell, because programmers wanted special higher-level utilities or functions that the existing shells did not have.

DETERMINING THE SHELL

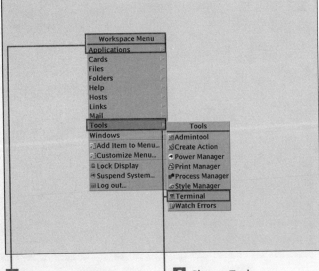

1 Open a new UNIX Terminal by right-clicking anywhere on the open desktop.

■ A pop-up menu appears.

2 Choose Tools.

3 Click Terminal.

■ A new Terminal window appears on the desktop.

4 Type **echo $SHELL** at the command prompt.

5 Press Enter.

Extra

Some intuitive options don't work

When you type `echo SHELL`, you're just telling the echo command to print out "SHELL" on the screen. It does this with commendable efficiency, but it doesn't tell you anything you can use.

Selecting command interpreter

If you ask ten different UNIX people this, you get ten different answers. This is because the higher-level tools that come with each type of command interpreter are useful to different people, such as administrators, programmers, and other specialized fields. Unless you're in (or planning to enter) one of these fields, you're best off sticking with your default command interpreter.

For many people, this is the `/sbin/sh`, or Bourne Shell. C-Shell, `/bin/csh`, is another popular choice. If you use Linux, the Bourne Again shell, `/bin/bash`, will likely be your default.

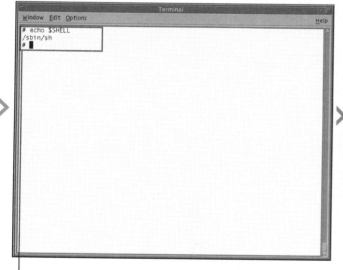

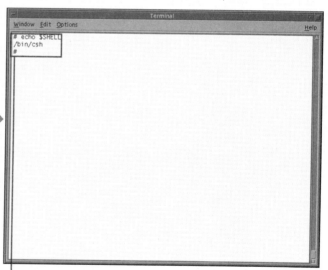

■ The shell you are using appears. The majority of the time, the shell that is your default is the ever popular Bourne shell, which is located in the `/sbin/sh` file.

6 Alternatively, if you're using a different shell, you'll get a slightly different result. For example, type **echo $SHELL** at the command prompt.

7 Press Enter.

STARTING A SHELL

Y ou can also start different shells, or command interpreters, from the command prompt if you want. You don't really have a practical need to do this unless you start working with more complex functions and commands that are shell-specific. (For example, the pipe symbol that I discuss in Chapter 7 exists in every shell that exists, and it works in an identical manner everywhere.) However, it's worthwhile to be familiar with this procedure.

You switch to different shells by typing the shell's name in at the command prompt. By "name" of the shell, you aren't going to be typing in Bourne, C-Shell, Korn, or Bourne Again. Instead, you use the command descriptors that you see when you show the shell in the `echo $SHELL` command.

So, Bourne is `sh`, C-Shell is `csh`, and Bourne Again is `bash`. You can also stack shells by going from the C-Shell, to Bourne, then to Korn, and so on. This procedure is called *nesting*. It isn't recommended as you can easily get confused about which shell you started in after a while.

STARTING A SHELL

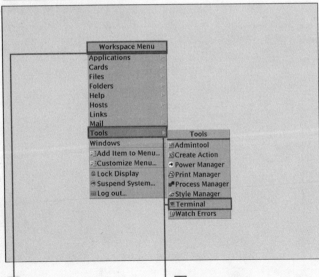

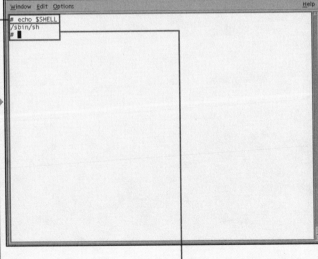

1 Open a new UNIX Terminal by right-clicking anywhere on the open desktop.

■ A pop-up menu appears.

2 Choose Tools.

3 Click Terminal.

■ A new Terminal window appears on the desktop.

4 Type **echo $SHELL** at the command prompt.

5 Press Enter.

■ Your default shell is the ever popular Bourne shell, which is located in the `/sbin/sh` file.

Extra

Some intuitive options don't work

When you type `echo SHELL`, you're just telling the echo command to print out "SHELL" on the screen. It does this with commendable efficiency, but it doesn't tell you anything you can use.

Selecting a command interpreter

If you ask ten different UNIX people this, you get ten different answers. This is because the higher-level tools that come with each type of command interpreter are useful to different people, such as administrators, programmers, and other specialized fields. Unless you're in (or planning to enter) one of these fields, you're best off sticking with your default command interpreter.

For many people, this is the `/sbin/sh`, or Bourne Shell. C-Shell, `/bin/csh`, is another popular choice. If you use Linux, the Bourne Again shell, `/bin/bash`, will likely be your default.

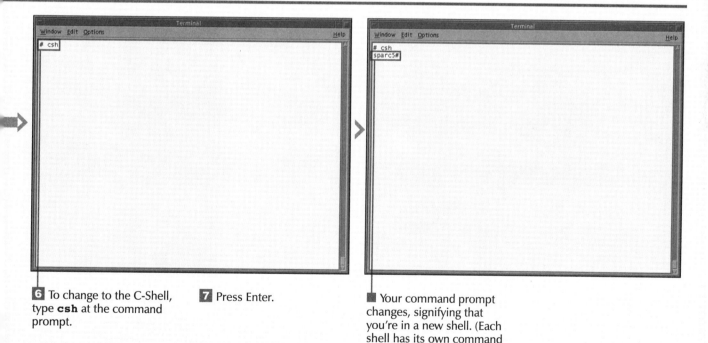

6 To change to the C-Shell, type **csh** at the command prompt.

7 Press Enter.

■ Your command prompt changes, signifying that you're in a new shell. (Each shell has its own command prompt conventions.)

EXITING A SHELL

You can exit any given shell in the UNIX Terminal window to switch back to an earlier shell, or your default shell. UNIX treats shells much like Terminal windows, except that it doesn't create a new window on the desktop to signify that you're in a new shell. Similarly, it doesn't close the Terminal when you exit a shell if it isn't the shell where you started.

If you try your hand at the *nesting* procedure, which I discuss in the preceding task, then you learn how to exit a shell. For example, you

nested a series of shells by starting in Bourne, jumping to Korn, then to the Bourne Again shell.

You can exit, in order, the Bourne Again shell, then the Korn shell, and then return to Bourne, where you started. You can't exit the shells out of order, and you can't exit shells more than one at a time, unless you close the Terminal window, which shuts down all command interpreters.

EXITING A SHELL

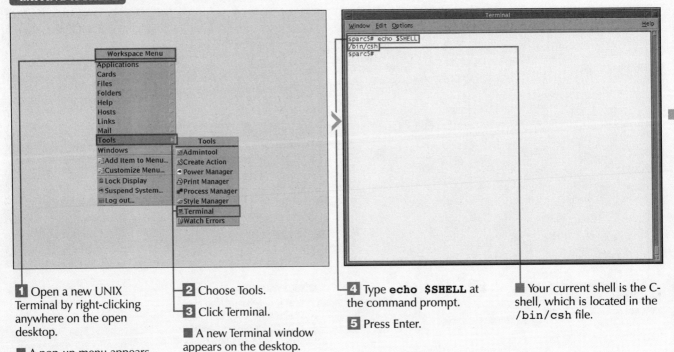

1 Open a new UNIX Terminal by right-clicking anywhere on the open desktop.

■ A pop-up menu appears.

2 Choose Tools.

3 Click Terminal.

■ A new Terminal window appears on the desktop.

4 Type **echo $SHELL** at the command prompt.

5 Press Enter.

■ Your current shell is the C-shell, which is located in the /bin/csh file.

Apply It

Exiting multiple shells

For example, you've logged in with the Bourne shell, nested inside the Bourne-Again shell, nested inside the C-Shell.

In order to exit the C-Shell and return to the Bourne-Again shell, type the following at the command prompt, then press Enter.

```
exit
```

You're now in the Bourne-Again shell. (You can check this by typing echo $SHELL at the command prompt and press Enter.) To exit from the Bourne-Again shell and return to your original Bourne shell, type the following at the command prompt and press Enter.

```
exit
```

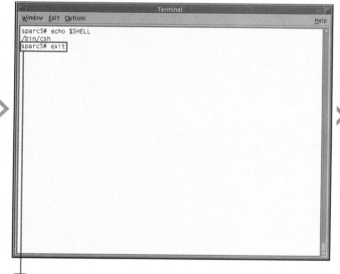

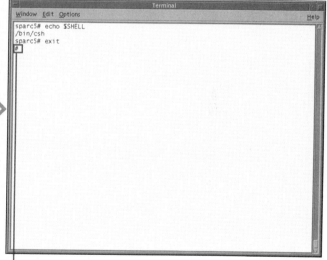

6 To switch back to your default Bourne shell, type **exit** at the command prompt.

7 Press Enter.

■ You know that you switched back successfully because the command prompt changes to what the Bourne shell normally shows.

EXECUTING A SHELL SCRIPT

You execute a shell script in UNIX by simply typing it in at the command prompt and pressing Enter, the exact same way you start a program or UNIX system utility. This is because to the UNIX operating system, every object on the system is a file — and is therefore treated similarly. Scripts are permissioned the same way as programs or utilities, so executing them is exactly the same.

A *shell script*, or *script* for short, is a file that contains a series of commands for the UNIX system to follow. Sometimes they come with the UNIX system, but more often they are put together by a UNIX system administrator to accomplish a system-specific task (such as cleaning out directories so they don't fill up a disk partition).

Incidentally, *executing* a script isn't as bad as it sounds. This is UNIX-speak for starting a shell script.

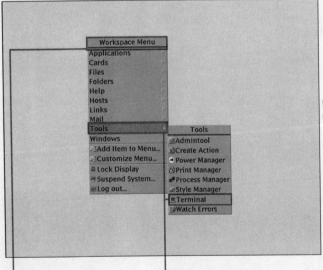

1 Open a new UNIX Terminal by right-clicking anywhere on the open desktop.

■ A pop-up menu appears.

2 Choose Tools.

3 Click Terminal.

■ A new Terminal window appears on the desktop.

4 In order to run a script called `testscript` in the `/usr/bin` directory, type `cd /usr/bin` at the command prompt.

5 Press Enter.

Apply
It

Executing a script in the background

When a script will take a long time to run, it's sometimes best to run it in the 'background.' Normally, when executing a script, you must wait for the script to finish before you can enter a new command at the command line. When you indicate that you want a script to run in the background, you can continue to use the command line; the script will finish normally and not notify you when it is complete. For example, to run the `testscript` script in the background, type the following at the command prompt and press Enter.

```
testscript &
```

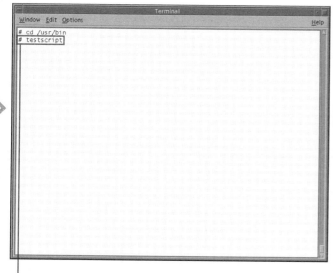

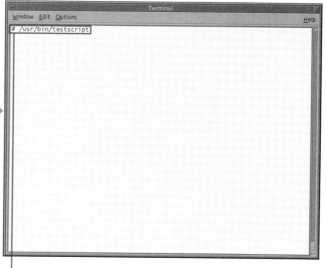

6 Now that you're inside the script's directory, you type **testscript** at the command prompt.

7 Press Enter.

8 Alternatively, you can run `testscript` by typing in the full file path to the script at the command prompt by typing `/usr/bin/testscript`.

9 Press Enter.

CHECKING YOUR ALIASES FOR SHELL SCRIPTS

You can check your aliases file in UNIX to see if you have any system shortcuts available. The aliases file is in the /etc directory, and it contains all of the aliases currently on your system. An *alias* in UNIX is simply a shorthand expression of a command. Think of it as a symbolic link not between files, but between commands.

You can save yourself a lot of typing in the long run by looking for *aliases* for the command strings that you use most frequently.

To execute an alias that's in the aliases file, simply type the alias at the command prompt, like any other UNIX command, then press Enter. Remember, if you go to a different UNIX system later in life, you may be stuck with a new set of aliases.

CHECKING YOUR ALIASES FOR SHELL SCRIPTS

Workspace Menu
- Applications
- Cards
- Files
- Folders
- Help
- Hosts
- Links
- Mail
- Tools
- Windows
- Add Item to Menu...
- Customize Menu...
- Lock Display
- Suspend System...
- Log out...

Tools
- Admintool
- Create Action
- Power Manager
- Print Manager
- Process Manager
- Style Manager
- Terminal
- Watch Errors

Terminal

Window Edit Options   Help

alias

1 Open a new UNIX Terminal by right-clicking anywhere on the open desktop.

■ A pop-up menu appears.

2 Choose Tools.

3 Click Terminal.

■ A new Terminal window appears on the desktop.

4 Type **alias** at the command prompt.

5 Press Enter.

Apply It

Creating your own aliases

Yes, you can do this on your UNIX system, and you don't even have to be the root administrator account. Use the alias command as specified in the man page for alias. (For information on how to use the man page, see Chapter 9.)

Names that you shouldn't give to the aliases you create

You shouldn't give your aliases certain names. If you name an alias the same as an existing command, you confuse the system. For example, you may create an alias `ls -ltr`, naming it `cp`. This can disable the `cp` *(copy)* command, the alias, or both.

Omitting these aliases from the `/etc/aliases` file

The aliases file in your `/etc` directory is a default system file, listing a number of aliases that come with your version of UNIX software.

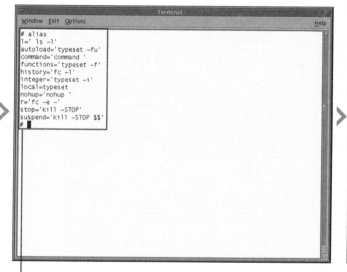

6 Your current aliases appear. For example, the first alias shows that if you type `l` at the command prompt, you execute the `ls @ndl` (long list) command.

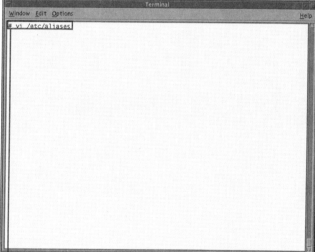

7 Alternatively, you can see your aliases by typing **vi /etc/aliases** at the command prompt.

8 Press Enter.

■ The aliases file opens in the vi editor.

DETERMINING YOUR SYSTEM VARIABLES WITH ENV

You can determine your system's environmental variables in your UNIX environment with the env command. *Environmental variables* are operating parameters or settings determined by your UNIX installation, whether Solaris, HP-UX, or another flavor.

These UNIX system variables provide the means to interface with the computer. They determine, among other things, your user name, user profile, shell account, and even what your command prompt looks like. For example, the environmental variable $SHELL, which you work with earlier in this chapter on the tasks "Exiting a Shell," "Starting a Shell," and "Determining the Shell," is what initially sets your command interpreter to be the default Bourne, Korn, or C-Shell.

The advantage to using the env command to see your environmental variables is that you see the big picture. This is because env lets you see all of your current variables at a single glance.

DETERMINING YOUR SYSTEM VALUES WITH ENV

1 Open a new UNIX Terminal by right-clicking anywhere on the open desktop.

■ A pop-up menu appears.

2 Choose Tools.

3 Click Terminal.

■ A new Terminal window appears on the desktop.

4 Type **env** at the command prompt.

5 Press Enter.

Apply It

Using env with the redirect command

You can use env with the redirect command to place the results generated by the env command into a text file. (For a review of the redirection commands, see Chapter 7.)

Placing the results from env into a text file is helpful because it allows you to refer back to your original set of variables if you plan to change any of the variables. To redirect the output of the env command into a text file, type the following at the command line and press Enter.

```
env > <file name>
```

■ Your environmental variables appear.

Note: The list may scroll off the top of the screen because there many be so many of these variables.

6 Click and drag the scroll bar on the right side of the Terminal.

■ You return to where you initially typed in the env command, enabling you to see the environmental variables that you couldn't see because they weren't on the screen.

DETERMINING ANY SINGLE VARIABLE

You can determine settings of individual variables by using the *echo* command. You first saw this command earlier this chapter, in the task "Determining the Shell." Remember that echo prints anything written after it back to the screen. If the word after echo has a dollar sign, UNIX interprets that as a *variable sign* and prints the variable.

Being able to see any single variable doesn't show you the whole picture that running env does. On the other hand, the output of the env command can sometimes be of such great

volume that it's difficult to focus on the one single variable that you want to learn about or change.

The most important setting, next to the $SHELL variable, is undoubtedly the $PATH variable. The $PATH variable tells the UNIX operating system which directories to find a given command. So, if the directories searched include /usr and /usr/bin, then a command in the /etc directory can't run unless you type the entire file path name — /etc/<command>.

DETERMINING ANY SINGLE VARIABLE

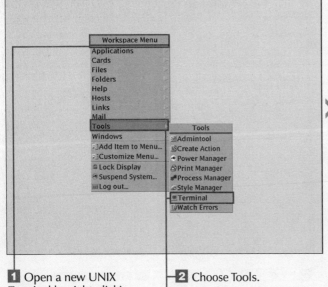

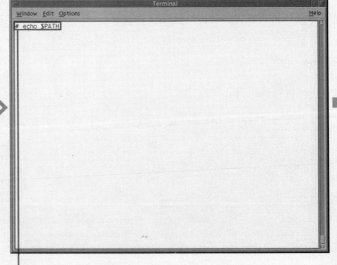

1 Open a new UNIX Terminal by right-clicking anywhere on the open desktop.

■ A pop-up menu appears.

2 Choose Tools.

3 Click Terminal.

■ A new Terminal window appears on the desktop.

4 To determine your $PATH variable, type **echo $PATH** at the command prompt.

5 Press Enter.

Extra

Selecting the $PATH

Usually, you should keep your path set to the system defaults. However, if you frequently use a utility from a directory that isn't in your path, you should edit your path to include that directory.

The difference between $PATH and the term *path*

$PATH is the term you use when you refer to the environmental variable that determines which directories that the UNIX operating system searches for a script, binary, or command that you execute. The term *path* refers to this list of directories as well. It also is a more colloquial phrase that can mean the general location of a file.

The longest a $PATH should be

Path lengths have no limits. However, remember that commands that come from the end of the path line take slightly longer to execute. Of course, this should only be noticeable if your system is running at peak capacity with many users on it at the same time.

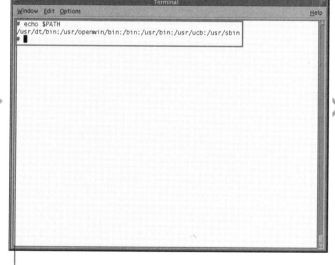

■ The path, or list of directories that the system searches when you execute a command appears.

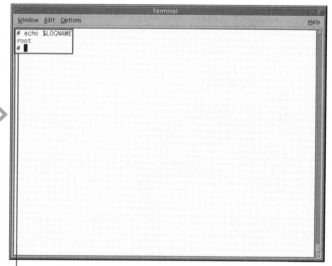

6 To see a different system variable, such as your Login Name, type echo $LOGNAME at the command prompt.

7 Press Enter.

■ The result appears in the next line.

SETTING THE $PATH VARIABLE

You can change the $PATH variable on your system to a completely custom setting that lets you run scripts or programs from nonstandard areas such as /tmp or /var.

The $PATH variable, or simply the *path* in UNIX terms, is the variable that determines where the UNIX operating system searches for programs and utilities to run. It also determines the order in which the search is conducted. For example, if the path is shown to be /bin:/usr:/usr/ucb, then UNIX first

checks in the /bin directory, followed by the /usr directory, then the /usr/ucb directory.

If you frequently use a program that exists outside your path, altering the $PATH variable makes it easier to use. You can set the $PATH variable with the setenv command. Setenv (*set environmental variable*) uses the syntax setenv <variable> <setting>.

SETTING THE $PATH VARIABLE

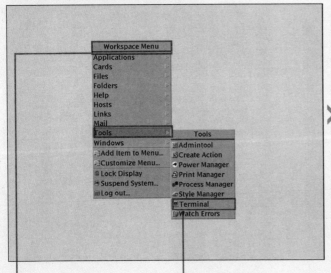

1 Open a new UNIX Terminal by right-clicking anywhere on the open desktop.

■ A pop-up menu appears.

2 Choose Tools.

3 Click Terminal.

■ A new Terminal window appears on the desktop.

4 To set your $PATH variable to simply /usr/dt/bin:/etc/mystuff, type **setenv PATH /usr/dt/bin:/etc/Ł mystuff**.

5 Press Enter.

Note: When using setenv, *you do not use the $ sign, as with the echo command.*

144

Apply It

Using the `setenv` command for other variables

You can use the `setenv` command to set different kinds of system variables other than the $PATH variable. (For a complete list of variables that you can change with `setenv`, type `env` at the command prompt and press Enter.)

For example, you can change the $USERNAME variable, which is the name of your user account, by typing the following at the command line and pressing Enter.

```
setenv USERNAME <new username>
```

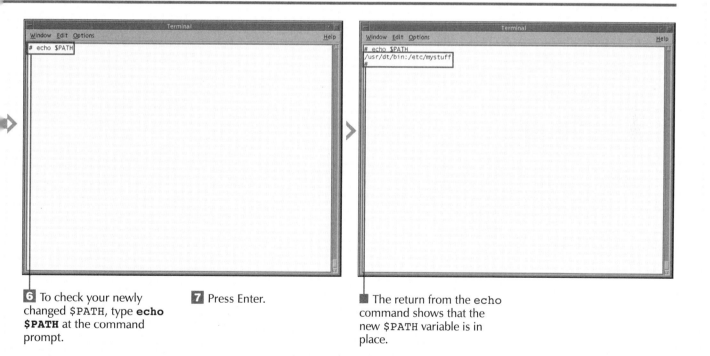

6 To check your newly changed $PATH, type **echo $PATH** at the command prompt.

7 Press Enter.

■ The return from the `echo` command shows that the new $PATH variable is in place.

ENTER THE ROOT USER ACCOUNT

You can become the root user account at any time, even if you haven't logged in as root. All you need is the root user account password. The *root user* account is the administrative account that is granted unilateral privileges over all the other accounts and files on the UNIX system. As root, you may edit any file or change any file's permission that you wish.

A UNIX system includes only one root account, but other accounts can have the same privileges as root if needed. For security purposes, however, root privileges should be granted sparingly, if at all. You can enter the root account from the typical login to performing the su command. The command su stands for *shift user*. Su is primarily used for the administrator to become root user account, though you can use su to shift into any other user account for which you have the password.

ENTER THE ROOT USER ACCOUNT

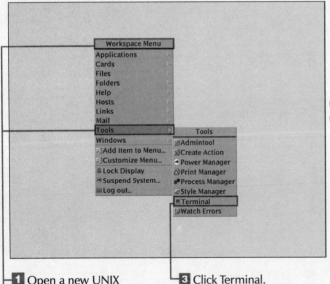

1 Open a new UNIX Terminal by right-clicking anywhere on the open desktop.

■ A pop-up menu appears.

2 Choose Tools.

3 Click Terminal.

■ After you select Terminal, the pop-up menu disappears and a new Terminal window appears on the desktop.

4 To change to the root user account, type **su** at the command prompt.

5 Press Enter.

Extra

Another way to double-check that the su command performed properly

You can use the id *(identification)* command to determine who you are at that point. Simply type id at the command prompt after you su to root, then press Enter. The command lists your current login name.

While typing in the password for the root account in the su'ing process, nothing appears on screen

During the su process, when you're required to type in a user account's password, that password doesn't appear on screen. This is a basic security precaution. It prevents a security breach if someone happens to be reading over your shoulder when you su to the root administrative account.

Canceling the su process if you forget the password

Press Control+C to cancel your su request.

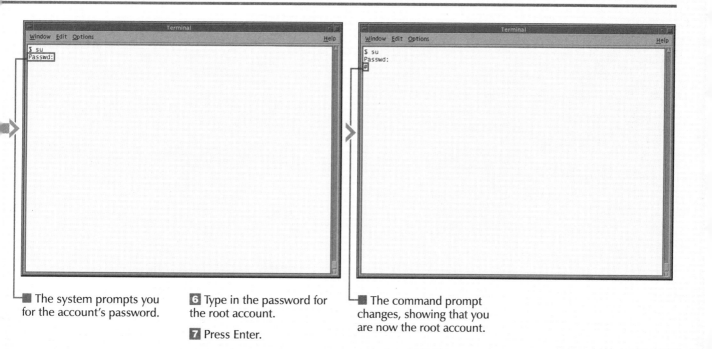

■ The system prompts you for the account's password.

6 Type in the password for the root account.

7 Press Enter.

■ The command prompt changes, showing that you are now the root account.

RERUN SU

Like several other UNIX commands, su can run more than once during one UNIX session. This phenomenon is *nesting*. I discuss nesting in more detail in Chapter 8.

You don't need to become root more than once when you're logged in as root, or become the root account with the su command.

Remember, the *shift user* command su runs with any user accounts, not just the root

administrative account. The only restriction on doing this is that anyone seeking to su into another account must know that new account's password.

This ability is most useful when you edit programs that affect all users on your system. After editing the file as root, you can switch into a user account to test the output and then return to root if further work is needed.

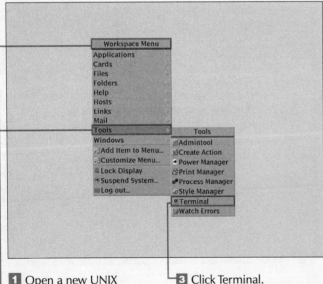

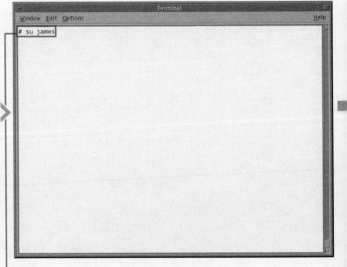

1 Open a new UNIX Terminal by right-clicking anywhere on the open desktop.

■ A pop-up menu appears.

2 Choose Tools.

3 Click Terminal.

■ After you select Terminal, the pop-up menu disappears and a new Terminal window appears on the desktop.

4 To su from the root account to another user, type **su** followed by the name of the other user account.

■ For example, to su from the root account to a user named "james," type su james at the command prompt.

5 Press Enter.

Apply It

Multiple su'ing to and from an account

Being able to use the su command multiple times allows you to test out a fix or change you have made to the system. For example, when you're logged in as the root account, say that you want to test a permissioning change you just made to a file owned by user james. Su to user account james by typing the following at the command prompt and pressing Enter.

su james

Next, test to see if anyone else on the system can view it. You do this by su'ing to kiko's account by typing the following at the command prompt and pressing Enter.

su kiko

Enter in the password for kiko's account and complete your testing.

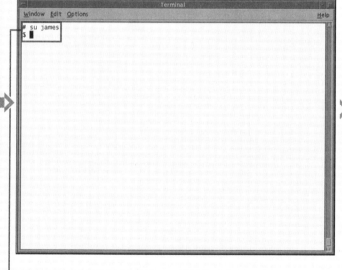

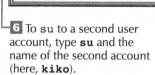

■ Because you are logged in as the root administrator account, you are not required to type in a password. Instead, you immediately enter james's account, as seen by the new command prompt.

■ Note that some systems ask for passwords, even if you are the root account.

6 To su to a second user account, type **su** and the name of the second account (here, **kiko**).

■ You are prompted for the account's password, as you are no longer root, but the first user account.

7 Type in the password for the second account, then press Enter.

8 The command prompt changes, showing that you are now the second user account.

RESEARCH MAN PAGES

Most UNIX system administration questions are answered by the man pages that come with every UNIX machine. The man (short for *manual*) pages are a listing of all the UNIX commands that have been passed down from earlier versions of the UNIX operating system. The syntax for the man command is man <command you want to learn about>.

Although they're at times written in very technical terms, the man pages are an invaluable source of information if you're

trying to determine what command option to use with a particular utility.

Remember, the man pages were created to provide assistance with commands that are executed inside the UNIX Terminal. As a rule, man pages don't cover help topics for the later, GUI-based utilities in CDE (Common Desktop Environment), such as the Main Toolbar and the Style Manager.

RESEARCH MAN PAGES

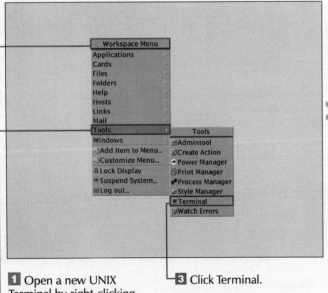

1 Open a new UNIX Terminal by right-clicking anywhere on the open desktop.

■ A pop-up menu appears.

2 Choose Tools.

3 Click Terminal.

■ After you select Terminal, the pop-up menu disappears and a new Terminal window appears on the desktop.

4 In order to find out more about the ls, or *list* command, type **man ls** at the command prompt.

5 Press Enter.

Apply It

Getting man pages

The man pages come automatically with all versions of UNIX. However, your version of man may be slightly more out of date than others if your system is six or seven years old. An older man page may not include some of the newer commands.

User accounts that can access the man pages

The man pages are available for all users, root and otherwise, by running the man command. Only the root account, however, really finds man pages helpful, because most users don't delve into UNIX as deeply as root. As an administrator, you sometimes use information from the man pages.

Deciphering the man page

Most man pages are not that technical, just wordy. Take your time and carefully read the man page if you're not sure what it says at first.

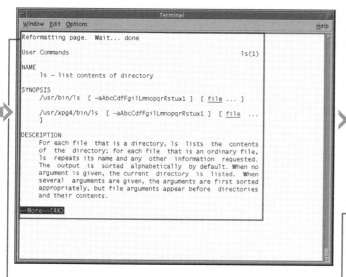

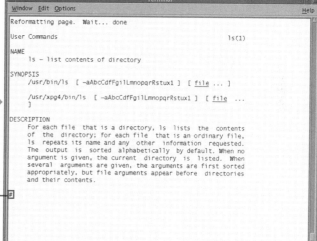

■ The man pages for `ls` appear in the Terminal. You can move from page to page by pressing the space bar.

6 In order to quit the man pages, press the space bar until the entry comes to the end.

■ To exit immediately, press Q on your keyboard. You return to the command prompt.

FIND ROOT FILE OWNERSHIP

The *list* command has the options to list detailed information. This is a useful function, because as root, you can grant or restrict access to files all over the UNIX system for the rest of the users. Determining which files to curtail access to and which to open up for the other users on the system is an important job.

Files containing information that more than one person or department needs should be as open as possible. On the other hand, system-critical files that control UNIX functions (such as passwords, printing, and basic commands) should be kept under the cybernetic equivalent of a lock and key. To make sure that they're not owned by user accounts that can affect your system by deleting these files, it's worthwhile checking whether they're owned by the root account.

FIND ROOT FILE OWNERSHIP

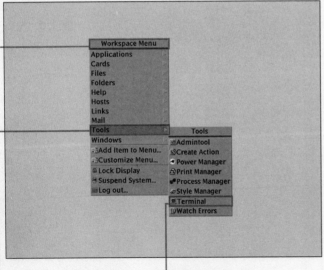

1 Open a new UNIX Terminal by right-clicking anywhere on the open desktop.

■ A pop-up menu appears.

2 Choose Tools.

3 Click Terminal.

■ After you select Terminal, the pop-up menu disappears and a new Terminal window appears on the desktop.

■ Several important system files such as `passwd` are kept in the `/etc` directory.

4 To see if these files are owned by root, type **cd /etc** at the command prompt to change directories to /etc.

5 Press Enter.

Apply It

Checking for root ownership on files in different locations

You can also check to see if root owns a file in a different directory than the location where you're running the command. For example, to list the owner of a file in another area, you can use any of the following commands:

```
ls -l /tmp

ls -l /var/tmp/

ls -l /usr/bin/tmp/testfile
```

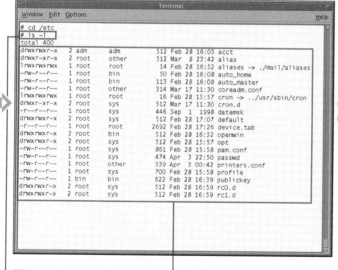

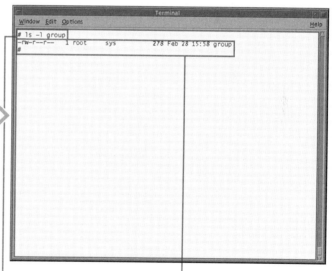

6 Type **ls -l** at the command prompt.

7 Press Enter.

■ The files appear in detailed list. Note that the third column from the left lists the file's owner. The owner of the passwd file is root.

■ If you want to see just one file, such as /etc/group, instead of the contents of the whole directory, type **ls -l group** while in the /etc directory, then press Enter.

■ The file appears in detailed form and is owned by root.

CHANGE PERMISSIONS TO RESTRICT ACCESS

You can change permissions on a sensitive file so that other user accounts can't edit or view it. You can set the read, write, and execute permissions on a file or directory in the CDE graphic desktop environment. By allowing you access to the properties that make up a given file's parameters, you can select the file to be visible to only the root account. Alternatively, you can make it visible only to root and one group of users who may

have an interest in the information, without allowing access to everyone on the system.

Restricting access is an effective way of preventing problems resulting from accidental editing. For example, if you have a file that is critical to the smooth operation of your UNIX system (such as /etc/password) left accessible to any user, serious problems can follow.

CHANGE PERMISSIONS TO RESTRICT ACCESS

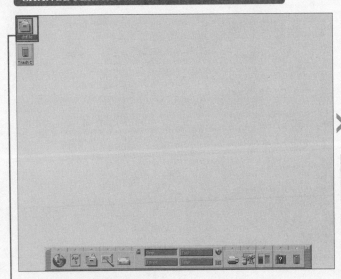

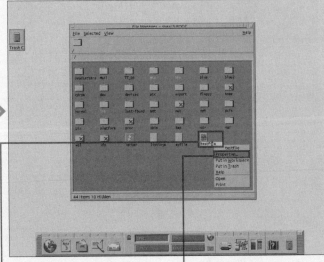

■1 Open the File Manager by clicking its desktop icon.

■2 In the File Manager, you can restrict permissions to a file by right-clicking the file's icon.

■ A pop-up menu appears.

■3 Click Properties from the pop-up menu.

154

Extra

Files to restrict reading and writing permissions

As a general rule, your best bet is to make sure that any files critical to the way your system operates are as heavily restricted as possible. Some of these files include, but are not limited to, the printer control file, /etc/printcap; the file system table, /etc/fstab; and most importantly, the password file, /etc/passwd. Luckily, the majority of these files are created with limited permissions by default, so you don't have to change them.

Files are best left with the most "open," or accessible, permissions

Files that you leave as open for everyone to look at or even edit are usually more site-specific in nature. For example, if your UNIX machine stores data at a university campus, all of the files containing research should be completely accessible to everyone.

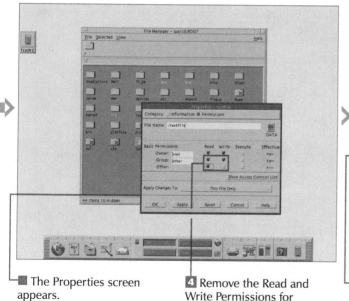

■ The Properties screen appears.

4 Remove the Read and Write Permissions for everyone except root by deselecting the checkmark boxes outside of the Owner row.

■ After you finish, the only selected checkboxes should be in the Owner row, which is root.

5 Click OK to apply these changes and return to the File Manager.

CHANGE PERMISSIONS TO RESTRICT TERMINAL ACCESS

You can use UNIX's ability to restrict access to a specific file in the UNIX Terminal by using the chmod command. Restricting access, whether through the CDE desktop GUI or through the UNIX Terminal, is a good idea.

If a system-critical file is permissioned so that anyone can edit it, a user can edit the file by himself to save time in changing his password. Worse, an experienced UNIX user can change the root account password, leaving you unable to restore the system.

An additional bit of file security is available in the UNIX Terminal through the idea of "security through obscurity." You can make a file more obscure if it is hidden from plain view. In UNIX, files starting with a single period (.) don't appear in a list command unless the -a option is used. An extra level of out-of-sight, out-of-mind security is available by renaming a file from topsecret to .topsecret.

CHANGE PERMISSIONS TO RESTRICT TERMINAL ACCESS

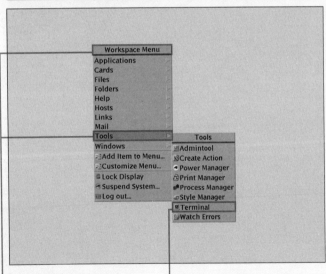

1 Open a new UNIX Terminal by right-clicking anywhere on the open desktop.

■ A pop-up menu appears.

2 Choose Tools.

3 Click Terminal.

■ After you select Terminal, the pop-up menu disappears and a new Terminal window appears on the desktop.

4 To restrict permissions to a file, type **ls −l** and the name of the file at the command prompt.

■ For example to restrict permissions to a file called testfile, type ls −l testfile.

5 Press Enter.

Extra

Reasons to restrict read permissions

Read-only permissions are good enough for some files, but not all. For example, if you work for a private company, it may not be good to allow people to read the files where you keep the records of people's salaries and bonuses.

Restricting access to a program or script

The easiest way to do this is to use the chmod command with the −x option. By revoking the file as an executable, no one can run the program. Of course, you can restore the executable permission if *you* want to run it.

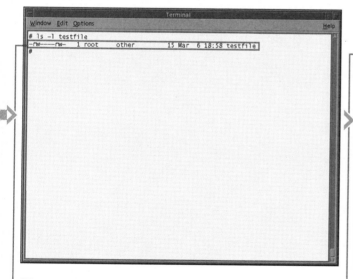

■ The current permissions for testfile appear. (For a quick review on how to read permissions, see Chapter 4.)

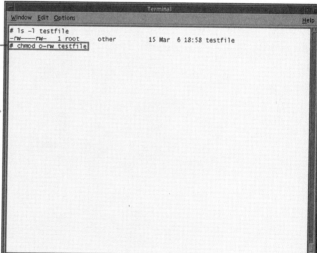

6 To remove other people's permission to read and write to the file, type **chmod o−rw** and the name of the file at the command prompt.

■ For example, to restrict permissions to a file called testfile, you would type chmod o−rw testfile at the command prompt.

7 Press Enter.

AUTOMATE TASKS

You can automate simple system tasks with the *cron* utility. Cron automates tasks by tracking time as kept on your UNIX machine. At a prearranged time, cron looks in the *crontab* file. If any tasks are listed in the crontab, cron runs the program specified just as if you'd typed it in at the command prompt. You list the contents of this file with the crontab command and the –l option, and edit it with the –e option.

In the crontab, you must specify the exact time you want a program to run. The time and tasks are written in the crontab in six fields:

<Minute>	0–59
<Hour>	0–23
<Day of Month>	1–31
<Month>	1–12
<Day of Week>	0–6
<Command to Run>	command

To run a command on every single unit in the field, use an asterisk (*). In the following example, the crontab is edited to run the ls command every Friday at 4 p.m. and redirect the output to a file called listme.

AUTOMATE TASKS

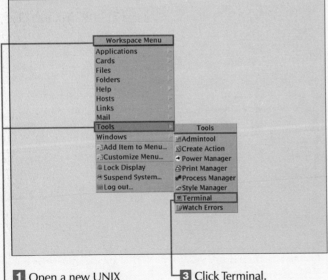

1 Open a new UNIX Terminal by right-clicking anywhere on the open desktop.

■ A pop-up menu appears.

2 Choose Tools.

3 Click Terminal.

■ After you select Terminal, the pop-up menu disappears and a new Terminal window appears on the desktop.

4 Type **crontab –e** to edit the crontab.

5 Press Enter.

Extra

Correcting if cron program ran at the wrong time

To begin with, double-check the time you enter into the crontab. The most common mistake is where people neglect to adjust the time to a military standard. Four in the afternoon isn't 04 — that's four in the morning. The appropriate number for the afternoon time slot is 16.

Correcting if the time is set correctly and the job still completes at the wrong time

The cron utility may be running fine, but the system time it's tracking is wrong. You can check what time your UNIX machine thinks it is by typing date and pressing Enter. The date program shows your system time. If it's off, correct the time setting.

Note that different machines on the same network can show different times! Just because the main server says it's noon doesn't mean that the outlying computers can't show 12:30 p.m., 2 p.m., or 6 a.m.

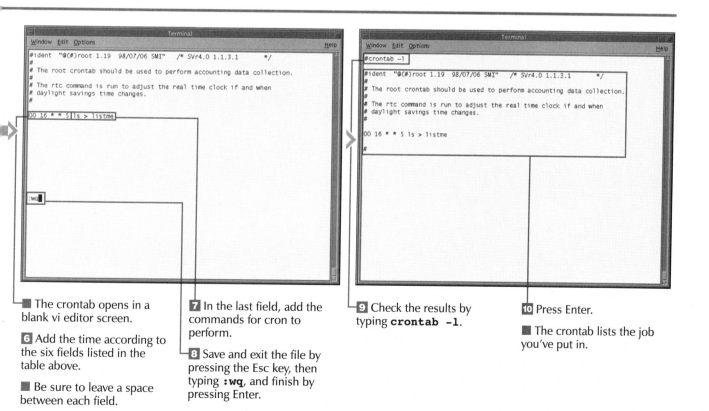

■ The crontab opens in a blank vi editor screen.

6 Add the time according to the six fields listed in the table above.

■ Be sure to leave a space between each field.

7 In the last field, add the commands for cron to perform.

8 Save and exit the file by pressing the Esc key, then typing :wq, and finish by pressing Enter.

9 Check the results by typing crontab -1.

10 Press Enter.

■ The crontab lists the job you've put in.

LIST USER ACCOUNTS

You can view the entire list of user accounts on your system with the graphics-based desktop utility, Admintool. Admintool is a standard offering with the Common Desktop Environment. This utility shows the account listings in alphabetical order. When you view the account listings this way, remember that you're seeing every single account that has been created on your UNIX system — not just every user account that is currently logged in. Remember, a user account may or may not have a person attached to it.

For example, you may see the user account `lp`, which is the dummy account the system uses when working with the line printer daemon that controls your print jobs. Whenever the operating system needs to perform an automated task on the print server, it uses this dummy account to do the work.

LIST USER ACCOUNTS

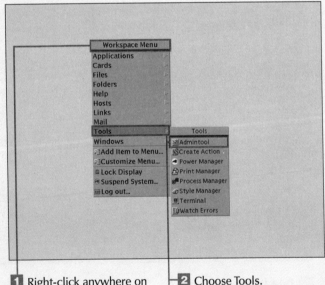

1 Right-click anywhere on the desktop.

■ The pop-up menu appears.

2 Choose Tools.

3 Click Admintool.

■ The Admintool window appears.

Note: By default, the Admintool window opens to the Admintool: Users display.

Extra

Expanding the Admintool screen more quickly than clicking and dragging

As with most of the other windows in the CDE desktop environment, you can maximize the Admintool window by clicking on the box in the upper right-hand corner of the window. To return the window to its normal size, click the box again.

Finding more information about the Admintool utility

The content of the man pages focuses on command-line utilities. To find out more about Admintool, click Help in the Admintool toolbar and choose About Admintool.

Listing users by UID (user ID) or name instead of account

Unfortunately, Admintool's User screen isn't quite as flexible as its nearest Windows counterpart. To find where a user is listed, scroll down the alphabetical list to locate the entry.

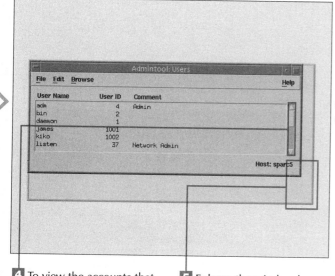

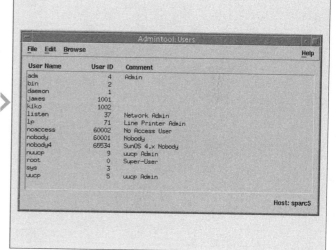

4 To view the accounts that you can't see initially, click and drag this scrollbar.

5 Enlarge the window by clicking the corner and dragging it to a new position.

■ The new outline of the window appears.

6 Release the mouse button.

■ The window expands to the size indicated by the outline. When enlarged, the window enables you to view the entire list of accounts.

CREATE USER ACCOUNTS

You can create user accounts for anyone on your UNIX system with the Admintool utility. Adding user accounts is one of the most basic of all administrative tasks in UNIX. If you administer a network with more than a few users, adding user accounts is a very common task. Luckily, it's neither difficult nor time-consuming.

As with the majority of the functions in the UNIX configuration tool, only the root user can

add a new user account. After the account is created, the user can reconfigure his account (unless the administrator decides to disable it). Remember, because user accounts are just the way a user logs into a UNIX system, a single user can have one account, or multiple accounts. However, it's best not to grant more than one account to any user. This limits the possible security breaches from an illegally gained password.

CREATE USER ACCOUNTS

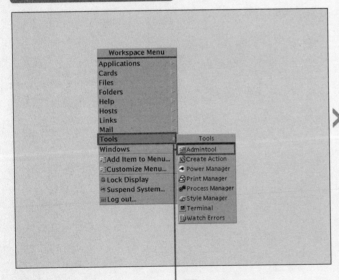

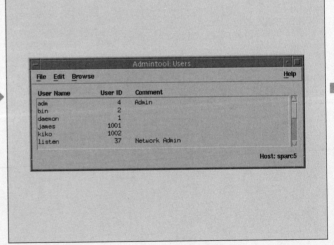

1 Right-click anywhere on the desktop.

■ The Workspace pop-up menu appears.

2 Choose Tools.

3 Click Admintool.

■ The Admintool window appears.

Note: By default, the Admintool window opens to the Admintool: Users display.

Extra

Naming a user's account

This really depends on how you decide to run your system. Some people let the users pick their own names, while others follow the "first initial, last name" scheme. This is where a user named James Smith gets the account name jsmith.

Names to avoid giving when creating a user account

Make sure that each name is unique, so don't award the same name twice. Also, don't create a user account with the same name as an automated system account (such as adm or bin) — you'll confuse your machine.

Selecting a shell for users

For consistency, use the shell that is predominant on your system. If you're starting from scratch, select the default setting in UNIX, the Bourne shell (sh).

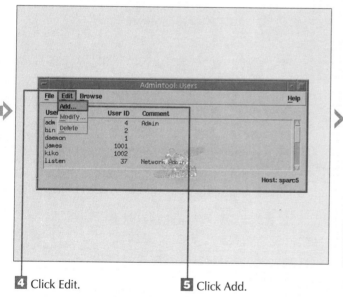

4 Click Edit.

5 Click Add.

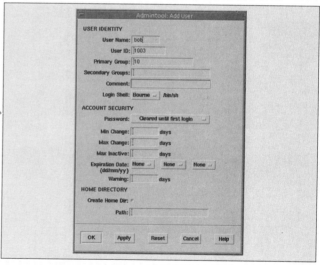

■ The Admintool: Add User screen appears.

Note: By default, Admintool automatically assigns the user the next free User ID (Identification Number), a group, and a default shell (Bourne).

CREATE USER ACCOUNTS (CONTINUED)

Y ou rarely have to change the default settings that Admintool assigns to each new user account that you create on the system. Admintool tailors each account that you create to avoid conflicts with other accounts and to place the account in a logical user group.

For example, each user account is assigned a unique User ID so the operating system can tell the accounts apart. Admintool starts numbering user accounts at 1001. As you add

each account, it increases the default number by increments up to 1002, 1003, and so on. This saves you from having to remember which numbers are available, and it provides a pattern to the numbers assigned.

In addition, Admintool assigns the Bourne shell as the default user account shell. Bourne is one of the most popular and convenient command interpreters, so it provides maximum benefit to a new account.

CREATE USER ACCOUNTS (CONTINUED)

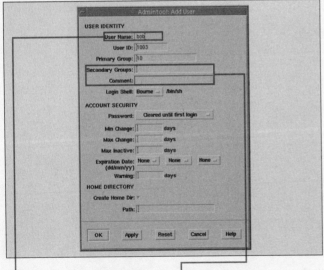

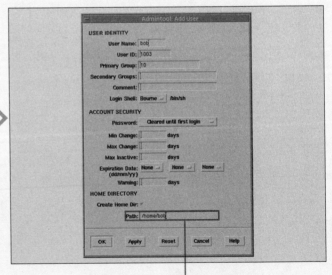

6 Type the user's account name in the User Name field; in this case, bob.

■ Optionally, you can also click in the Secondary Group and Comment fields to type additional information.

7 Click the Path field.

8 Type the path of the user's home directory. Usually, this is /home.

Extra

Entering for a comment in the Comment field

This is an optional field, so you don't need to enter anything. However, you may want to put in the user's real name, so you can contact that person if you need to edit something on his account.

Finding how to do something for the User Accounts in Admintool

The man pages don't cover the Admintool functions. If you need additional help or information, click Help and choose About Managing Users from the pop-up menu.

Selecting a group for users

Unless you have strong preference, allow Admintool to enter user accounts in the default user group, which is number 10. The important point here is to never put users in the root group. This grants them administrative privileges, which is not what you want on a secure system.

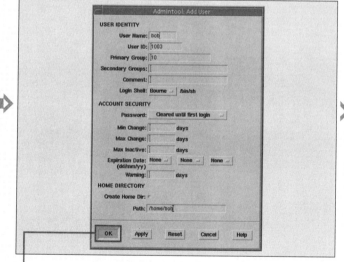

9 Click OK to apply your new changes.

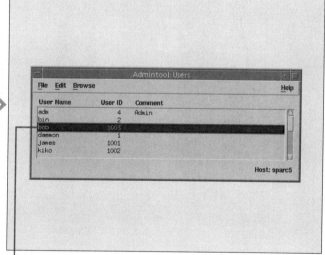

10 The new user, in this case, bob, appears in the list.

CHANGE USER ACCOUNTS

You can make changes to any user account and the information that configures it from the Admintool: Users screen. Because only the root account can use Admintool, this centralizes the control that changes user accounts. However, users on the system can change their passwords and pertinent information via the `passwd` command or the vi editor.

Of course, you can encourage people to see you if they want to change any aspect of their account. However, remember that if you

choose to set yourself up as the primary source of user account administration, prepare for a lot of requests. If you have more than a dozen users on your system, you can easily become swamped by relatively mundane administration chores.

As a general rule, if you find yourself in an administration position and you're allocating more than an hour or two to handle Admintool-based tasks, you're spending too much time administering user accounts.

CHANGE USER ACCOUNTS

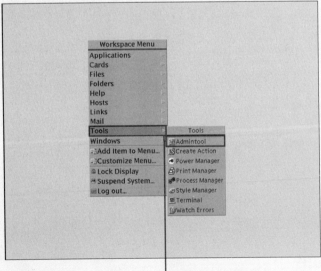

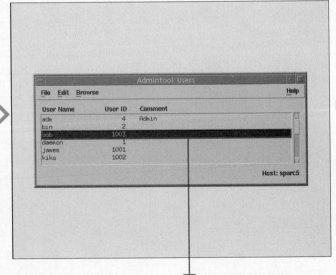

1 Right-click anywhere on the desktop.

■ The Workspace pop-up menu appears.

2 Choose Tools.

3 Click Admintool.

■ The Admintool window appears.

Note: By default, the Admintool window opens to the Admintool: Users display.

4 Click the user account bob to edit it.

166

Extra

Common fields to modify for the user accounts in Admintool

If you manage a group of advanced users, such as programmers, you may be asked to change the default shell, or command interpreter. This is because different shells have special utilities that programmers find useful. Another commonly modified field is the password area, although many users are confident enough of their own abilities in UNIX to use the `passwd` command.

A final area you can change is the user account name. Whether people change their names after marriage or whether they change their user name when switching departments, you may have to edit this to keep your naming scheme consistent.

Advantages to a consistent naming scheme

If you have a consistent naming scheme, it's easier to organize, locate, and recognize users on your system. For example, if you have two James Smiths in different departments of the same company, you can call one js-personnel and the other js-research.

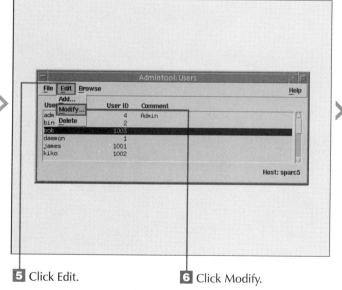

5 Click Edit.

6 Click Modify.

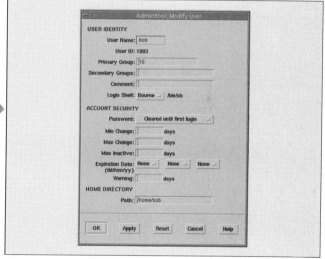

■ The Admintool: Modify User screen appears. You can make changes to any attribute of the user account listed on this screen.

CHANGE USER ACCOUNTS (CONTINUED)

Y ou can easily change a user account's password in Admintool to improve the level of security on the system. Normally, because users can set their passwords whenever they want, you only have to edit their passwords in special situations.

The most common case is when you're having a security problem where someone is *hacking* (gaining illegal access) onto your system through a specific user account. If the user is on vacation or is not using his or her account, it's up to you to make the password change.

You can also improve the security on your system by requiring regular user password changes. You can set the interval by typing the number of days in the Min Change field of the Modify user screen, or you can set a specific date for changing the passwords on the system. Changing passwords improves security, because a hacker who has gained illegal access no longer has a valid password.

CHANGE USER ACCOUNTS (CONTINUED)

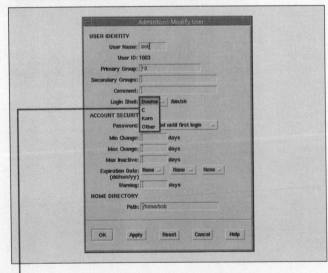

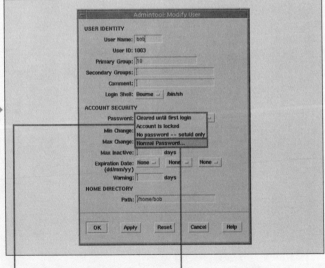

■7 To change a user account's default shell, click the Login Shell button.

■8 Click a shell from the pop-up menu.

■9 To change a user account's password, click the button to the right of Password.

■10 Click Normal Password.

Extra

Requiring users to change their passwords

This is up to you — it really depends on the level of security you realistically need on your system. For example, if you work at a top secret government laboratory where valuable research goes on, you may want to change the passwords quarterly.

On the other hand, if this system is in your home, it may be less likely that someone will try to hack your system. In that case, you may change passwords once a year, if that.

Duplicating user account names

You shouldn't enable users to change their names to duplicate system accounts. This can cause both UNIX and a new administrator some confusion. User account names by necessity should be unique. In any case, Admintool has built-in safeguards that won't let you duplicate a user account name.

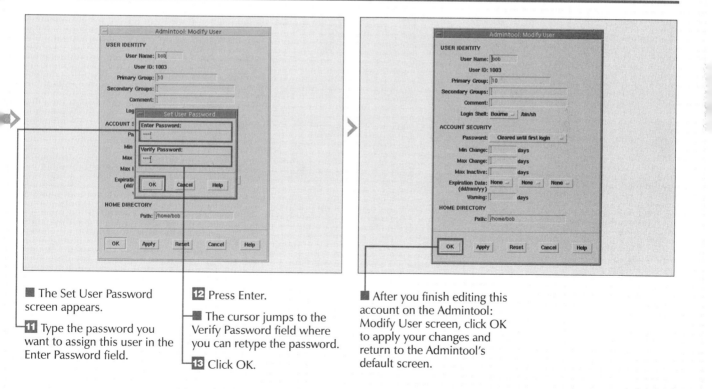

■ The Set User Password screen appears.

11 Type the password you want to assign this user in the Enter Password field.

12 Press Enter.

■ The cursor jumps to the Verify Password field where you can retype the password.

13 Click OK.

■ After you finish editing this account on the Admintool: Modify User screen, click OK to apply your changes and return to the Admintool's default screen.

DELETE USER ACCOUNTS

Y ou can delete user accounts from the Admintool: Users screen. Admintool makes this task as easy as the creation or editing of user accounts in the Common Desktop Environment. An additional advantage is that in Admintool, deciding what level of account removal you want is easy. You can remove the account outright, or you can save the user's home directory and just leave it in place.

You should delete user accounts only in certain instances. If an employee leaves your company, or a student is graduating from the institution that runs the UNIX network, remove that user's account.

On the other hand, deleting accounts is not a cure-all. For example, if a user is going away for an extended vacation but will return, your best option is to disable the account, not to delete it.

DELETE USER ACCOUNTS

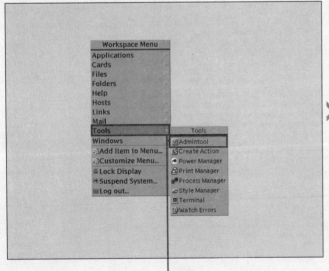

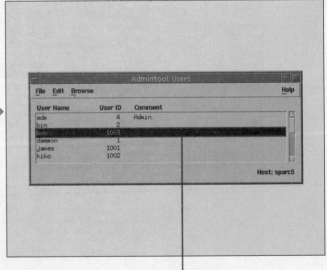

1 Right-click anywhere on the desktop.

■ The Workspace pop-up menu appears.

2 Choose Tools.

3 Click Admintool.

■ The Admintool window appears.

Note: By default, the Admintool window opens to the Admintool: Users display.

4 Click the user account bob to highlight it.

Extra

Selecting the Delete Home Directory option when deleting a user account

By default, Admintool does not let you delete a user's home directory, because you cannot easily reverse this step. You should keep this default if you feel the user has information that you need in the user's home directory. Remember, if you accept this option, then you should immediately go into the user's directory, copy what you need, and remove the directory with the `rm` command, which I discuss in Chapter 3.

Use this option whenever you want to free up the maximum space on the hard drive. It's the most commonly used option, because important information rarely resides in a personal user account. Special accounting or research information is normally kept in more public areas, such as a departmental directory.

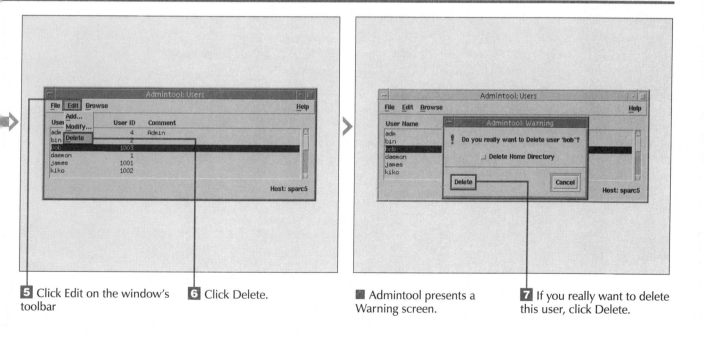

5 Click Edit on the window's toolbar

6 Click Delete.

■ Admintool presents a Warning screen.

7 If you really want to delete this user, click Delete.

DISABLE USER ACCOUNTS

You can disable user accounts in the Admintool utility by *locking* the account password. You should know the process of disabling user accounts because this gives you more options when controlling members of your user community.

For example, if you delete a user account every time an employee goes on an extended vacation, you're effectively doubling your

workload because you have to recreate the account when the user returns. Disabling the user's account is less work.

Also, disabling user accounts gives you some middle ground when it comes to disciplining errant users. Any user who tries to gain access to administrative files or root privileges can be disabled.

DISABLE USER ACCOUNTS

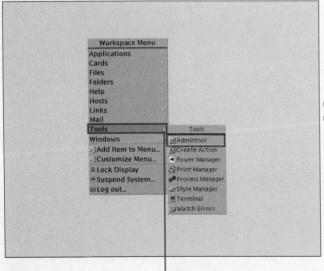

■1 Right-click anywhere on the desktop.

■ The Workspace pop-up menu appears.

■2 Choose Tools.

■3 Click Admintool.

■ The Admintool window appears.

Note: By default, the Admintool window opens to the Admintool: Users display.

■5 Click the user account.

■6 Click Edit.

■7 Click Modify.

Extra

Establishing accounts for remote users

You should disable user accounts only when people won't use them for some time. If a person uses the account (even if she is physically absent), then you should leave the account alone.

Addressing disabled user accounts

Find out if the user recently changed his password. If not, then you should edit his account and change his password to something he can remember.

Actions when users change passwords

First, try to give him a new password. If that doesn't do the trick, you may have to delete the account and start from scratch.

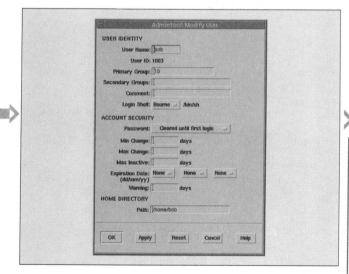

■ The Admintool: Modify User screen appears.

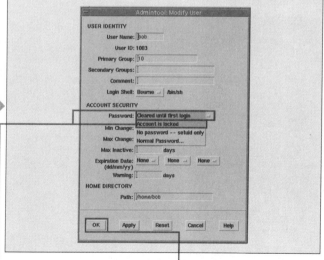

■ 8 To lock a user account, click the Password button.

■ 9 Click Account is Locked.

■ 10 Click OK to apply your changes and return to the Admintool default screen.

LIST USER GROUPS

You can use the Admintool utility to view the entire list of user groups on your system. A *group* is a logical collection of user accounts. When you log in as a user (even as root) you are part of a group of accounts that share file permissions, e-mail aliases, and probably the same slice of hard disk that holds data. Admintool enables you to view this group information in alphabetical order in a friendly, graphic mode.

When Admintool lists all groups, it's not just listing groups that contain user accounts. Admintool shows you all the groups, which may or may not contain users. For example, you can have a user group called *staff* that has no users in the group. Just because there are no users in the group doesn't mean that the group ceases to exist. The *staff* group is just an empty logical container where you can place users.

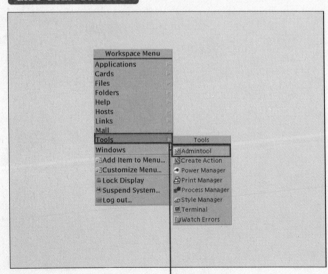

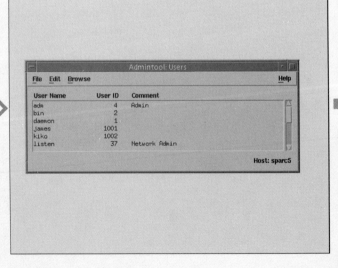

1 Right-click anywhere on the desktop.

■ The Workspace pop-up menu appears.

2 Choose Tools.

3 Click Admintool.

■ The Admintool window appears.

Note: By default, the Admintool window opens to the Admintool: Users display.

Extra

Listing users by Group ID (GID) or Members alphabetically

Admintool's Groups screen isn't as flexible as its Microsoft Windows counterpart. To find where a group is listed, click and drag on the scroll bar to the right of the screen to locate the entry.

Naming a group after a user

You can, but you shouldn't get into the habit of doing this. It causes you confusion if you have to start remembering who is called what.

Automatically installed groups

Such groups as daemon, tty, and uucp are automatically created during the UNIX installation. UNIX uses these groups (sometimes called *system groups*) to run systems processes and maintenance procedures, such as disk defragmentation. These groups usually contain only the root account and a system account, such as ad, bin, or lp.

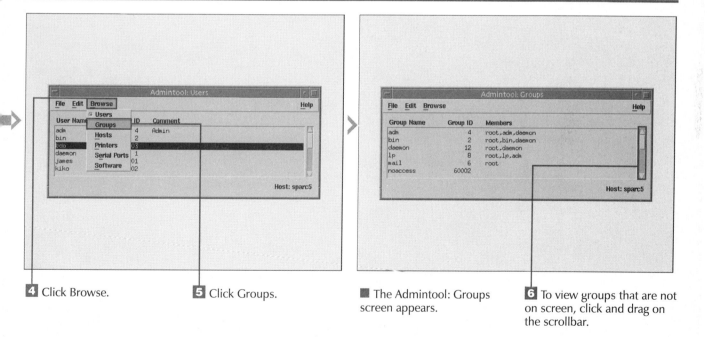

4 Click Browse.

5 Click Groups.

■ The Admintool: Groups screen appears.

6 To view groups that are not on screen, click and drag on the scrollbar.

ADD USER GROUPS

You can add user groups with the Admintool utility. This is a particularly important task if you work on a network with more than a few user accounts. Creating new user groups helps you to keep large numbers of users organized. In the corporate world, you can organize your groups by department, such as Accounting, Marketing, or Human Resources. Similarly, in an academic environment, you can organize your groups by discipline, such as Biology, Social Studies, or Computer Science.

Remember, no set ratio exists between users and user groups. Because user accounts are just the method by which a user can log into a UNIX system, a single user can have one or multiple user groups. Similarly, a group can have one user, two users, a million users, or no users at all — the logical grouping still exists and works just as well.

ADD USER GROUPS

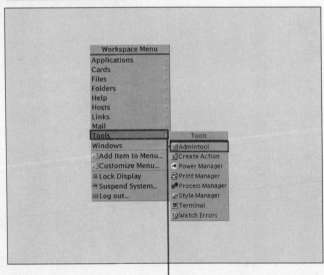

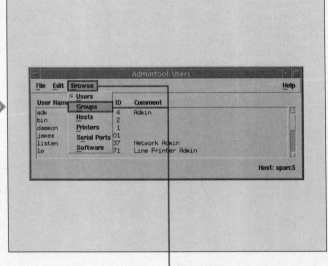

1 Right-click anywhere on the desktop.

■ The Workspace pop-up menu appears.

2 Choose Tools.

3 Click Admintool.

■ The Admintool window appears.

Note: By default, the Admintool window opens to the Admintool: Users display.

4 Click Browse.

5 Click Groups.

Extra

Deleting user groups if there are no user accounts in the group

You shouldn't do this unless you're sure that *you* created the group. Having an extra group doesn't hurt your system. But you can delete a system group that's important to the operation of your computer and cause some problems. For example, deleting the `lp` group, which controls print functions, can leave you without the ability to send documents to any of the printers on your network.

Selecting groups for my users

Most users should be in the group that Admintool selects as the default. Most importantly, never put users in the root group. Doing so gives them administrative authority, which is not what you want on a secure system.

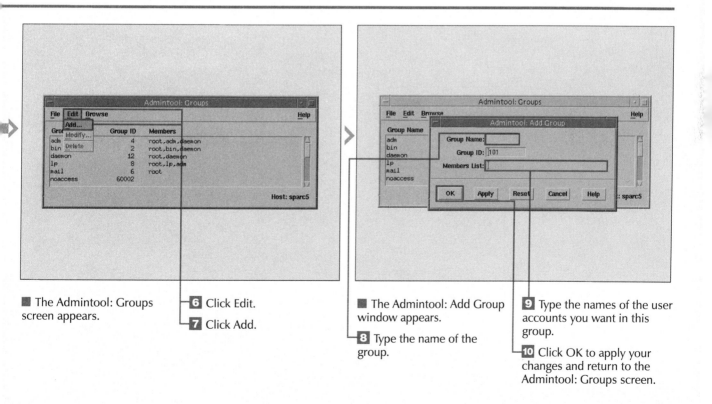

■ The Admintool: Groups screen appears.

6 Click Edit.

7 Click Add.

■ The Admintool: Add Group window appears.

8 Type the name of the group.

9 Type the names of the user accounts you want in this group.

10 Click OK to apply your changes and return to the Admintool: Groups screen.

DELETE USER GROUPS

You can delete user groups through the Admintool utility as easily as creating or editing user groups. However, you should delete user groups only in certain instances. If a group of users like to receive information on games — and are therefore part of the *games* group, you can delete the *games* group when none of the users in it are part of your organization anymore.

However, you shouldn't delete groups whenever you feel like it. For example, don't delete the group *consultants* just because your consultants have completed their tasks and moved on. You may need this group again if your company decides to hire more consulting services. Consider deleting a group when you have more than three groups that have no users in them. This prevents your groups list from getting cluttered with obsolete data.

DELETE USER GROUPS

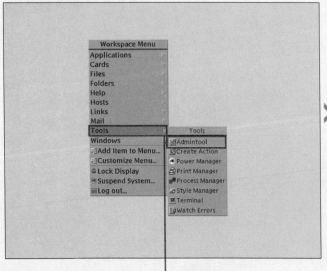

1 Right-click anywhere on the desktop.

■ The Workspace pop-up menu appears.

2 Choose Tools.

3 Click Admintool.

■ The Admintool window appears.

Note: By default, the Admintool window opens to the Admintool: Users display.

4 Click Browse.

5 Click Groups.

Extra

Users without groups

This isn't possible under UNIX. A user account must be in at least one group. Trying to remove a user from all groups — or editing the user account so that the Groups field is blank — isn't allowed by the Admintool utility.

Disabling user groups

User groups don't contain actual data themselves, so you can't put them into stasis the way you can with a user account. Being a logical grouping file, the best you can do is delete it or leave it alone.

Disabling groups without deleting

Your best bet in this case is to remove every user account that's in the group, leaving it empty.

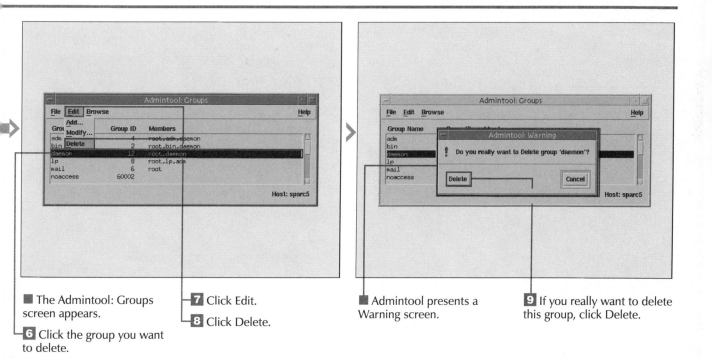

■ The Admintool: Groups screen appears.

6 Click the group you want to delete.

7 Click Edit.

8 Click Delete.

■ Admintool presents a Warning screen.

9 If you really want to delete this group, click Delete.

DETERMINE AVAILABLE DISK SPACE

You can determine approximately how much disk space you have on your machine with the df *(disk free)* command. In its most popular form, df works with the -k command option (which reports the total amount of both used and available space in kilobytes).

UNIX divides disk space into *partitions* (think of partitions as sections of the hard drive). If any partition fills, your UNIX machine slows or stops.

As a general rule, allow about 10 percent of your partition's size as unused "breathing room." This allows some leeway should a process log grow quickly and fill the drive. A full drive almost always leads to a system slowdown and crash.

DETERMINE AVAILABLE DISK SPACE

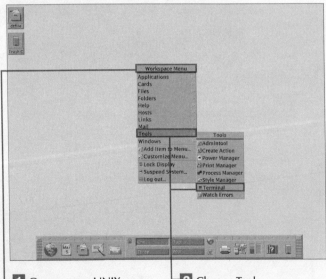

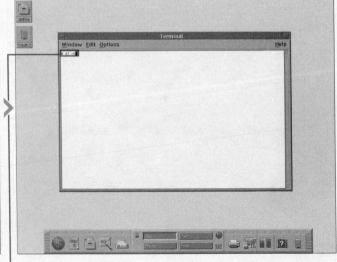

1 Open a new UNIX Terminal by right-clicking anywhere on the open desktop.

■ A pop-up menu appears.

2 Choose Tools.

3 Click Terminal.

■ After you click Terminal, the pop-up menu disappears and a new Terminal window appears on the desktop.

4 Type **df -k** at the command prompt.

5 Press Enter.

Apply It

Using the Human Option with `df`

One popular (and cleverly named) option for the `df` command is the `-h` option. The `-h` is also known as the *human* option, because it displays the disk space results in the most familiar format to new users: in MB (megabytes). To use this option, type the following at the command line and press Enter:

```
df -h
```

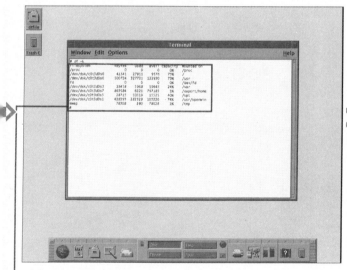

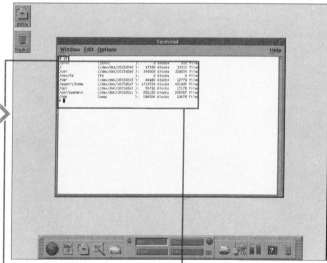

■ The results of the `df -k` command appear. The most important column is the Capacity column. This shows the percentage of the partition that is filled. When this reaches 100 percent, the partition is full.

■ Alternatively, you can type **df** at the command prompt and press Enter.

■ This reports similar information, but the space is listed in *blocks* of 512K.

READ FLOPPY DISKS

You can read floppy disks on today's UNIX machine more easily than on earlier forms of the operating system. In the earlier forms of UNIX, there was no GUI (Graphical User Interface) to provide you with an icon of a floppy disk or disk drive to click on.

Also, earlier forms of UNIX required the `mount` command, together with arcane command options, to use a floppy disk.

This is still true for some recent forms of UNIX and Linux. Solaris automatically mounts the floppy disk when you read it, so you're spared the hassle of typing "mount." This increases your flexibility in creating, transferring, and storing files between computers.

You can view files, directories, and information from floppy disks on a UNIX machine by using the Open Floppy utility in the CDE (Common Desktop Environment) desktop.

READ FLOPPY DISKS

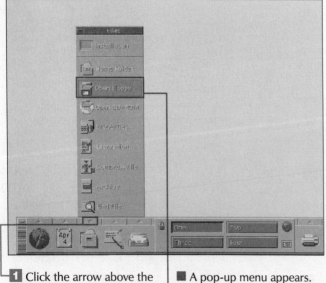

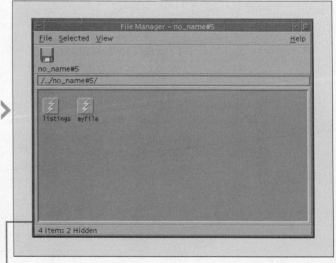

1 Click the arrow above the Files button on the desktop toolbar.

Note: For a review of the desktop toolbar buttons, see Chapter 1.

■ A pop-up menu appears.

2 Click Open Floppy on the pop-up menu.

■ A window on your desktop displays the floppy disk's contents.

Extra

Compacting file displays to see more

The method of file display from a floppy is controlled from the View menu on the File Manager display. Click View and choose Set View Options to change the display controls in the floppy's window the same way you use it for your home directory. Set the display to List or Small Icons and you have more space.

Displaying the contents of an empty disk

The most common problem is that the disk doesn't have anything saved to it yet. When nothing is on the disk, UNIX doesn't create any icons to represent files on the disk.

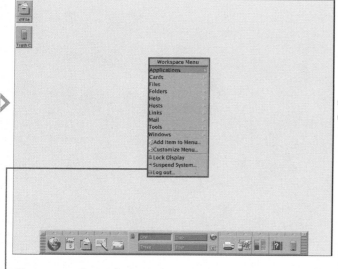

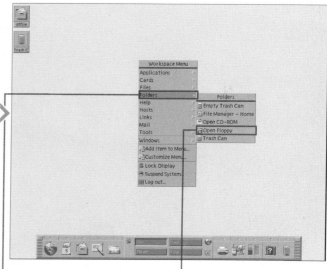

■ Alternatively, you can open a floppy disk by right-clicking anywhere on the open desktop. The Workspace Menu appears.

■ Choose Folders. A submenu appears.

■ Click Open Floppy from the submenu. The File Manager creates a window of the floppy disk's contents.

COPY FILES TO AND FROM THE FLOPPY DISK

You can copy files to a floppy disk for transporting data to UNIX or Windows-based computers. Of course, copying files to a floppy is a simple, efficient form of backup if you aren't saving more than 1.4MB of data. After you start stacking the floppies, consider investing in a *tape drive* or a *writable CD-ROM drive*.

You can select a file to copy with a single click. When you want to select a whole range of files to copy at one time and they're in the same directory, you can do that. Simply click and drag the mouse over the entire group of files you want to copy. You can easily tell which files you select because they're highlighted. After selection, you can perform the copy process to the location you want.

COPY FILES TO AND FROM THE FLOPPY DISK

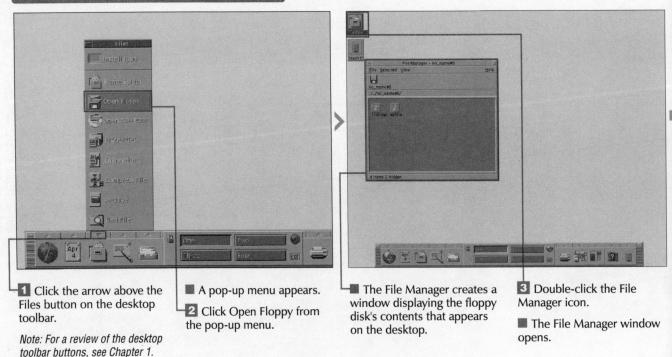

1 Click the arrow above the Files button on the desktop toolbar.

Note: For a review of the desktop toolbar buttons, see Chapter 1.

■ A pop-up menu appears.

2 Click Open Floppy from the pop-up menu.

■ The File Manager creates a window displaying the floppy disk's contents that appears on the desktop.

3 Double-click the File Manager icon.

■ The File Manager window opens.

Extra

Slow display of newly copied files

CDE very slowly updates the icon count during a file transfer. If you want, you can click View and select Update from the drop-down menu to see the newly copied contents.

Working in Microsoft Word or WordPerfect and saving a document that works on a UNIX machine

Word processors insert a lot of hidden data when you save a word document. A simpler text editor, such as UNIX's vi editor, usually translates this extra data as garbage characters. To combat this problem, save a Word document in Text format. (Text format deletes special formatting, such as bold print.)

Choosing to save pictures as GIFs instead of BMPs

Either format is acceptable in UNIX. However, BMPs often use more disk space because they don't have built-in compression.

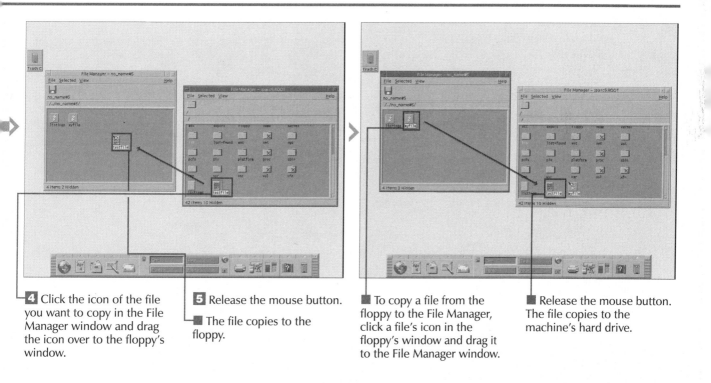

4 Click the icon of the file you want to copy in the File Manager window and drag the icon over to the floppy's window.

5 Release the mouse button.

■ The file copies to the floppy.

■ To copy a file from the floppy to the File Manager, click a file's icon in the floppy's window and drag it to the File Manager window.

■ Release the mouse button. The file copies to the machine's hard drive.

EJECT FLOPPY DISKS

You eject floppy disks from your UNIX machine by using the `eject` command. This contrasts the usual PC method, which allows you to simply remove a floppy from the floppy drive by pushing a release button.

The eject process in the UNIX operating system is more complex than the simple "pop and go" philosophy of a PC. UNIX still performs the relatively cumbersome tasks of *mounting* and *unmounting* floppy disks.

It mounts and unmounts disks automatically in the newer versions of the operating system.

By mounting and unmounting disks automatically, the File Manager utility in CDE makes your life easier. File Manager automates these functions as part of the window that displays the floppy disk's contents. Of course, if you ever suffer a power outage and can't use these commands, keep a paper clip handy to manually eject the floppy disk from the drive.

EJECT FLOPPY DISKS

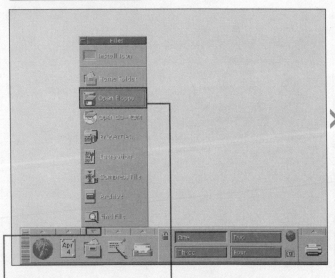

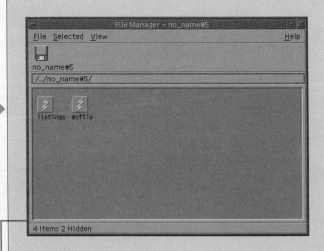

1 Click the arrow above the Files button on the desktop toolbar.

Note: For a review of the desktop toolbar buttons, see Chapter 1.

■ A pop-up menu appears.

2 Click Open Floppy from the pop-up menu.

■ The File Manager creates a window of the floppy disk's contents on the desktop.

Extra

Retrieving floppy disks when the drive refuses to unmount or eject

If your machine refuses to eject the floppy disk, reboot the computer and see whether the trouble persists.

In addition, all PC-based UNIX machines have a physical method in order to eject the disk. If you're running UNIX on a Sun Microsystems machine or a Macintosh, you need a paper clip or thin pencil to force-eject the floppy disk.

Using a paper clip to retrieve a floppy disk

This is a bit of UNIX and Macintosh lore that everyone should know in case of a major power failure. Some Macintosh and UNIX computers lack the manual release button for the disk, but they have a small hole below the floppy drive. By straightening one bend of the paper clip so that it forms a straight spike, you can stick it into the hole and push in the spring that activates the eject mechanism.

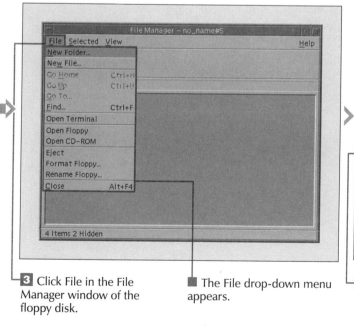

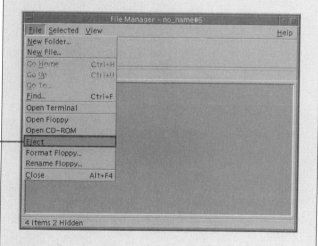

3 Click File in the File Manager window of the floppy disk.

■ The File drop-down menu appears.

4 Click Eject on the drop-down menu.

■ The floppy disk ejects from the drive so that you can remove it.

READ CD-ROMS

You can read CD-ROMs on your UNIX machine much more easily today than on earlier versions of UNIX. In the earlier forms of UNIX, there was no GUI like the Common Desktop Environment to provide you with an icon of a CD-ROM drive to click.

Also, to read CD-ROMs then, you used the `mount` command, together with special command options, to use the information on the CD. Now, you can view files, directories, and information from a CD on a UNIX machine by using the Open CD-ROM utility on the Common Desktop Environment area.

Always prepare for longer copy times when moving files from the CD-ROM to your local hard drive. Usually, you're copying large files from a CD-ROM, such as whole applications or utilities.

READ CD-ROMS

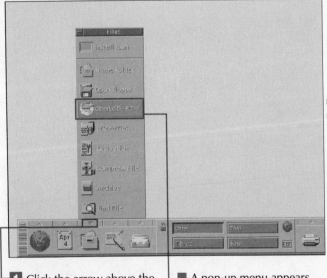

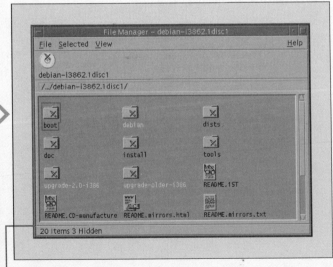

1 Click the arrow above the Files button on the desktop toolbar.

Note: For a review of the desktop toolbar buttons, see Chapter 1.

■ A pop-up menu appears.

2 Click Open CD-ROM from the pop-up menu.

■ The File Manager creates a window displaying the CD-ROM's contents that appears on the desktop.

Extra

Delays in the copy process from the CD-ROM to the hard drive

If you have an old, double-speed drive, you need more copy time than you do with a faster CD-ROM.

The meaning of "speed" in CD-ROM drives

Speed is how fast the CD-ROM rotates in the drive. Usually, the faster the CD spins, the faster the data transfers.

Other delays when copying from a CD drive

When you install a super-fast CD-ROM drive in a slow machine, you transfer the data bottleneck from one area to another. If you have an old information bus or a small amount of RAM, your bottleneck is on the computer's hard drive. This is called *disk bound*. On the other hand, if you have a fast machine and a slow CD-ROM drive, you're *drive bound*.

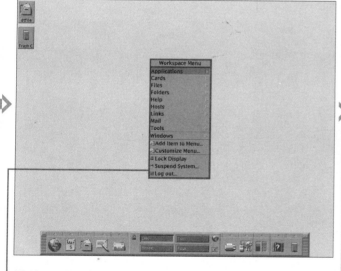

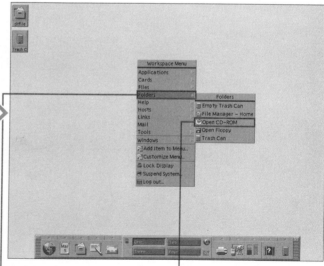

■ Alternatively, you can open a CD-ROM by right-clicking anywhere on the open desktop. The Workspace Menu appears.

■ Choose Folders. A submenu appears.

■ Click Open CD-ROM from the submenu. The File Manager creates a window of the CD-ROM's contents.

EJECT CD-ROMS

You eject CDs from your UNIX machine with the same `eject` command as with a floppy disk. This is unlike ejecting a CD-ROM from a PC, which allows you to simply remove a CD-ROM from the drive by pushing an eject button.

The eject process in the UNIX operating system is more cumbersome than on a PC because UNIX performs the relatively cumbersome tasks of mounting and unmounting the CD. However, much of the process in UNIX is automated, behind the scenes, in the newer versions of the operating system.

In this case, the CDE File Manager utility makes your life much easier by automating these functions as part of the window that displays the contents of the CD-ROM.

EJECT CD-ROMS

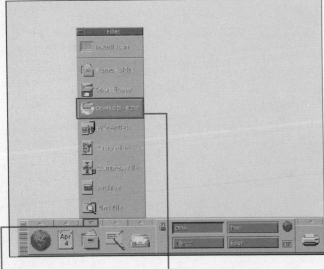

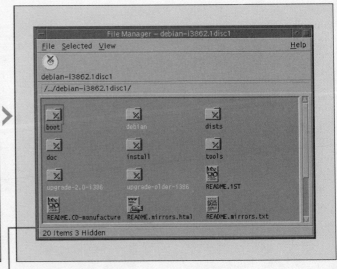

1 Click the arrow above the Files button on the desktop toolbar.

Note: For a review of the desktop toolbar buttons, see Chapter 1.

■ A pop-up menu appears.

2 Click Open CD-ROM from the pop-up menu.

■ The File Manager creates a window of the CD-ROM's contents on the desktop.

Extra

Using unlabeled CD-ROMs with UNIX

UNIX doesn't require a label on the CD-ROM to run. When an unlabeled CD-ROM doesn't play, usually you've inserted the disk upside down by mistake because there is no sticker label to mark the top. Eject the disk, flip it over, and insert it again.

Retrieving CD-ROMs when the CD-ROM drive tray refuses to open

First, back up your system before proceeding any further. Check whether any lights on the drive flash when you press the Eject button on the CPU. When you do, make doubly sure that the drive has been dismounted. If not, the drive may be hung; you have to reboot the machine to free it.

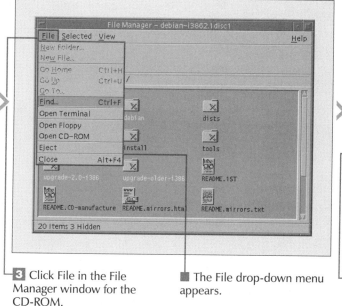

3 Click File in the File Manager window for the CD-ROM.

■ The File drop-down menu appears.

4 Click Eject on the drop-down menu.

■ The CD-ROM ejects from the drive so that you can remove it.

OPEN THE PRINT MANAGER

You can open the Print Manager on the UNIX desktop to see printers and print jobs on your system. *Printers* are devices that punch, spray, burn, or fuse ink onto paper. Next to actually starting the UNIX operating system, administering Print Manager is the most important task in running a UNIX machine in a public environment.

The volume of printing in any office, college, or laboratory far outweighs any other request. So

it's worthwhile to learn how to effectively add and configure printers in UNIX.

The Print Manager shows which print jobs go to each printer. When a print job must wait for the printer to finish another job, it is *spooled* (stored) on the hard drive or the printer itself. When many jobs spool on one printer, send more print jobs to the less-used printers.

OPEN THE PRINT MANAGER

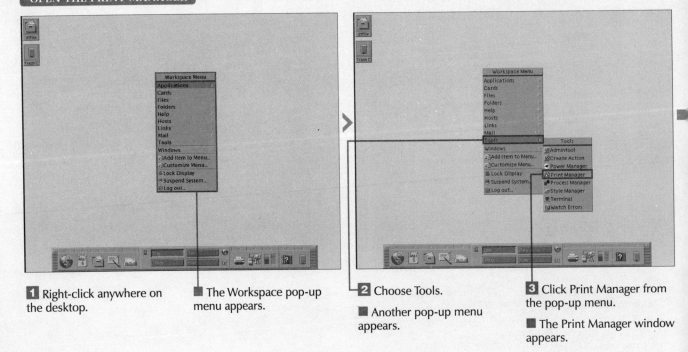

1 Right-click anywhere on the desktop.

■ The Workspace pop-up menu appears.

2 Choose Tools.

■ Another pop-up menu appears.

3 Click Print Manager from the pop-up menu.

■ The Print Manager window appears.

Apply It

Using the lpc Command to Check Printer Status

Another option to check on the status of printers and print jobs is the `lpc` command. `lpc` stands for line printer control and can only be used in the Linux terminal.

To view the status of all printers, print daemons, and print jobs on your system, type the following at the command line and press Enter:

```
lpc status
```

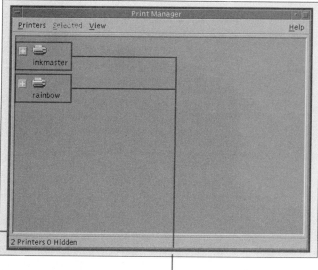

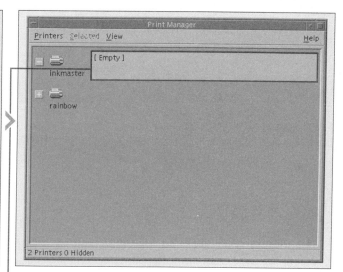

■ The Print Manager screen shows the printers currently on the system. In this example, the Print Manager shows the two printers on this system, Inkmaster and Rainbow.

■ To view the print jobs currently spooled on a printer, click the box marked with a plus sign to the left of each printer.

■ No print jobs currently exist on Inkmaster because the field listing this information to the right of the printer shows as Empty.

ADD PRINTERS

You can add printers to your UNIX system easily in the Admintool utility. Contrary to what you may think, printers aren't added in the UNIX operating system through the Print Manager. Instead, you use the Print Manager primarily for managing print job queues. You add and remove printing hardware in Admintool.

Usually, you're working with a printer known as a *local* printer. A local printer attaches directly to a given machine. Although the name *local* implies that the printer only handles local print jobs, that isn't the case. A printer can be local, but if it's networked, it can still receive print jobs from all corners of the network.

ADD PRINTERS

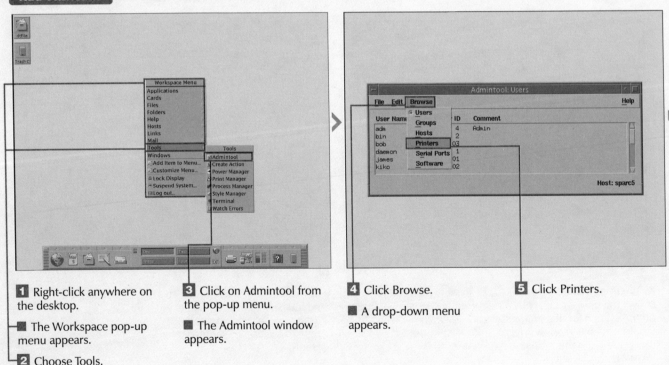

1 Right-click anywhere on the desktop.

■ The Workspace pop-up menu appears.

2 Choose Tools.

3 Click on Admintool from the pop-up menu.

■ The Admintool window appears.

4 Click Browse.

■ A drop-down menu appears.

5 Click Printers.

Extra

Choosing a printer port in the Add Local Printer screen

Normally, you accept the default setting, which is the lp1 parallel port. However, if your printer documentation recommends attaching the printer to a different port, click the field next to Printer Port. Select a printer port from the drop-down menu to change ports.

Setting Write to Superuser under Fault Notification in the Add Local Printer screen

This means that when the printer fails, an e-mail is automatically sent to the system administrator. If you want to change this, click the field next to Fault Notification. Choose a different setting from the drop-down menu. Your other options are to have no notification

sent to anyone, or to have a notification sent to a specific user account.

Using the buttons Default Printer and Always Print Banner in the Add Local Printer screen

Selecting a printer as a *default* means that jobs always go to that printer unless you specify otherwise. A *banner* is an extra page that prints before a document with the user's name and information on it. This helps when many users print to a printer, but otherwise it just wastes paper and time.

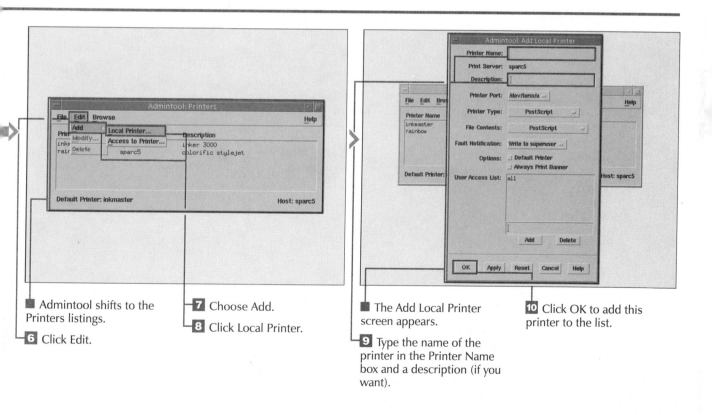

■ Admintool shifts to the Printers listings.

6 Click Edit.

7 Choose Add.

8 Click Local Printer.

■ The Add Local Printer screen appears.

9 Type the name of the printer in the Printer Name box and a description (if you want).

10 Click OK to add this printer to the list.

DELETE PRINTERS

You can delete printers from the list of print machines in the Print section of Admintool. When a printer is removed from the network, remove it from the printer list. Otherwise, users see a viable printer and try to send print jobs to it.

Also, some of the more advanced word processors work more actively with printer servers and try to balance printing jobs across a network. Not updating the list of printers in Admintool confuses these programs — they send jobs where they will never print!

After a printer is scheduled for temporary or permanent downtime, remove it from the Admintool list of printers as soon as possible. Luckily, Admintool makes this task exceptionally easy for you.

DELETE PRINTERS

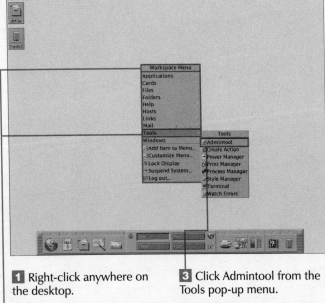

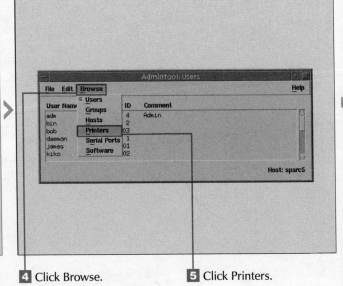

1 Right-click anywhere on the desktop.

■ The Workspace pop-up menu appears.

2 Choose Tools.

3 Click Admintool from the Tools pop-up menu.

■ The Admintool window appears.

4 Click Browse.

■ A drop-down menu appears.

5 Click Printers.

Extra

Renaming a printer

While in the Printer screen of Admintool, highlight the printer by clicking it and then click Edit. Choose Modify from the drop-down menu and the Modify screen appears. You can change aspects of the printer on the Modify screen, such as the fonts it uses and the darkness of the print. Click OK to apply the changes.

What happens to documents sent to a printer which isn't receiving print jobs

Often, these jobs don't just go away or get reassigned. Instead, they're stored, or stacked, in the print queue. The print jobs just pile up. When users on the system complain that jobs disappear after being sent to the printer, check your print queues — ensure that print jobs aren't just stacking up and sitting there.

What happens to the print jobs stacked on a broken printer when the printer is removed

After a printer is removed, it has no print queue. All print jobs stored in that queue are permanently deleted.

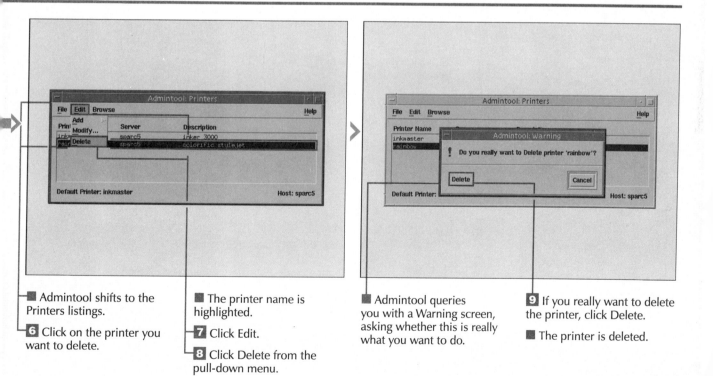

■ Admintool shifts to the Printers listings.

6 Click on the printer you want to delete.

■ The printer name is highlighted.

7 Click Edit.

8 Click Delete from the pull-down menu.

■ Admintool queries you with a Warning screen, asking whether this is really what you want to do.

9 If you really want to delete the printer, click Delete.

■ The printer is deleted.

GET BASIC HOST INFORMATION

You can get the basic information on your UNIX machine, or *host*, most conveniently with the graphically-based Admintool. (For a quick review of Admintool's capabilities, see Chapter 10.) Admintool allows you to view and edit information from the graphic desktop. However, the most basic task is still the same in the GUI as in the original UNIX Terminal — delivering basic host information.

You need your own machine's host name as a base point of reference when you start any networking task in UNIX. When you install UNIX, you start with the default host name, `localhost`. Normally, you go into the UNIX Terminal and use the vi editor to change the default host name to something else, but you can also perform this task in the Admintool utility.

GET BASIC HOST INFORMATION

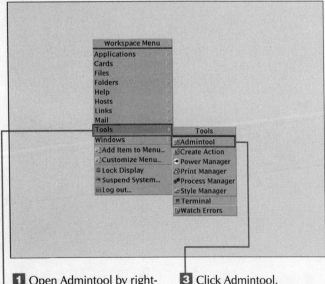

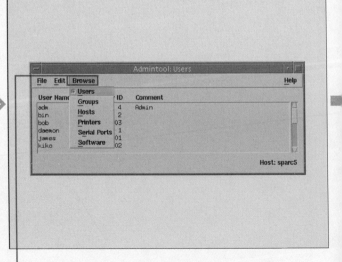

1 Open Admintool by right-clicking anywhere on the open desktop.

■ A pop-up menu appears.

2 Choose Tools.

■ A submenu appears.

3 Click Admintool.

■ The pop-up menu disappears and the Admintool window appears on your desktop.

4 In the Admintool window, click Browse.

■ A drop-down menu appears.

Extra

How to check for local host information when Admintool isn't working

Your best bet in that situation is to bring up a UNIX Terminal. Change directories to `/etc` and vi the hosts file. The first entry in the file is the local host's address, host name, and domain.

Guidelines to follow when changing the host name

When you really want to change your machine's host name, don't use any characters except numbers and letters. Your best bet is to stick to letters. When you have a group of machines, name them by a *theme*.

For example, you can name all your mail servers after planets and the clients after moons. Be sure not to make names long. Retyping `ganymede_moon_of_jupiter` again and again is both tedious and prone to error.

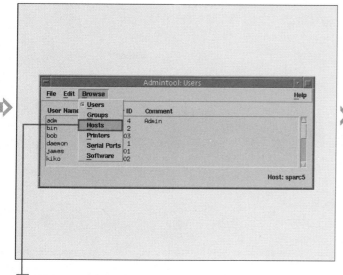

5 Click Hosts from the drop-down menu.

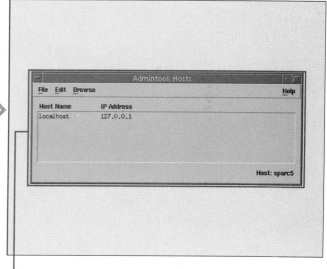

■ The Admintool window lists the hosts. By default, the localhost appears.

CHECK NETWORK CONNECTIVITY WITH `PING`

You can check whether machines on the network communicate by using the `ping` command. `Ping` is one of the oldest and most useful commands in the UNIX networking world.

Basically, the `ping` command sends a TCP packet between two machines. The TCP (Transport Control Protocol) packet is also called the *virtual circuit* because it provides feedback after it is received at its destination.

`Ping` uses TCP's feedback mechanism to report whether a host is working or not.

When `ping` sends a stream of TCP packets that are returned, `ping` reports the number of packets returned. When `ping` doesn't return any packets, either the network or the machine isn't running or configured correctly.

CHECK NETWORK CONNECTIVITY WITH PING

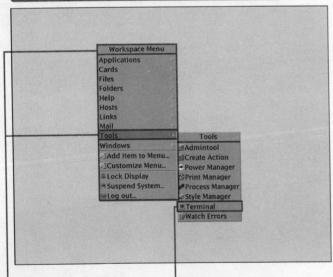

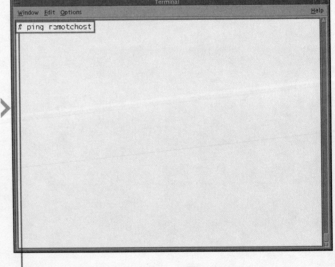

■1 Right-click anywhere on the open desktop to open a new UNIX Terminal.

■ A pop-up menu appears.

■2 Choose Tools.

■ A submenu appears.

■3 Click Terminal.

■ The pop-up menu disappears and a new Terminal window appears on your desktop.

■4 To ping a machine, type **ping remotehost** at the command prompt, then type the name of the machine.

■5 Press Enter.

Extra

Machine connectivity checked with `ping`

Any machine that connects to another machine can be checked with the `ping` command. You can *ping* from PCs, UNIX servers, and laptops to routers, mail servers, and remote hosts. Generally, if you can remotely log into it, you can *ping* it.

When `ping` doesn't respond

There are too many possibilities to give an exact answer as to why connectivity failed. It can be due to heavy network traffic, or a machine that is hung on a process. However, the most common cause is when a cord or wire is disconnected somewhere.

Other `ping` outputs

When you use `ping  -v` for *verbose output,* network statistics help you estimate the speed of your network and whether it's bogging down. Packet transmission times usually are reported in milliseconds.

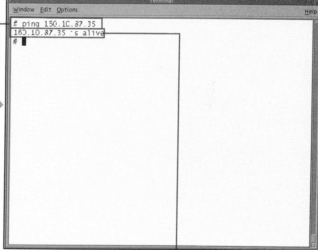

■ `Ping` reports the number of `ping` packets that are returned.

■ Alternatively, if you know the machine's Internet Protocol address, you can ping the machine by typing **ping** at the command prompt, then typing the IP address, then pressing Enter.

■ Again, a `ping` message reports the number of `ping` packets that are returned.

LOG IN WITH **RLOGIN**

You can connect to other UNIX clients and servers on your network and give them remote commands after you log in with the `rlogin` command. With a *remote login* (which is where `rlogin` gets its name), you have complete access to all the resources of the remote computer as if you are at the keyboard. This holds true whether you're down the hall or a whole continent away. While there are several different kinds of remote login tools, the most commonly used one in the UNIX world is `rlogin`.

`Rlogin` is on your UNIX network as part of the TCP/IP connection protocols utilities. It's also fairly flexible. You can remotely log into another machine via either the machine's name or the machine's Internet Protocol (IP) address. Either method connects to a remote machine.

LOG IN WITH RLOGIN

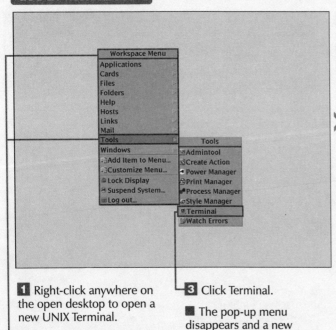

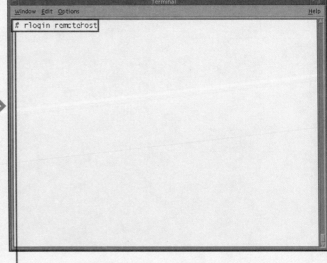

1 Right-click anywhere on the open desktop to open a new UNIX Terminal.

■ A pop-up menu appears.

2 Choose Tools.

■ A submenu appears.

3 Click Terminal.

■ The pop-up menu disappears and a new Terminal window appears on your desktop.

4 To remotely log into a machine, type **rlogin** at the command prompt, then type the machine name.

5 Press Enter.

Extra

rlogin doesn't work for some machines

Some UNIX machines remain on a network but refuse rlogin attempts. Machines set up in this manner are known as *restricted hosts*. This option was more valuable when there weren't as many security safeguards you could implement, but today it's more inconvenient than anything else.

The only way to get onto a restricted host is to try a different login tool, such as telnet, or to ask the machine's administrator to remove the restriction.

What to do when rlogin "hangs"

When the rlogin prompt hangs (stays on the screen without connecting), you don't return to your command prompt. You can either wait five minutes for the rlogin process to automatically time out, or you can attempt to kill the process. You can also try pressing Ctrl+C — you may be able to cancel the rlogin process from the screen.

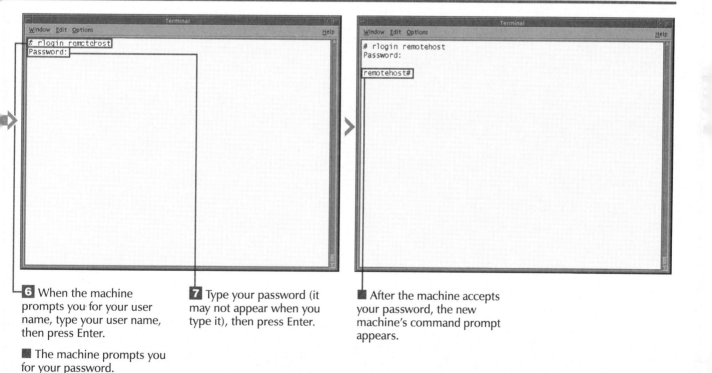

6 When the machine prompts you for your user name, type your user name, then press Enter.

■ The machine prompts you for your password.

7 Type your password (it may not appear when you type it), then press Enter.

■ After the machine accepts your password, the new machine's command prompt appears.

USE THE -1 OPTION WITH **RLOGIN**

You can connect to other UNIX machines as a different user account than the one you're currently logged in as. You can do this with the help of the most powerful of the `rlogin` command options, `-l`. The `-l` option starts the remote login process as a completely different user account. This is especially helpful when the user account has special privileges, such as the root account. When you `rlogin` to clients and servers on your network as root, you can give commands remotely that only the administrative account is allowed.

For example, when you're logged in as a user and want to edit the `/etc/passwd` files on a remote machine, you log in as root. By using the `-l` option, you can actually log on to that computer as the root account (if you have the password) and edit the `passwd` file without touching the remote machine.

USE THE -1 OPTION WITH RLOGIN

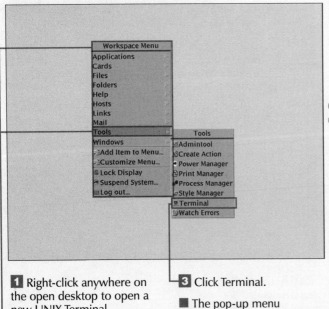

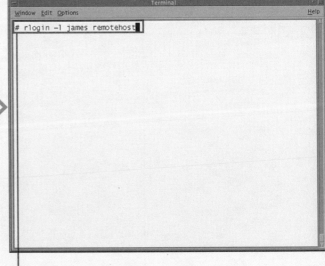

1 Right-click anywhere on the open desktop to open a new UNIX Terminal.

■ A pop-up menu appears.

2 Choose Tools.

■ A submenu appears.

3 Click Terminal.

■ The pop-up menu disappears and a new Terminal window appears on your desktop.

4 When you're logged in as root and want to log in as a different user account, type **rlogin -1** at the command prompt, then type the account name.

5 Press Enter.

Apply It

Using `rlogin` with the IP Address

If you don't know the name assigned to the machine that you want to remotely log into, you can use `rlogin` with the machine's IP address. An IP, or Internet Protocol, address is a set of numbers, such as 160.101.80.91, that indicate the location of a computer on a network. To use this option, use the following format at the command line, then press Enter:

```
rlogin -l <machine's IP address>
```

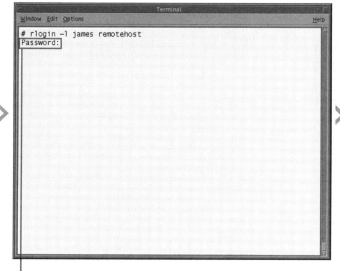

4 You're prompted for the account's password. Type the password (it may not appear when typed), then press Enter.

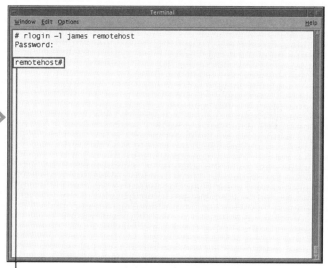

5 After the machine accepts your password, the new machine's command prompt appears.

CONNECT WITH RSH — THE REMOTE SHELL

You use the *remote shell*, or rsh command, to connect a remote host with your local group of machines. By typing **rsh <hostname>**, your command logs you into the machine and lets you work remotely. You can also use the rsh command through the IP (Internet Protocol) address of a machine when you're not sure of a machine's name. Although rsh is less sophisticated than telnet or rlogin, it's effective for a quick login and limited remote work on other machines.

Rsh is used less commonly than telnet or rlogin. It's used mostly for intra-system remote logins (within the network) versus inter-system logins (outside the network). Also, rsh only works on machines running UNIX and other variants of the UNIX operating system, such as Linux. You can't rsh into a machine that runs Novell or Microsoft Windows NT, 95, 98, or 2000.

CONNECT WITH RSH — THE REMOTE SHELL

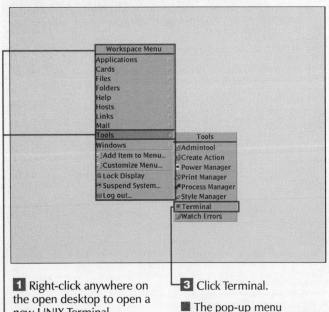

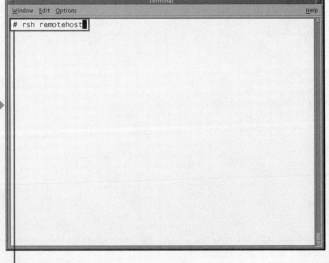

1 Right-click anywhere on the open desktop to open a new UNIX Terminal.

■ A pop-up menu appears.

2 Choose Tools.

■ A submenu appears.

3 Click Terminal.

■ The pop-up menu disappears and a new Terminal window appears on your desktop.

4 To log into a machine, type **rsh** at the command prompt, then type the name of the machine.

5 Press Enter.

Apply It

Using the -1 Option with `rsh`

You can save yourself some typing by using the -1 command option with `rsh`. The -1 option works in the same way as the `rlogin` command — it sends the remote machine your user name so that you type in only your password to remotely log on. To use `rsh` with the -1 option, type the following at the command line, then press Enter:

`rsh -l <username> <remotehost>`

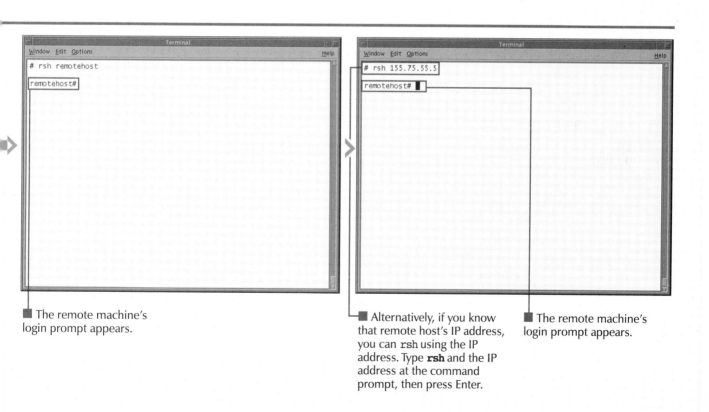

■ The remote machine's login prompt appears.

■ Alternatively, if you know that remote host's IP address, you can `rsh` using the IP address. Type **rsh** and the IP address at the command prompt, then press Enter.

■ The remote machine's login prompt appears.

LOG IN WITH TELNET

You can remotely log into other machines on your network with `telnet`. Like `rlogin`, `telnet` is automatically installed on your UNIX network as a remote connection system.

When you execute the `telnet` command, your UNIX box starts a daemon called `telnetd`. Telnetd controls the specific byte-to-byte operations of a `telnet` session with the remote host of your choice. Telnet is more popular than `rlogin` or `rsh`. The main

reason is that all other computers running UNIX use `telnet` to communicate. In addition, computers running Linux, Macintosh, and Windows 95, 98, and NT use the `telnet` utility. To use `telnet`, double-click the `telnet` icon located in the Communications or Accessories directory.

TCP/IP-based `telnet` sessions are the most widely accepted method of opening communication between different computers. Telnet is simple, reliable, and easy to use.

LOG IN WITH TELNET

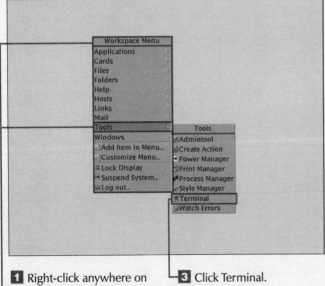

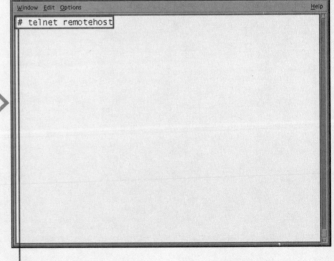

1 Right-click anywhere on the open desktop to open a new UNIX Terminal.

■ A pop-up menu appears.

2 Choose Tools.

■ A submenu appears.

3 Click Terminal.

■ The pop-up menu disappears and a new Terminal window appears on your desktop.

4 To log remotely into a machine, at the command prompt type **telnet remotehost**, then type the name of the machine.

5 Press Enter.

Extra

When `telnet>` doesn't appear where the prompt used to be

Telnet is a more complete program than `rlogin`. When activated, it displays its own command prompt. To begin a login session, type a host name or IP address.

Exiting the `telnet>` prompt and returning back to the command prompt

In order to exit the `telnet` prompt, type `exit` or `quit`, then press Enter. This returns you immediately to the command prompt.

Equivalents to `rlogin -l` in `telnet`

Telnet can attempt an automatic login, though it's not exactly the same as `rlogin -l`. Typing `telnet` with the `-a` option attempts an automatic login to a remote machine you specify, but as the same user name. This saves you some typing, but doesn't let you `telnet` in as a different user account.

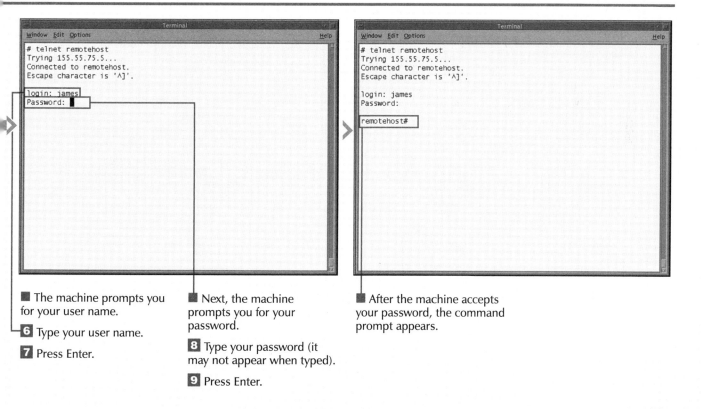

■ The machine prompts you for your user name.

6 Type your user name.

7 Press Enter.

■ Next, the machine prompts you for your password.

8 Type your password (it may not appear when typed).

9 Press Enter.

■ After the machine accepts your password, the command prompt appears.

REVIEW SETUP FOR NETSCAPE COMMUNICATOR

You can install the Netscape Web browser on your UNIX machines from CD-ROM or disk. A Web browser is a program that provides you with a graphical interface for the Internet. By clicking the appropriate fields and buttons, you can navigate to any point or Web site on the World Wide Web, search for any information, or bookmark a site that you like so that you can return to it with a single click.

Most UNIX systems have the Netscape Web browser pre-installed. If you don't have this Web browser available, you can install it from CD-ROM or floppy disk. Before you actually start the installation procedure, your first step should be to read the documentation that comes with Netscape to ensure that you have the right version, and that you have a machine with enough space and memory to handle Netscape.

REVIEW SETUP FOR NETSCAPE COMMUNICATOR

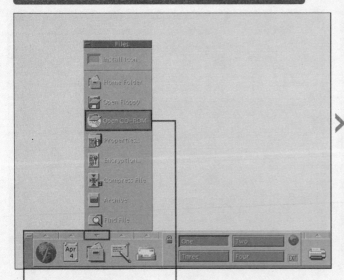

■1 After inserting the CD-ROM containing the Netscape Web Browser in your CD-ROM drive, click the upward-facing arrow above the Files button on the desktop toolbar.

■ The Files panel slides out.

■2 Click Open CD-ROM from the panel.

■ A File Manager window for the CD-ROM appears.

■3 Before you install Netscape, double-click the readme_en.txt file.

Extra

Printing the information in the readme file

You can do this by choosing File⇨Print in the Text Editor menu. (For this to print properly, you must have at least one printer properly configured for your system. See Chapter 11, "Adding Printers," for more information.)

Finding readme files in other languages

The en suffix stands for the language that the file is written in. En is for English, fr for French, and so on.

Applying Release Notes

Release Notes are final bits of documentation that the software company places on a disk or CD-ROM that were completed too late to be included in the software manual (if there is one). It's always a good idea to skim through a Release Notes document in case a bug for your specific setup was discovered at the last minute.

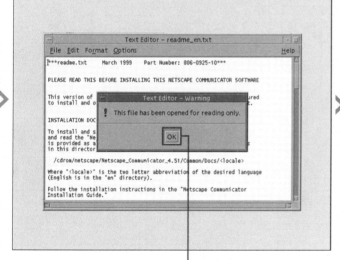

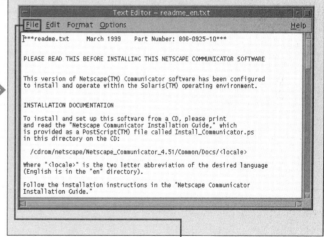

■ A text editor window appears, along with a warning window, telling you that the file is *read only*, meaning that you cannot edit it.

4 Click OK to close the warning window so you can read the text.

■ This readme file describes the documentation on the CD-ROM and the requirements for this version of Netscape to be installed properly. Read the information carefully.

5 Close the window by choosing File, then Close.

INSTALL THE NETSCAPE WEB BROWSER

Most UNIX workstations come with a Web browser installed. In the case of Solaris, one of two Web browsers normally is available to you. You may have Netscape already installed for you. However, if you do not, a Sun-based Web browser is normally included — HotJava. HotJava works well on all types of computers that run a version of Solaris, Sun's "flavor" of UNIX. However, it's best to be familiar with installing and working with Netscape's Web browser — this program is commonplace in the UNIX world.

The Netscape Web browser now is packaged with an installation program (also called an installation engine in some circles) that makes installing Netscape very easy. Starting the installation program and accepting the default locations for Netscape to install its components works for nearly every UNIX machine.

INSTALL THE NETSCAPE COMMUNICATOR WEB BROWSER

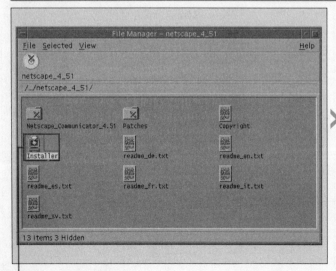

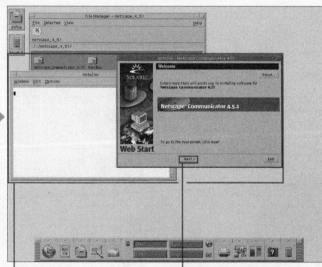

1 In the File Manager window displaying the contents of the CD-ROM, double-click the Installer icon.

■ A Terminal window opens, followed by an Installer screen. The Installer screen may take a few seconds to appear.

2 Click Next to begin the Installer process.

■ The Installer guides you through the installation process, much like a Windows Wizard program.

Extra

Installing Netscape from a floppy disk

The procedure for installing the Netscape Web browser from a floppy disk is exactly the same as installing from a CD-ROM, with one exception. To open the CD-ROM and view the `readme` and installation files, you must open the Files drawer and choose Open Floppy instead of Open CD-ROM.

Installing Netscape from the Web

This is slightly more difficult because you need two computers for this task. Unless you use HotJava, you need another computer with a working Internet connection to get to the Netscape Web site. On the site, there are directions to download the installation information to a floppy disk. Take this floppy disk to your UNIX machine and open the Netscape Web browsing program as I describe in the prior tip. Then install the browser as I describe in this chapter's task "Installing the Netscape Web Browser."

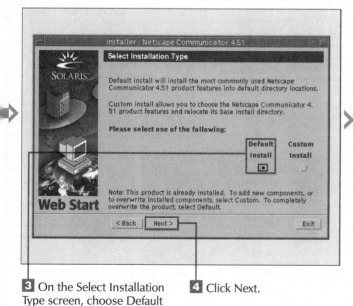

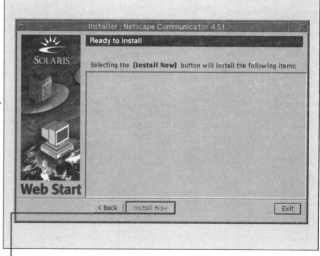

3 On the Select Installation Type screen, choose Default Install by clicking the Default Install button.

4 Click Next.

5 Finally, on the Ready to Install screen, click Install Now.

■ Netscape installs automatically, and you are returned to the desktop.

START THE NETSCAPE WEB BROWSER

Y ou can start the Netscape Web browser on your desktop immediately, but you need to configure it so that you can start browsing the World Wide Web. Your UNIX installation provides you with a couple of different ways you can access Netscape. These include starting your Web browser from the desktop toolbar, from a desktop pop-up menu, or directly from the command line of a UNIX Terminal.

Whichever way you choose, there is no difference in how the Web browser functions when it starts. In each case, the Netscape program is activated and a new Web browsing window launches on your desktop.

As a whole, Netscape's version of a Web browser is as easy to use as the competing Microsoft application.

START THE NETSCAPE WEB BROWSER

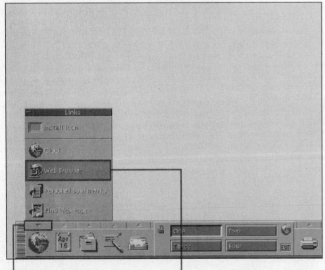

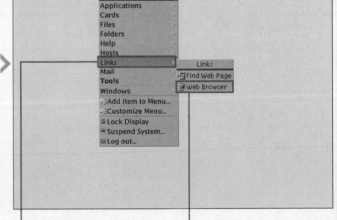

1 Click the arrow above the Links button on the desktop toolbar.

■ The Links panel slides out.

2 Click Web Browser from the panel to start Netscape.

■ Alternatively, right-click anywhere on the open desktop and choose Links from the pop-up menu. A submenu appears.

■ Choose Web Browser from the submenu.

Extra

Using my Terminal after launching Netscape from the Terminal window

After you start Netscape from the Terminal, the Netscape program acts like a newly started daemon, refusing to relinquish the screen until you shut Netscape down. Until Netscape does this, the command line where you can enter in new commands doesn't appear.

Continuing to work in a Terminal while running Netscape

Your best bet is to simply work in another UNIX Terminal window (this task explains how to open a new Terminal window). Alternatively, you can start Netscape on the Terminal command line, followed by an ampersand (&). By typing netscape & and pressing Enter, you start the Web browser in the background, which allows you to return to the command line after starting Netscape.

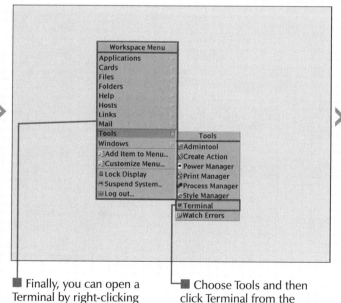

■ Finally, you can open a Terminal by right-clicking anywhere on the open desktop. This brings up the main pop-up menu.

■ Choose Tools and then click Terminal from the submenu. After you select Terminal, the pop-up menu disappears and a new Terminal window appears on the desktop.

■ At the command prompt, type **netscape** and press Enter. In a few seconds, Netscape starts.

CONFIGURE YOUR WEB BROWSER TO CONNECT TO THE INTERNET

You can configure your Web browser, whether you use Netscape or a different program, using the same standard information for each. If you're running UNIX at home, you need to sign up with an ISP (Internet Service Provider), such as America Online, to get your connection to the Internet. To complete your connections for both Internet and electronic mail access, ask the provider for this information:

1) Name of the Internet proxy server, if there is one, and the port to connect to it.

2) Name of your mail server.

A *proxy server* is one method by which an ISP allocates a single machine to handle your connection to the Internet. Similarly, a *mail server* is a machine that is set up, or *dedicated*, to handling and storing your e-mail for retrieval when you log in via your ISP.

More commonly, you're on a UNIX network with other machines; in this case, ask your network administrator for the ISP information.

CONFIGURE YOUR WEB BROWSER TO CONNECT TO THE INTERNET

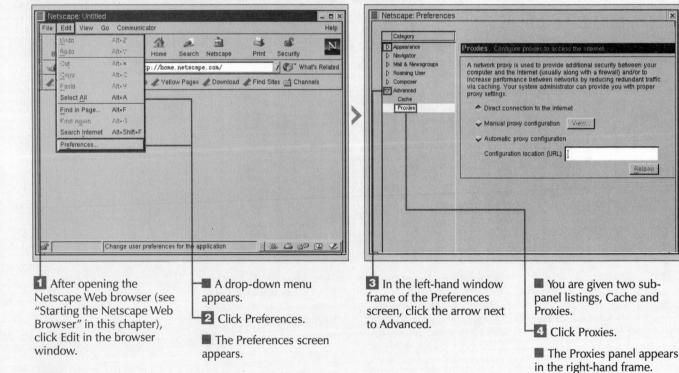

1 After opening the Netscape Web browser (see "Starting the Netscape Web Browser" in this chapter), click Edit in the browser window.

■ A drop-down menu appears.

2 Click Preferences.

■ The Preferences screen appears.

3 In the left-hand window frame of the Preferences screen, click the arrow next to Advanced.

■ You are given two sub-panel listings, Cache and Proxies.

4 Click Proxies.

■ The Proxies panel appears in the right-hand frame.

Extra

Setting up Netscape browser to use automatic proxy configuration

Automatic proxy configuration is the third of the three settings in the Proxies screen. By selecting this option, you tell Netscape where the proxy configuration is located. Though rarely used, your network administrator is able to tell you whether you need to use this setting, and what to enter in the Configuration Location field.

Networks using proxy servers

Networks with large user groups and demands use proxy servers to spread network load and increase access speed. Rather than overload one server that needs to handle printing, ftp transfers, and Web access, many organizations spread these functions by allocating one machine per use. They often refer to these machines by their task, such as *print server*, *ftp server*, or *Web server*.

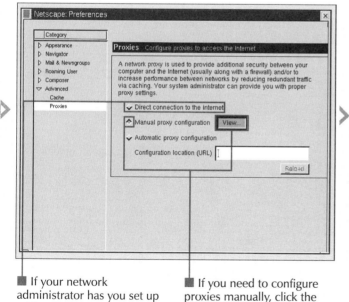

■ If your network administrator has you set up with a direct connection to the Internet, click the Direct Connection to the Internet button.

■ If you need to configure proxies manually, click the Manual Proxy Configuration button and click the View button to bring up the View Manual Proxy Configuration screen.

■ Type the proxy information in the fields on the left, and the port number for connecting in the fields to the right. Click OK when you finish.

5 When you have made your selections, close the Preferences window by clicking the Close button – the X in the upper right-hand corner.

■ You return to the Netscape browser.

USE NETSCAPE FOR WEB BROWSING

You'll probably use your Web browser for its primary function, which is visiting different Web sites on the Internet. When you first start Netscape, you go to a default home page, which is usually the Netscape home page, www.home.netscape.com. Your current *location* on the Web, which is the address of the Web page you're currently viewing, always appears in the Location field in the upper center of your screen.

When you browse or *surf* through several Web sites, your Netscape Web browser keeps a

cache, or list, of the sites you visit. By clicking on the Back or Forward buttons, you can move to different points on the list, saving you from bookmarking every single site or typing it in again and again. Much like the CDE environment as a whole, Netscape tries extra-hard to be user friendly, so look for button icons like the forward and back arrows, or the printer picture on the Print button.

USE NETSCAPE FOR WEB BROWSING

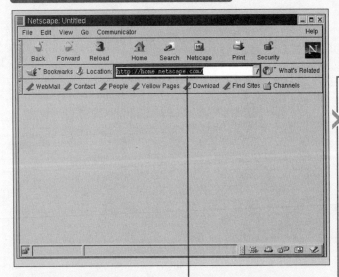

■ After opening the browser (see "Starting the Netscape Web Browser," earlier in this chapter), you start at Netscape's default Web page, home.netscape.com.

1 To view a different Web site, click the Location field to highlight the contents.

2 Type in the new Web address.

3 Press Enter.

■ Netscape locates the site, displaying its information in the window.

Extra

Printing a Web page

When you have a printer set up in UNIX, simply click the Print button whenever you want to print the site you're visiting.

Jumping to a site visited before

You have two options available. You can either hit the Back button three or four times, or you can bookmark the site. While on the page you plan to return to, click the Bookmarks button on the left side of the screen and choose Add Bookmark. The Web page's name appears in the list of bookmarks that show whenever you click the Bookmark button.

Sources of all those other bookmarks in the Bookmark utility

The Bookmark utility is pre-loaded with sites that Netscape thinks you may find useful. For example, clicking the Search button gives you a choice of different search engines recommended by Netscape. You can also find the Search setting under your Bookmarks menu.

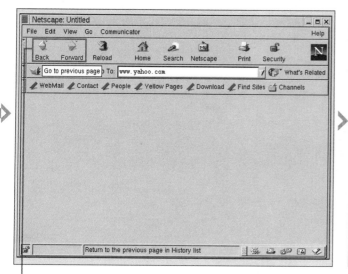

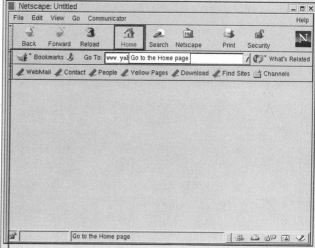

■ The Back and Forward buttons enable you to move among the multiple Web sites you visit during your Internet session.

■ As with most of the buttons in the Netscape window, you can place your mouse pointer over the button for a few seconds and read the button's function from the pop-up text.

■ The final button you need to be familiar with at the start is the Home button. This button acts like the cd command in the UNIX Terminal. When you need to return to your starting point, also called your *home page*, click here.

SET UP NETSCAPE TO RECEIVE E-MAIL

Y ou can also configure Netscape to handle your electronic mail (e-mail) for you, both when sending and receiving e-mail. Although not as efficient as some UNIX-based e-mail programs that come with UNIX, most people find the graphic style easier to use.

To send and receive e-mail, your Web browser must be set up to connect to a specific machine that is set up to handle e-mail, normally called a *mail server*. This kind of

server is also sometimes called a *POP* server, due to the specific protocols it uses to hold and send e-mail.

In this configuration area, you can also edit what *identity* you plan to give over the Web via e-mail. While you can't send e-mail anonymously, you can choose to remove your given name, or, on the other extreme, provide detailed personal or business information.

SET UP NETSCAPE TO RECEIVE E-MAIL

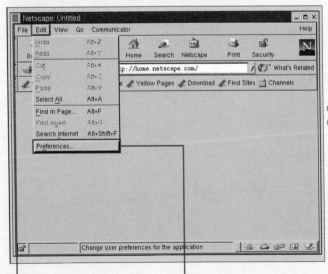

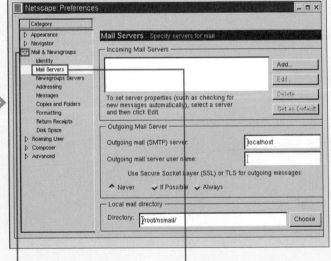

1 After opening the browser (see "Starting the Netscape Web Browser," earlier in this chapter), click Edit in the browser window.

2 In the menu that appears, click Preferences.

■ The Preferences screen appears.

3 Click the arrow next to Mail & Newsgroups in the left-hand window frame.

■ A submenu appears.

4 Choose Mail Servers from the submenu.

■ The Mail Servers panel appears in the right-hand frame.

220

Extra

Setting up an IMAP server

POP and IMAP are different mail servers in that they use slightly different protocol systems to handle the data that makes up your electronic mail. By default, Netscape adds a POP server, as noted on the dialog box when you add a new server.

To add an IMAP server, simply click the POP button next to Server Type in the dialog box. You can select IMAP from the pop-up menu.

Changing a server from POP to IMAP without changing the server's name

Instead of clicking Add in the Mail Servers screen, highlight the current mail server by selecting the listing in the Incoming Mail Servers screen. Next, click Edit instead of Add. In the dialog box, you can change the setting as I describe in the previous tip.

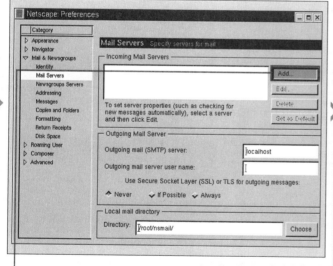

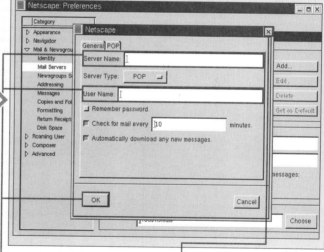

5 Click Add to add the name of a mail server.

■ A dialog box appears where you can type the server name in the open field, and when the server requires it, a User name.

6 Type in the appropriate information for your situation.

7 Click OK when you finish.

8 Close the Preferences window by clicking the Close button – the X in the upper right-hand corner – to return to the Netscape browser.

SEND E-MAIL IN NETSCAPE

You can start sending e-mail after you finish setting up Netscape to connect to the Internet and locate a mail server. Sending e-mail in Netscape is a very simple task, as it requires a couple clicks of the mouse and some reasonable typing skills to put together a letter. The actual utility to send e-mail via Netscape is a program called Netscape Messenger, which works the exact same way on all versions of Netscape.

Note that unlike some e-mail programs, Netscape on UNIX normally doesn't get your mail for you. To save CPU cycles and reduce your annoyance level, Netscape doesn't pull mail from the mail server every 10 to 15 minutes. Instead, when you want to check for mail, you click the Get Mail button on the toolbar.

SEND E-MAIL IN NETSCAPE

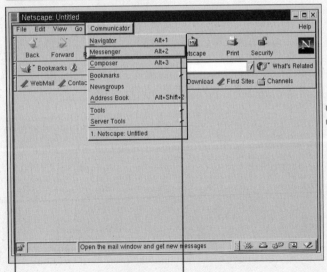

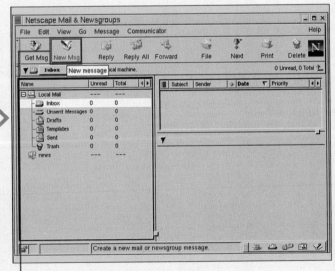

1 After opening the browser (see "Starting the Netscape Web Browser," earlier in this chapter), click Communicator in the browser window.

2 In the menu that appears, click Messenger.

■ The Netscape Messenger screen appears.

3 In the Messenger screen, click the New Msg button on the toolbar.

■ The Compose screen appears.

Extra

Reviewing e-mail.

In the Messenger screen, click Sent in the left-hand pane. Any e-mail that you have sent in Netscape Messenger is stored here until you decide to delete it.

Other ways of getting to the Messenger from the main Netscape screen.

Look down to the lower right-hand corner of your Netscape window. You can see an icon that looks like a letter in a slot. Clicking this icon brings up the Netscape Messenger.

Sending an e-mail attachment

An *attachment* is a picture or file that you choose to send with your e-mail. When you begin to compose an e-mail, click the paper clip icon below and to the left of where you enter the recipient's e-mail address. Click the open field that appears, and you're taken to a navigation screen where you can locate and select the file to attach by clicking it once.

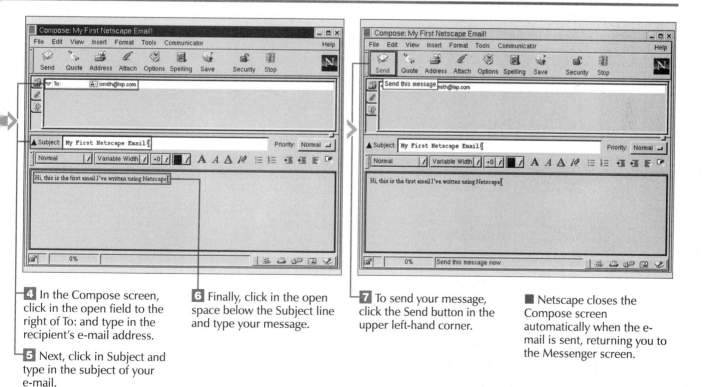

4 In the Compose screen, click in the open field to the right of To: and type in the recipient's e-mail address.

5 Next, click in Subject and type in the subject of your e-mail.

6 Finally, click in the open space below the Subject line and type your message.

7 To send your message, click the Send button in the upper left-hand corner.

■ Netscape closes the Compose screen automatically when the e-mail is sent, returning you to the Messenger screen.

OPEN THE MAILX PROGRAM

You can use mailx as your e-mail program if your version of UNIX doesn't come with the Netscape web browser, or you run UNIX without a graphic desktop. *Mailx* is a very basic e-mail program that works in all versions of UNIX. It's as old as the hills — it predates Netscape's mail program, and doesn't use a GUI of any kind. When you work with mailx, you type commands in the UNIX Terminal. You don't use your mouse to work any part of mailx.

The advantage to choosing mailx as your e-mail program is that it's completely native to UNIX, making it very stable. It's also faster, on average, than Netscape mail because it has no pictures to display. On the other hand, you may experience difficulties when receiving pictures as e-mail attachments or even HTML fragments in mailx mail. If you get a lot of .jpg or .bmp files, you may want to use Netscape Messenger instead.

OPEN THE MAILX PROGRAM

1 Right-click anywhere on the open desktop.

■ A pop-up menu appears.

2 Choose Tools.

3 Click Terminal.

■ A new Terminal window appears on the desktop.

4 At the command prompt, type **mailx**.

5 Press Enter.

Extra

Gettting more help in mailx with a new command

Mailx gives you the appropriate reminder when starting; it tells you to type a question mark, or ?, at the mailx prompt and press Enter. This provides you with a list of commands that you can use.

Sending Microsoft Word documents or MP3 sound files to mailx

Mailx has less trouble handling properly packaged sound formats, such as MP3. Word files sent to mailx don't display properly unless you save the files on your hard drive and open them with a UNIX-based word processor, such as WordPerfect or Applix. Your best bet when sending mailx text attachments is to save the document as Text Only.

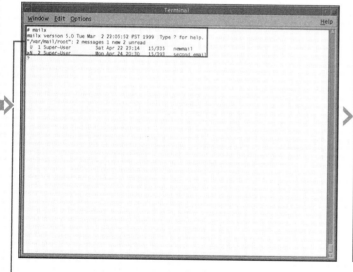

■ The mailx program starts, displaying its version and the mail in your inbox.

Note: You can always tell when you're still in the mailx program by its distinctive command prompt, a question mark, ?.

⑥ Alternatively, you can start mailx by typing **Mail** at the command prompt.

⑦ Press Enter.

RECEIVE E-MAIL

You can receive e-mail automatically in mailx whenever you start the program. Additionally, you can reply to an e-mail immediately upon receiving and reading it in mailx.

Mailx has its own conventions for receiving and replying to e-mail. In most UNIX installations, mailx works with a notification program called biff. *Biff* is a small program that automatically beeps whenever mail arrives.

However, if your system is not equipped with speakers — or the biff program itself — a message at the base of the screen also tells you that a message has arrived.

The mailx program automatically sends a command to your mail server to download any new mail that you've received since the last time you started mailx. This new mail appears in the opening mailx screen.

RECEIVE E-MAIL

1 Right-click anywhere on the open desktop.

■ A pop-up menu appears.

2 Choose Tools.

3 Click Terminal.

■ A new Terminal window appears on the desktop.

4 At the command prompt, type **mailx**.

5 Press Enter.

Apply It

Inputting new commands for the mailx program to read a new e-mail

Whenever you view an e-mail in mailx, you're still able to perform different commands within the program. The mailx command prompt appears after the message, allowing you to input other commands for mailx after you finish with the e-mail.

Inputting new commands for the mailx program when replying to or composing a new message

Unlike reading a message, mailx requires you to finish writing (or quit from) a message that you're composing. I detail this further in the next task section.

Changing the order of the messages in the inbox

Unlike newer, graphics-based mail programs, you can't change the order of the messages by user name, priority, or reverse chronology. Mailx displays messages stored in the inbox strictly by chronological order.

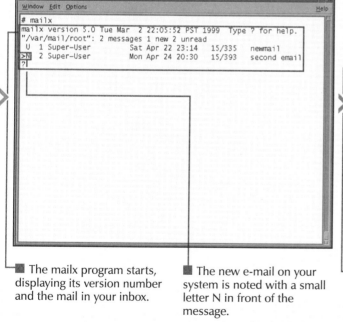

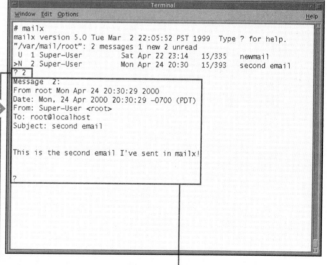

■ The mailx program starts, displaying its version number and the mail in your inbox.

■ The new e-mail on your system is noted with a small letter N in front of the message.

6 To read a new e-mail, type the number of the message at the command prompt.

7 Press Enter.

■ The new message's text appears onscreen.

REPLY TO E-MAIL

You can use mailx's partially automated reply command to respond to e-mail that you receive. When it comes to replying to e-mail, it's easiest to do when you finish reading the incoming e-mail. Mailx is primed to send a reply to whichever e-mail address is part of the currently read message.

Mailx is able to do this because when you read a message in the mailx program, mailx loads the message into a text buffer. This buffer is a sort of memory cache that keeps a segment of text available for use or copying in a program.

You use this buffer when you cut, copy, or paste any text segment in word-processing programs ranging from the UNIX vi text editor to the Microsoft Word program in Windows.

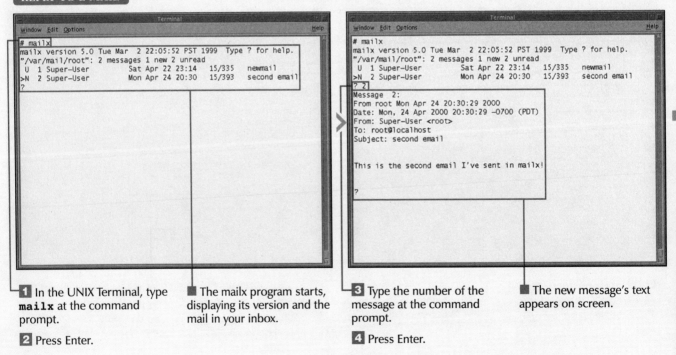

1 In the UNIX Terminal, type **mailx** at the command prompt.

2 Press Enter.

■ The mailx program starts, displaying its version and the mail in your inbox.

3 Type the number of the message at the command prompt.

4 Press Enter.

■ The new message's text appears on screen.

Apply It

Replying to an E-mail without Reading it a Second Time

If you've read an e-mail and have moved on to another message, you can reply to the e-mail without going back and rereading it. To do this, type the following at the mailx command prompt:

```
r <message number>
```

The e-mail composition screen appears, with the return address and the subject filled in for you. You can begin composing your reply.

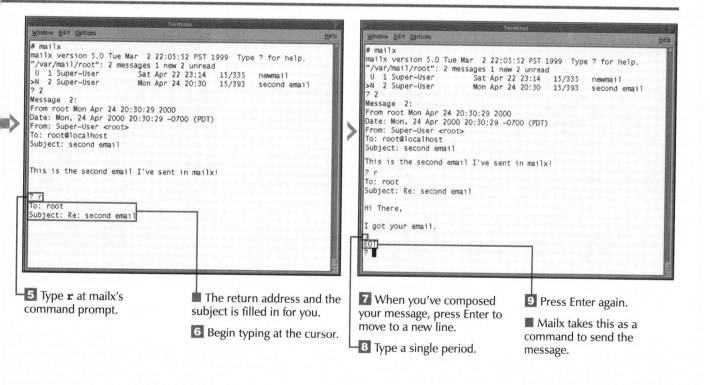

5 Type **r** at mailx's command prompt.

■ The return address and the subject is filled in for you.

6 Begin typing at the cursor.

7 When you've composed your message, press Enter to move to a new line.

8 Type a single period.

9 Press Enter again.

■ Mailx takes this as a command to send the message.

COMPOSE E-MAIL
TO SPECIFIC USERS

You can compose e-mail to other users on your system or across the Internet, even when you aren't replying to a previously sent message in the mailx inbox. Be aware that unless the e-mail recipient is on your same local network, you must know the full e-mail address of the person for the message to be sent properly. For example, if you need to send a message to jsmith@isp.com, simply typing jsmith doesn't send the message properly. The isp.com section of the address

denotes the *domain*, or general address, where user jsmith keeps his or her user account and electronic mail.

Remember, mailx is a relatively primitive text editor, designed to send short text messages between user accounts. If you want to send e-mail with graphics, attachments, or fancy formatting, you're best off using the Netscape application's mail program.

COMPOSE E-MAIL TO SPECIFIC USERS

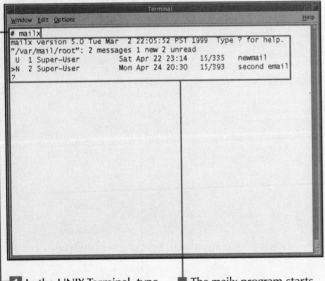

1 In the UNIX Terminal, type **mailx** at the command prompt.

2 Press Enter.

■ The mailx program starts, displaying its version and the mail in your inbox.

3 Type **mail <user name>** at the mailx command prompt. For example, to send mail to the root account, type **mail root**.

4 Press Enter.

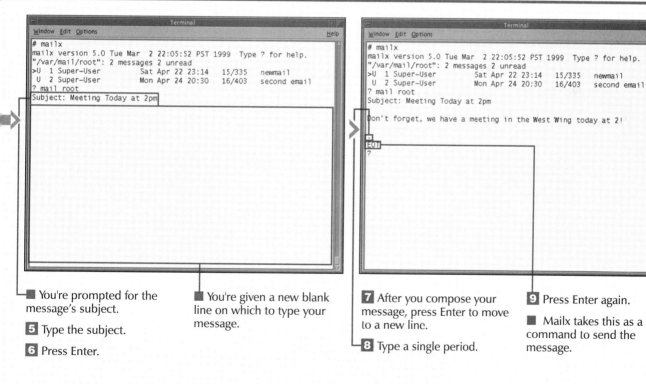

Apply It

Mailing to Multiple Users

If you want to send the same email message to multiple users, compose your message, then press Enter to move to a new line, and type a single period. Mailx will display `cc:`, or 'carbon copy.' Type in all of the addresses of the people you want to send copies to. Be sure that a comma and a space as follows:

```
cc: user@isp.com,
user2@isp.com,
user3@isp.com
```

When you're finished, press Enter and the email will be sent.

■ You're prompted for the message's subject.

5 Type the subject.

6 Press Enter.

■ You're given a new blank line on which to type your message.

7 After you compose your message, press Enter to move to a new line.

8 Type a single period.

9 Press Enter again.

■ Mailx takes this as a command to send the message.

DELETE E-MAIL

You can delete e-mail messages in mailx after you read them by using the *delete* command on the mailx command line. Deleting mail in mailx is both quicker and more dangerous than performing the same task in other mail programs, such as the UNIX Pine program or the Netscape Messenger application.

The process of deleting e-mail in mailx is both quick and dangerous for the same reason: there is no warning message when you delete an e-mail, and there is no way to retrieve the

message after it is removed. (In contrast, Netscape simply moves the e-mail to the Deleted folder until you delete it a second time.)

On the plus side, if you're careful about which messages you remove, this makes the mailx program very useful in pruning your e-mail file if you receive a large number of disposable messages in a day.

DELETE E-MAIL

1 Right-click anywhere on the open desktop.

■ A pop-up menu appears.

2 Choose Tools.

3 Click Terminal.

■ A new Terminal window appears on the desktop.

4 At the command prompt, type **mailx**.

5 Press Enter.

Apply It

Deleting Multiple Messages

You can delete several e-mails at one time in mailx. Type d at the mailx command prompt, then press the space bar.

Type the numbers of the e-mails you want to delete. Separate the numbers with spaces, but not using commas, as follows:

```
d 1 2 6 7 11 15
```

Press Enter. The e-mails are deleted and you're returned to the mailx command prompt.

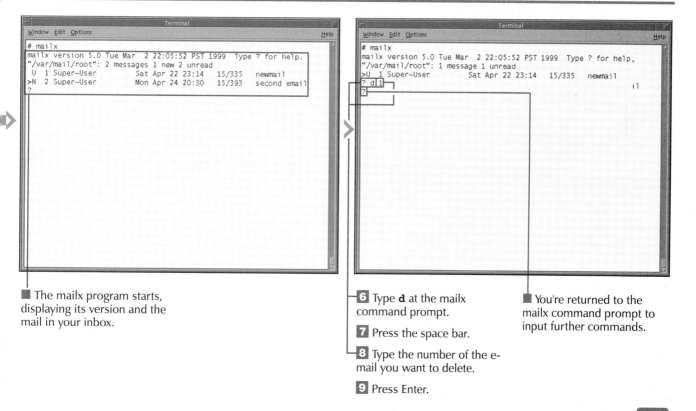

```
Terminal
Window  Edit  Options                                              Help
# mailx
mailx version 5.0 Tue Mar  2 22:05:52 PST 1999  Type ? for help.
"/var/mail/root": 2 messages 1 new 2 unread
 U  1 Super-User          Sat Apr 22 23:14   15/335    newmail
>N  2 Super-User          Mon Apr 24 20:30   15/393    second email
?
```

```
Terminal
Window  Edit  Options                                              Help
# mailx
mailx version 5.0 Tue Mar  2 22:05:52 PST 1999  Type ? for help,
"/var/mail/root": 1 message 1 unread
>U  1 Super-User          Sat Apr 22 23:14   15/335    newmail
? d 1                                                           i1
?
```

■ The mailx program starts, displaying its version and the mail in your inbox.

6 Type **d** at the mailx command prompt.

7 Press the space bar.

8 Type the number of the e-mail you want to delete.

9 Press Enter.

■ You're returned to the mailx command prompt to input further commands.

EXIT THE MAIL PROGRAM

You can exit the mailx program in several ways. Whenever you finish working with e-mail for the day, or even if you plan to be away from your computer for a while, it's best to quit mailx. This prevents extra CPU cycles from being used on a busy network, and it lessens the chance of a malicious prankster sending rude or inappropriate e-mails from your mail account.

Exiting mailx is a little easier than with other e-mail programs, such as UNIX's Pine or Elm, because of the program's lack of built-in

safeguards. In both of the aforementioned programs, nothing is truly deleted until you leave the program entirely. Mailx never asks for confirmation upon exiting each time that you mark some file or folder to be deleted. This increases the risk of accidental deletions, but it does make your life easier.

EXIT THE MAIL PROGRAM

1 Right-click anywhere on the open desktop.

■ A pop-up menu appears.

2 Choose Tools.

3 Click Terminal.

■ A new Terminal window appears on the desktop.

4 Type **mailx** at the command prompt.

5 Press Enter.

■ The mailx program starts, displaying its version and the mail in your inbox.

Apply It

The Absolute Quickest Method of Exiting Mailx

You can save yourself some typing by using the q command in mailx. To exit the program, type the following at the mailx command prompt and press Enter.

q

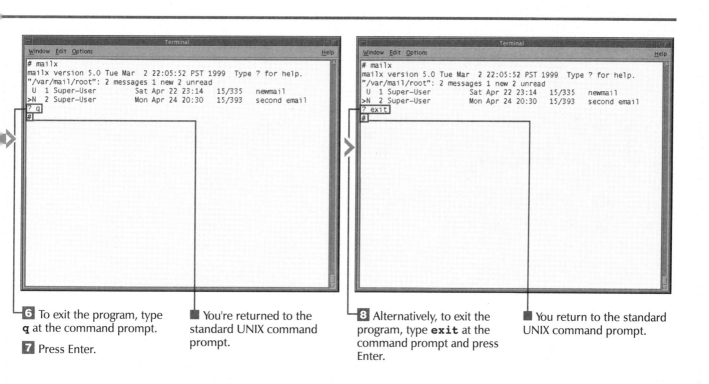

■6 To exit the program, type **q** at the command prompt.

■7 Press Enter.

■ You're returned to the standard UNIX command prompt.

■8 Alternatively, to exit the program, type **exit** at the command prompt and press Enter.

■ You return to the standard UNIX command prompt.

ARCHIVE FILES WITH TAR

You can save large files in a smaller, compressed format if you have limited disk space with the tar command. Compressing files for the purpose of saving them in a different location is also known as *archiving*.

The *tar* command is actually an acronym for "tape archive resource." It was originally designed to store files directly to a tape unit. However, tar has since then expanded its role, and you can use it to compress text files, programs, executables, sound files, and even

picture graphics like bitmaps and JPEGs. The command syntax for using tar to compress files is `tar -cvf <new location> <original filename>`.

The tar utility backs up and restores files on your system either after a system crash or as a regular part of your system maintenance. tar is a very reliable and effective way to compress and store many large files into an area of finite space, such as a magnetic tape unit.

ARCHIVE FILES WITH TAR

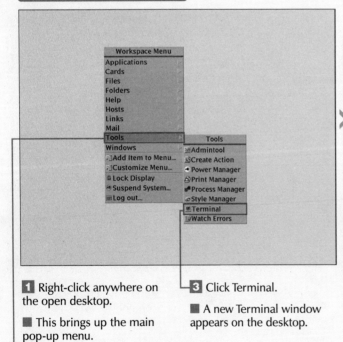

■ **1** Right-click anywhere on the open desktop.

■ This brings up the main pop-up menu.

■ **2** Choose Tools.

■ **3** Click Terminal.

■ A new Terminal window appears on the desktop.

■ **4** List your files in the directory by typing **ls**.

Extra

Naming the newly created tar file

If you don't name the file with a .tar extension, you can't restore the file back to its normal size. As a rule, always name a tar file like the original file — with a .tar extension.

What the cvf command option used with the tar command stands for

The `cvf` command option is actually three command options used together: c, for compress, v for verbose, and f for file name.

What it means if the tar command is set to use the verbose command option

In tar, or any command in the UNIX operating system, verbose means that if the command runs into a problem or an error, it returns an error message instead of just exiting without telling you what's wrong.

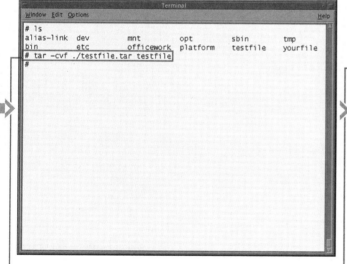

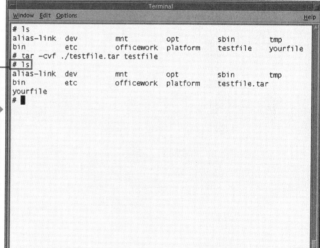

5 To compress a file, type **tar –cvf** at the command line, followed by the filename and the path where you want to store the file.

6 To check the result, type **ls**.

7 Press Enter to view the contents of your directory again.

ARCHIVE FILES WITH TAR TO A DIFFERENT LOCATION

You can save large files in a smaller, compressed format to a different location than your current directory. This is especially useful when you have limited disk space and you need to archive large numbers of files with the tar command. By far, the most common problem that a user can encounter when using the tar utility is running out of disk space when tar is backing up a file in a directory.

Because tar has since expanded its role into compressing text files, programs, executables, sound files, and even picture graphics like bitmaps and JPEGs, the space problem can be acute. Even when compressed, for example, image files can take up an entire megabyte of space or even more.

By storing a file of this size to a different partition, or slice of the hard disk, you can avoid the problems caused by trying to save to a full area. As a rule, your best bet is to back up your files to the /tmp directory, which is usually empty.

ARCHIVE FILES WITH TAR TO A DIFFERENT LOCATION

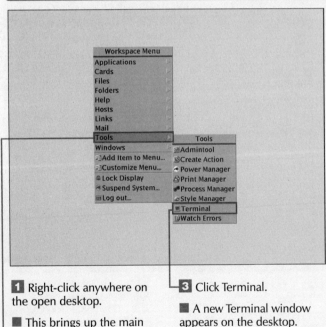

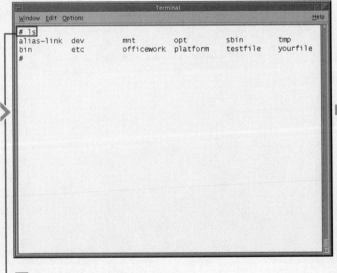

■1 Right-click anywhere on the open desktop.

■ This brings up the main pop-up menu.

■2 Choose Tools.

■3 Click Terminal.

■ A new Terminal window appears on the desktop.

■4 List your files in the directory by typing **ls**.

Extra

Applying the cvf command option with the tar command

The `cvf` command option is actually three command options used together: *c* for compress, *v* for verbose, and *f* for file name.

Setting the tar command to use the verbose command option

In tar, or any command in the UNIX operating system, verbose means that if the command runs into a problem or an error, it returns an error message instead of just exiting without telling you what's wrong.

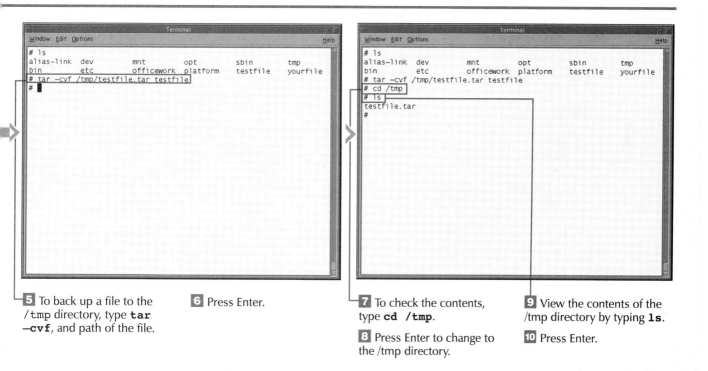

5 To back up a file to the /tmp directory, type **tar –cvf**, and path of the file.

6 Press Enter.

7 To check the contents, type **cd /tmp**.

8 Press Enter to change to the /tmp directory.

9 View the contents of the /tmp directory by typing **ls**.

10 Press Enter.

RESTORE FILES WITH TAR

You can restore files that you've backed up with the tape archive utility by using the same tar command. However, you'll be using tar with different command options. The key difference is that the restoration process uses the *x* command option, which stands for *extract*.

You'll be restoring files most frequently after you've completed some major system upgrade. Another possibility is that you're restoring the entire UNIX system from a system crash. Untarring files for this purpose is also called *restoring the system*.

The most important task you should complete before you begin restoring a compressed file with tar is to make sure that you have enough space on your hard drive to accommodate the restored file. When you restore a file with the tar command, keep in mind that you're returning the file to its full size. A compressed tar file can expand up to 50 percent larger when you restore it.

RESTORE FILES WITH TAR

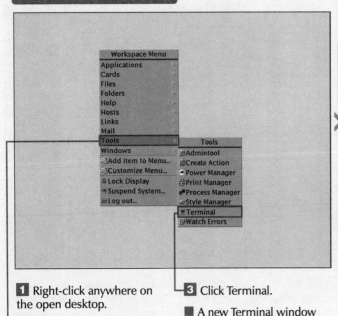

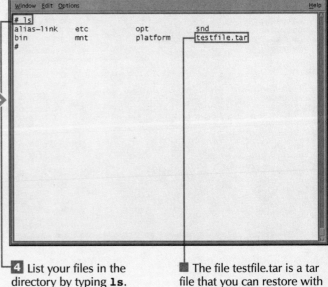

1 Right-click anywhere on the open desktop.

■ This brings up the main pop-up menu.

2 Choose Tools.

3 Click Terminal.

■ A new Terminal window appears on the desktop.

4 List your files in the directory by typing **ls**.

■ The file testfile.tar is a tar file that you can restore with the tar command.

Extra

Untarring a file to a different location

To untar a file to a different location, such as /root, type the following at the prompt, then press Enter.

```
tar -xvf backup.tar /root
```

If you read the preceding task spread on archiving files to a different location, you'll see that the command syntax is exactly the same, save for the use of the x command option instead of the c command option.

Determining how often to use tar to back up the system

This depends on two factors: (1) how much you have to spend in time and money and (2) how important the data is. How will a loss of, say, a day's worth of data affect people versus a week's worth of data loss? When you've determined those factors, you can set up a backup schedule. As a rule, unless you're working on an important system where things change daily or weekly, you can tar the important files once every three to four months.

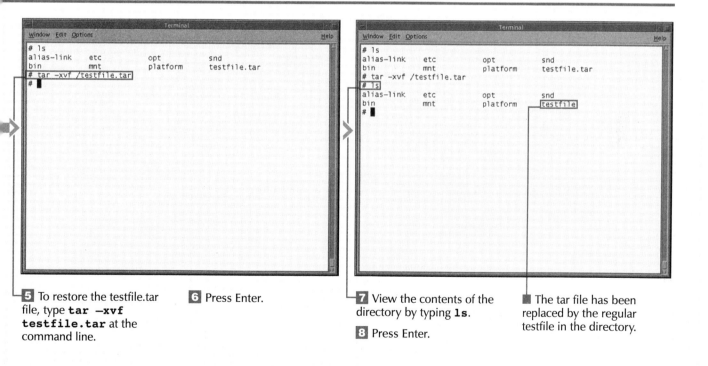

5 To restore the testfile.tar file, type **tar -xvf testfile.tar** at the command line.

6 Press Enter.

7 View the contents of the directory by typing **ls**.

8 Press Enter.

■ The tar file has been replaced by the regular testfile in the directory.

COMPRESS FILES

Y ou can use the *compress* utility as an alternative to tar. Compress is usually faster and compresses more space out of text files on average than the tar process. Like tar, compress has the main advantage of being available on all UNIX platforms, regardless of the flavor or age of the operating system. Compress is also slightly less cryptic than tar, particularly when you specify compress to operate in what is called *verbose mode,* which is described in the task spread following this one.

When it comes to compressing binaries, pictures, and other files, compress is not as efficient a compression process as is tar. Therefore, compress is not as suited for backing up large files or an entire system. In addition, compress isn't designed to work as closely with tape storage as tar. Your best use of compress is as a storage utility to place large amounts of text into a directory set aside for compressed files.

COMPRESS FILES

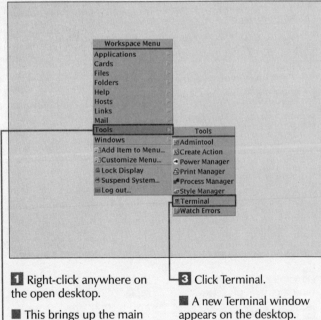

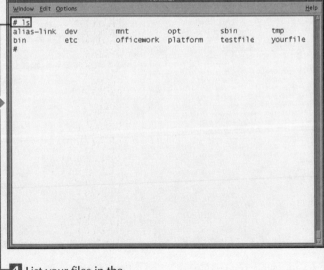

1 Right-click anywhere on the open desktop.

■ This brings up the main pop-up menu.

2 Choose Tools.

3 Click Terminal.

■ A new Terminal window appears on the desktop.

4 List your files in the directory by typing **ls**.

Extra

Compressing multiple files with the compress command at one time

You can compress multiple files at once by simply listing the files after the compress command, placing a space between each file instead of a comma. For example, to compress both files X and Y, you type compress X Y at the command prompt and press Enter.

Limitations to compressing multiple files at one time

There are no real limitations to compressing multiple files at one time. For example, you could compress six files at once by typing compress a b c d e f at the command prompt and pressing Enter.

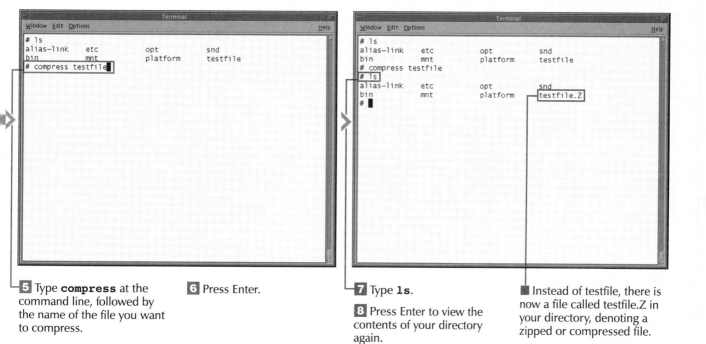

5 Type **compress** at the command line, followed by the name of the file you want to compress.

6 Press Enter.

7 Type **ls**.

8 Press Enter to view the contents of your directory again.

■ Instead of testfile, there is now a file called testfile.Z in your directory, denoting a zipped or compressed file.

COMPRESS FILES IN VERBOSE MODE

You can use the compress command with specific command options to further control the way compress is used. One of the most popular command options is –v. While the –v is optional, it invokes the useful verbose mode of the compress command. When running the verbose mode, the compress command enables you to see, among other things, how much space you're saving by compressing a file.

Since the compress utility is similar to tar, you may use it to back up and restore files on your system either after a system crash or as a regular part of your system maintenance. While not as suited to this task as tar, if you use it, the issues of limited space are exactly the same. Because you're using compress to compress and store many large files into an area of finite space, it's helpful to know how much space you're saving each time you use it.

COMPRESS FILES IN VERBOSE MODE

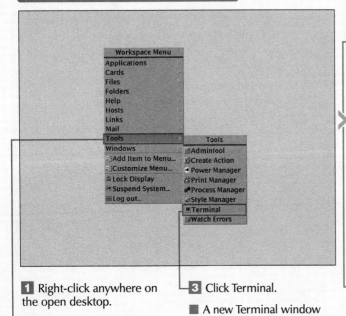

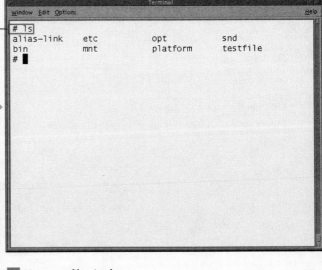

1 Right-click anywhere on the open desktop.

■ This brings up the main pop-up menu.

2 Choose Tools.

3 Click Terminal.

■ A new Terminal window appears on the desktop.

4 List your files in the directory by typing **ls**.

Extra

Watch how much space you are saving when you use the compress command

If you're short on disk space, it may help you to budget your remaining space based on how much room on the disk you are 'regaining' by compressing files.

Limitations to compressing multiple files verbosely

There are no real limitations, but the process of compressing multiple files in the verbose mode may seriously slow down a computer that is not very powerful or one that is currently handling many other jobs. If you're running compress on a busy system, then you might break the jobs down into compressing one file at a time.

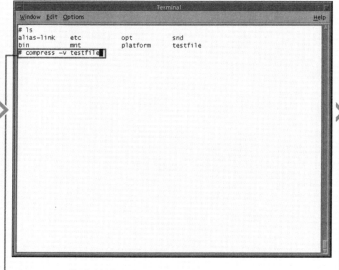

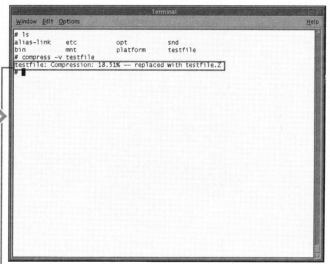

5 Type **-v** at the command line, followed by the name of the file you want to compress.

6 Press Enter.

■ When activated, the compress command notes how much the file has been compressed in a percentage.

UNCOMPRESS FILES

You can restore files that you've backed up with the compress command with the intuitive counter-command *uncompress*. This is in distinct contrast to restoring a file compressed with tar, where you would use the same command with different command options. Instead, your .Z files need an entirely different command to unpack them properly, and uncompress is the tool you need. Luckily, wherever you find compress as a command (which is 99.9 percent of all UNIX platforms), you'll also find its alter ego, uncompress.

As with restoring tar files, the most important task you should complete before you begin restoring files right and left is to make sure that you have enough space on your hard drive to accommodate the restored files. If you've recently compressed (in verbose mode) the file you're planning to restore, you can figure out whether a restoration is possible by reading the percentage that the file has been compressed by.

UNCOMPRESS FILES

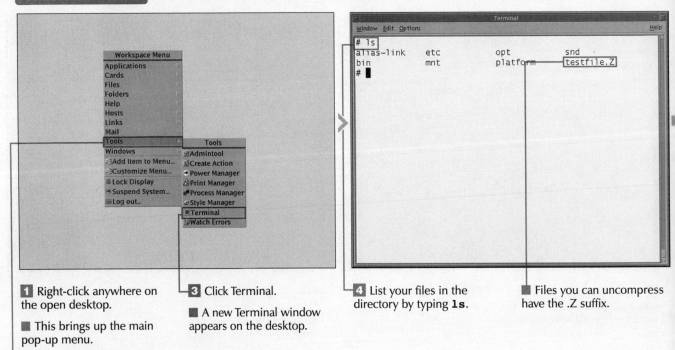

1 Right-click anywhere on the open desktop.

■ This brings up the main pop-up menu.

2 Choose Tools.

3 Click Terminal.

■ A new Terminal window appears on the desktop.

4 List your files in the directory by typing **ls**.

■ Files you can uncompress have the .Z suffix.

Extra

Uncompressing multiple files with the uncompress command at one time

As with compressing multiple files, you can uncompress multiple files at one time by simply listing the files after the uncompress command, placing a space between each file instead of a comma. For example, to uncompress both files a.Z and b.Z, you would type uncompress a.Z b.Z at the command prompt and press Enter.

Limitations to uncompressing multiple files at one time

There are no real limitations to uncompressing multiple files at one time. However, uncompressing multiple files at once will take slightly longer than if you uncompress one file at a time, because you are uncompressing a larger amount of information at once.

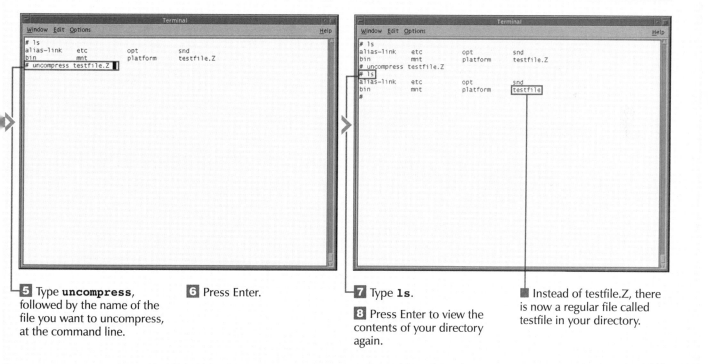

5 Type **uncompress**, followed by the name of the file you want to uncompress, at the command line.

6 Press Enter.

7 Type **ls**.

8 Press Enter to view the contents of your directory again.

■ Instead of testfile.Z, there is now a regular file called testfile in your directory.

ARCHIVE AND COMPRESS FILES

You can also archive files on your system for backing up your system or saving space by using the tar command in conjunction with the compress command. Together, both utilities can gain you additional room (on either a crowded hard drive or a backup magnetic tape) by compressing an already compressed file a little more.

You should be aware that this task, also called a *dual-compression* scheme, is not a cure-all to the problem of limited drive (or tape) space. Compressing a file that has already been compressed will generally save you only an additional two to five percent of space, depending on the type of file you're dealing with.

In addition, you'll need to follow a slightly more complex process to restore the file in question. However, if a two-percent gain in compressing is worth your while, it can be done between the two commands.

ARCHIVE AND COMPRESS FILES

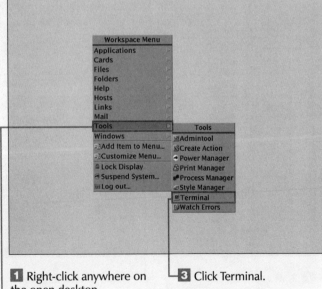

1 Right-click anywhere on the open desktop.

■ This brings up the main pop-up menu.

2 Choose Tools.

3 Click Terminal.

■ A new Terminal window appears on the desktop.

4 Type **tar –cvf**, the destination of the compressed file, and the name of the file you want to compress at the command line

5 Press enter.

Extra

Saving multiple files with the tar and compress command at one time

Although you can't do everything with one command, you can certainly use tar to compact the files you want to save, then use the compress command to compress all the tar files you've created at once.

Remember that you can compress multiple tar files at once by simply listing the tar files after the compress command, placing a space between each file instead of a comma. For example, to compress the tar files X.tar and Y.tar, you would type compress X.tar Y.tar at the command prompt and press Enter.

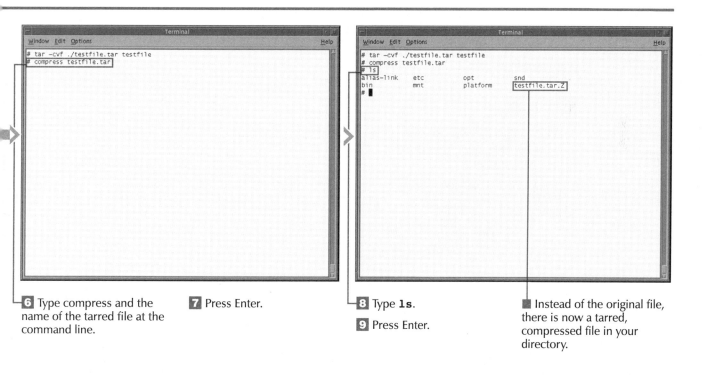

6 Type compress and the name of the tarred file at the command line.

7 Press Enter.

8 Type **ls**.

9 Press Enter.

■ Instead of the original file, there is now a tarred, compressed file in your directory.

RESTORE ARCHIVED AND COMPRESSED FILES

You can restore a file that has been both archived with tar and compressed with the compress command by using the proper commands and command options in order. Whenever you're using what's called a dual-compression scheme to back up your system, you'll need to follow a slightly more complex process to restore the file in question.

The key to restoring a file that has been doubly compressed is to use the right commands in the proper sequence. The clue for this is in the file's two suffixes. For example, if a file's name

is bigreport.tar.Z, then the file was first tarred with the tar command, then compressed with the compress command. This is because the .tar suffix was added first, then followed by the .Z suffix on the outside.

To restore properly, work from the outside in. Begin by decompressing the file to remove the .Z, then restore it the rest of the way with the proper tar options described earlier in this chapter.

RESTORE ARCHIVED AND COMPRESSED FILES

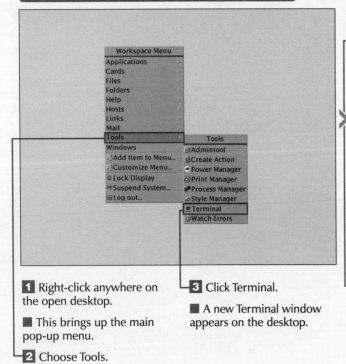

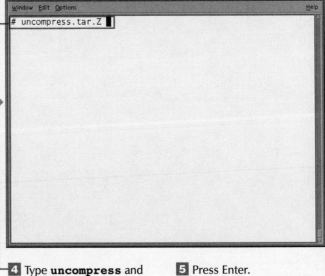

1 Right-click anywhere on the open desktop.

■ This brings up the main pop-up menu.

2 Choose Tools.

3 Click Terminal.

■ A new Terminal window appears on the desktop.

4 Type **uncompress** and the name of the tarred, compressed file at the command line.

5 Press Enter.

■ The file is now a plain .tar file.

What to do when you are restoring archived and compressed files and you get a No space left on device message

When you are restoring files and get a No space left on device message, the UNIX system is telling you that your hard drive (or whatever device you are restoring files on) is 100 percent full.

First, if the restoration process hasn't automatically exited, press Ctrl-C to exit the process.

Second, list the current contents of your device and delete any files that have been created since you started the restoration. These files will likely be only half-restored and will cause problems if you try to access them.

Finally, move the archived files to a different disk or machine where you have enough space to handle the restored files, and restart the restoration process.

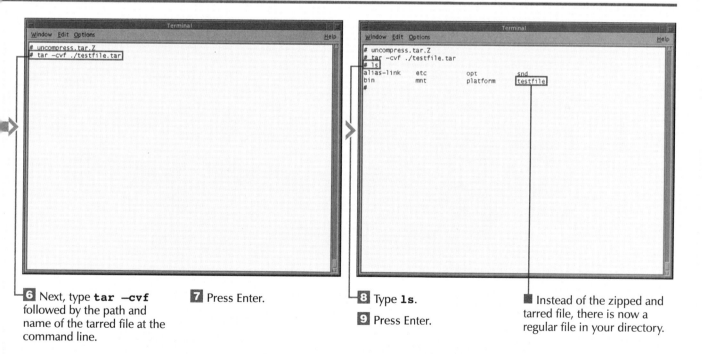

6 Next, type **tar —cvf** followed by the path and name of the tarred file at the command line.

7 Press Enter.

8 Type **ls**.

9 Press Enter.

■ Instead of the zipped and tarred file, there is now a regular file in your directory.

TEST A NETWORK CONNECTION VIA HOST NAME

You can test whether your UNIX machine can talk to other computers on the network with the *ping* command. Ping is one of the oldest and most useful commands in UNIX, and is found on all flavors and versions of the operating system. You'll want to use ping when checking on or hooking up machines so you can see if there is connectivity between two computers on your network.

Ping works by sending a TCP packet between two machines. The TCP (Transport Control Protocol) packet is also called the virtual circuit because it provides feedback once it is received at its destination. Ping harnesses the power of TCP's feedback mechanism to report whether a host is up and working. If there is connectivity between two machines, you'll get a response back from the ping command; if not, then ping won't return anything at all. The syntax for the ping command is `ping <hostname>`.

TEST A NETWORK CONNECTION VIA HOST NAME

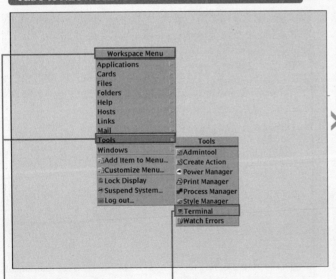

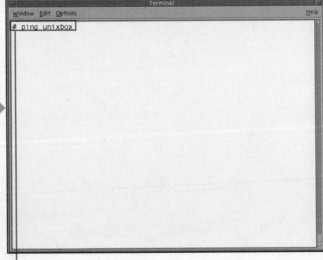

1 Open a new UNIX terminal by right-clicking anywhere on the open desktop.

■ The Workspace Menu appears.

2 Choose Tools.

3 Click on Terminal in the submenu that appears.

■ When you select Terminal, the pop-up menu disappears and a new Terminal window appears on the desktop.

4 At the command prompt, type **ping** and the host name of the machine you want to contact.

5 Press Enter.

Extra

Command options with ping

Command options for ping vary between different flavors of UNIX. The most commonly found command option that can be used with ping is –v, for *verbose output*. If you use ping –v, you get network statistics that help you estimate the speed of your network and whether it's bogging down. Packet transmission times are usually recorded in milliseconds.

Machine connectivity to check with ping

You can check any machine that hooks up to another machine with ping. You can ping from PCs, UNIX servers, and laptops to routers, mail servers, and remote hosts. Basically, if you can remotely log into it, you can ping it.

Other commands that can test network connectivity

Other commands that perform a similar function include *spray* and *telnet*. However, spray doesn't provide you with a verbose option, and using telnet can hang your machine if a connection fails. Ping is still your best option.

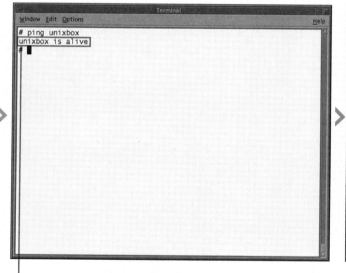

■ If there is connectivity between the two machines, then a response is sent back from the ping command, usually something like *host is alive*.

■ If ping can't establish a connection with another machine, then you either get no response or a message like *host not responding*.

TEST A NETWORK CONNECTION VIA IP ADDRESS

You can use ping to test whether your UNIX machine can talk to other computers on the network if you don't know the name of the machine you're trying to connect to. Whether you simply lack (or forget) the name of the host machine, or if it is not correctly registered in your network's local network maps, you can still use ping to your benefit. Therefore, you can see if there is connectivity between two computers on your network.

Since ping is based on the TCP (Transport Control Protocol) packet, it can read an IP address (Internet Protocol) that you give it and locate a machine in that fashion. An IP address is a quartet of numbers, such as 117.56.3.11, that helps computers determine which machine is located exactly where on a network. If there is connectivity between two machines, you get a response back from the ping command; if not, then ping won't return anything at all. The syntax for the ping command is `ping <IP address>`.

TEST A NETWORK CONNECTION VIA IP ADDRESS

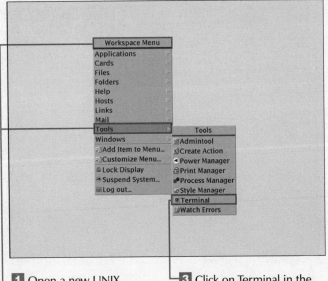

1 Open a new UNIX terminal by right-clicking anywhere on the open desktop.

■ The Workplace Menu appears.

2 Choose Tools.

3 Click on Terminal in the submenu that appears.

■ When you select Terminal, the pop-up menu disappears and a new Terminal window appears on the desktop.

4 Type **ping** and the IP address of the machine you want to contact on the command line.

5 Press Enter.

Extra

Problems that cause the host not to respond

A hardware or software problem could be interfering with the machine's ability to respond to your pings. If the operating system has a bug where it has 'frozen,' it may need to be restarted. More commonly, a network cable may be broken or loose, causing the machine to be disconnected from the rest of the network.

What to do if a host is not responding, and you are either unable to reach the host or have no control over the host

There are times when the host that does not respond is either out of your control (under another network's administrator) or too physically remote for you to reach. In either case, the only thing you can do is to contact the person(s) responsible for taking care of the machine at that network or physical location.

Absolutely, you should perform a backup of the system before you perform any troubleshooting procedure. This will prevent you from losing data in any repair the system makes. (For a review of how to compress and archive your data, see Chapter 15).

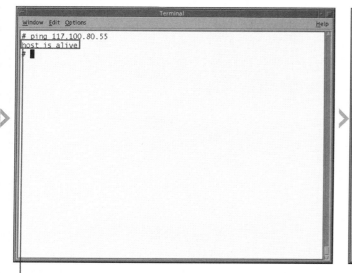

■ You get the same response back from this method as you would from pinging a host name. If there is connectivity between the two machines, then a response is sent back from the ping command, usually something like *host is alive*.

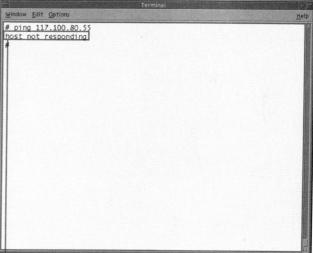

6 If ping can't establish a connection with another machine, then you either get no response or a message like *host not responding*.

FIX DEVICE PROBLEMS ON REBOOT

You can fix device problems on your machine if you're having trouble shutting your computer down or rebooting it. If your computer hangs when you shut it down, your machine might not be unmounting all of the disks. A telltale sign of this is when the message *device busy* appears on-screen the next time you reboot. Device problems are a serious malfunction of your UNIX system and could mean that you have either a physical problem or a software problem.

A software problem could mean that you have corrupted files or sectors on the disk drive. You normally get this if you've had a power outage or you haven't been shutting the machine down properly.

A hardware failure could be a scratched disk drive, an aging disk head, or even a speck of dust that has demagnetized a portion of the disk.

FIX DEVICE PROBLEMS ON REBOOT

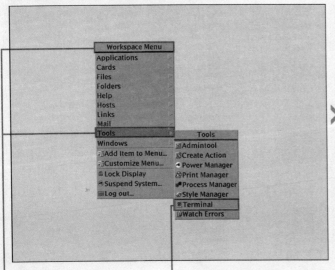

1 Open a new UNIX terminal by right-clicking anywhere on the open desktop.

■ The Workspace Menu appears.

2 Choose Tools.

3 Click on Terminal in the submenu that appears.

■ When you select Terminal, the pop-up menu disappears and a new Terminal window appears on the desktop.

4 Edit the file that controls the dismounting of your devices by typing `vi /etc/rc.d/init.d/halt` at the command line.

5 Press Enter.

Note: For a quick review of the `vi` editor, see Chapter 5.

Extra

Should I perform a backup before I complete the task outlined above?

Absolutely. You should perform a backup of the system before you perform any troubleshooting procedure. This will prevent you from losing data in any repair the system makes. (For a review of how to compress and archive your data, see Chapter 15.)

Why might I lose data in a repair?

The data might be corrupt, causing the problem. Often, the only way to correct the data is to remove it so the disk as a whole can function. Additionally, when you change device settings on your machine, you may lose access to portions of the hard disk. It's better to be safe than sorry.

What if I continue to have problems with the devices after this repair?

If the following fix does not work, consider backing up the contents of the drive and replacing it.

```
#!/bin/sh
# rc.halt     This file is executed by init when it goes into runlevel
#                 0 (halt) or runlevel 6 (reboot). It kills all processes,
#                 unmounts file systems and then either halts or reboots.

mount -o remount, ro /mount.dir


# Set the path.
PATH=/sbin:/bin:/usr/bin:/usr/sbin

. /etc/rc.d/init.d/functions

runcmd() {
    echo -n "$1 "
    shift
    if [ "$BOOTUP" = "color" ]; then
        $* && echo_success || echo_failure
    else
        $*
    fi
    echo
```

6 While in the vi editor, type in the following line: **mount –o remount, ro /mount.dir**.

```
#!/bin/sh
# rc.halt     This file is executed by init when it goes into runlevel
#                 0 (halt) or runlevel 6 (reboot). It kills all processes,
#                 unmounts file systems and then either halts or reboots.

mount -o remount, ro /mount.dir


# Set the path.
PATH=/sbin:/bin:/usr/bin:/usr/sbin

. /etc/rc.d/init.d/functions

runcmd() {
    echo -n "$1 "
    shift
    if [ "$BOOTUP" = "color" ]; then
        $* && echo_success || echo_failure
    else
        $*
    fi
    echo

:wq
```

7 Write and quit the file by pressing Esc, typing **:wq**, and then pressing Enter.

8 Reboot the machine.

FIND DISK HOGS

Y ou can locate users or even files that are becoming disk hogs with a special combination of UNIX commands. A *disk hog* is a person that takes up an inordinate amount of space on your hard drive. A disk hog can even be an automated file that keeps on growing and taking up more and more of your disk space. For example, certain programs can store messages and updates in special files called *log files*, which keep on growing until a program is shut down.

A shortage of disk space is more than just a minor annoyance. If a given disk partition such as /root or /etc fills up to 100 percent of its capacity, your UNIX machine may hang, or even crash, destroying or corrupting valuable data in the process.

To prevent this, you'll be using the *du* (disk usage) command and the *sort* command together. These two commands will work together via a pipe that is discussed as a method of linking command output together in Chapter 7.

FIND DISK HOGS

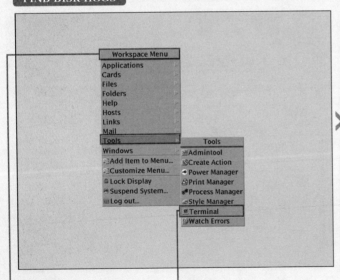

■1 Open a new UNIX terminal by right-clicking anywhere on the open desktop.

■ The Workspace Menu appears.

■2 Choose Tools.

■3 Click on Terminal in the submenu that appears.

■ When you select Terminal, the pop-up menu disappears and a new Terminal window appears on the desktop.

■4 Type **du | sort −n** at the command line.

■5 Press Enter.

Extra

My machine appeared to hang when I ran the du command listed above; it won't accept commands but the hard drive is working. What is going on?

You have probably run the du and sort combination described above from the root directory, /. Since du will search for and calculate the size of each directory beneath where you started the command, you may have to wait a few minutes for du to complete its task. In the future, you may want to start du in a location further down the directory tree; if /usr/tmp looks like it's filling up, then start du there instead.

What if I need the command prompt right away and I don't want to wait for the du and sort process to finish?

In this case, you can kill the process in midstream by pressing Ctrl+C. Alternatively, you can use the kill command, as described in Chapter 7.

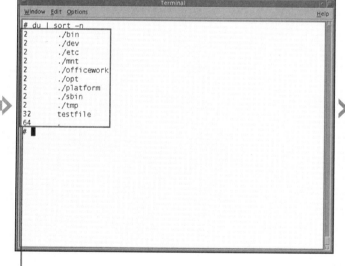

■ The disk usage command returns the sizes of all the files in your current directory; the sort command places them in order for easy viewing.

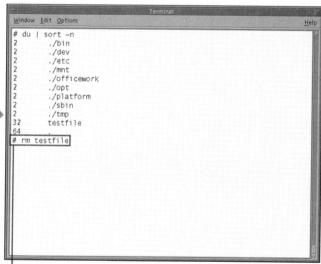

6 If the largest file is one that can be safely removed, type **rm** and the filename.

7 Press Enter to remove the file.

KILL HUNG PROCESSES

You can stop hung processes with the appropriately named *kill* command. A *hung* process is one that simply refuses to exit once you start it. Hung processes can slow down or stall your system, and they usually deprive you of the command prompt if you've started the process in a UNIX terminal.

Kill will terminate a process by sending it a special signal that UNIX programs understand as a "terminate now" signal. This signal is also called SIGHUP, for "signal — hang up", which indicates that a process should exit as soon as it is able.

However, even the garden-variety kill command, as discussed in detail in Chapter 7, will sometimes not work on a command that is hung. In this case, you need to use the variant of kill called *kill –9*. Kill –9 sends a much stronger signal to the process, essentially acting as a Force Quit command in Microsoft Windows.

KILL HUNG PROCESSES

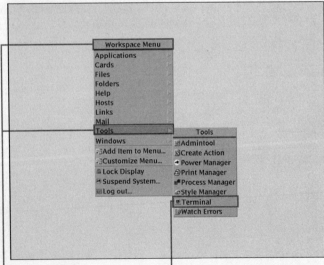

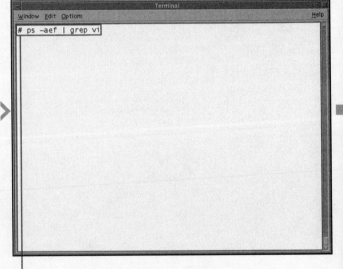

1 Open a new UNIX terminal by right-clicking anywhere on the open desktop.

■ The Workspace Menu appears.

2 Choose Tools.

3 Click on Terminal in the submenu that appears.

■ When you select Terminal, the pop-up menu disappears and a new Terminal window appears on the desktop.

4 If the hung process is a vi process, search for it by typing **ps –aef | grep vi** at the command prompt.

5 Press Enter.

Extra

Why is the kill –9 option more powerful than the regular kill command?

Kill essentially sends an electronic signal to a given process. It tells it to "hang up," or gently shut down. With kill –9, the process will shut down, but it won't go through its polite shutdown procedures. It might core dump or otherwise leave its work unfinished. Therefore, when you use kill –9, so you should always do so sparingly.

What is a core dump?

A process core dumps when it exits abruptly. When a core dump occurs, the process creates a file of jumbled data called a core file. Programmers who are testing new software can untangle core files, but for the general user, they simply take up a lot of space and should be promptly removed.

Are there other kill options, like –6 or –8?

Yes. Each performs different functions, but they're a little more esoteric than the most common ones. As a general rule, the higher the number, the more powerful the shutdown signal becomes.

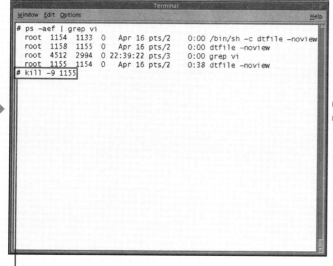

6 After you locate the PID (process ID number), type in **kill –9** and the PID.

7 Press Enter.

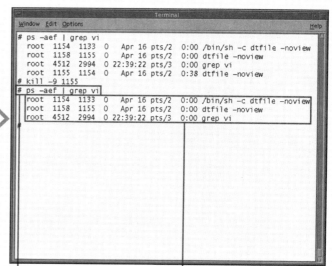

8 You can double-check that the process has been killed by typing **ps -aef | grep vi** again, then pressing Enter.

■ If the process has been successfully killed, it will not show up on the new search.

KILL SPAWNING PROCESSES

You can use a variant of the kill command to combat processes that have started "spawning" uncontrollably. Processes that spawn out of control will slow a system down and eventually cause a major system failure or a crash of your machine.

Spawning is the UNIX terminology that in popular parlance has come to mean any process that creates a new copy of itself. For example, some processes, like the print daemon (lpd) or telnet (telnetd), do this routinely. In each case, the daemon will spin

off a new copy of itself each time a new print job or telnet request comes along.

However, finding a few dozen telnet or other processes running amok on your system means you have to use the *killall* command. This variation of the kill command will kill all processes of the same name. Use killall before the spawning print, telnet, or other processes begin to act as a drag on how fast your system can run.

KILL SPAWNING PROCESSES

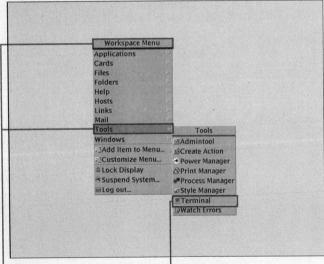

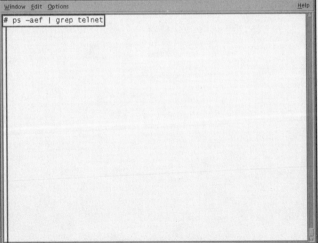

1 Open a new UNIX terminal by right-clicking anywhere on the open desktop.

■ The Workspace Menu appears.

2 Choose Tools.

3 Click on Terminal in the submenu that appears.

■ When you select Terminal, the pop-up menu disappears and a new Terminal window appears on the desktop.

4 If network connections are slow, check to see how many telnet daemons are running by typing `ps –aef | grep telnet` at the command prompt.

5 Press Enter.

Extra

Processes that respond to the killall command

All processes should respond to the 'killall' command. The only time that this is not true is when the process itself refuses to listen to the command — in which case you may need to use kill –9, which is the strongest level of the kill command.

Processes out of control

Two factors determine the likelihood of a process spawning out of control: the number of processes that are normally started on a machine, and how buggy the process normally is. For example, the telnet daemon can spawn out of control because on systems with multiple users, it's likely that many telnet connections will be started as people do their work. Print daemons historically go out of control because their design is considered slightly unstable.

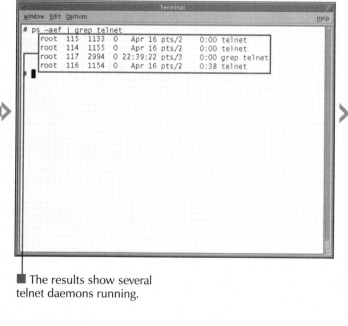

■ The results show several telnet daemons running.

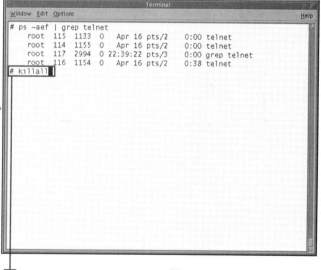

6 To kill all processes with the same name, type **killall** and the name of the process.

7 Press Enter.

RESET THE DATE

You can reset the date and time on a UNIX machine directly from the terminal. Resetting the date and time on your machine is relatively important, since many automated processes that maintain your system work better when they are allowed to work in the early morning or late at night when no one is using the system. Providing the system with the proper time ensures that this will take place.

The *date* command allows you to do this. Unfortunately, the date command can appear

confusing, because the date and time are entered numerically in one long string of text.

The date is set out with pairs of numbers in the following order: month, day, year, hour, minute. For example, January 1, 2000, at 11:15 p.m. would be written as: 0101002315. Note that the time 11:15 is expressed in the date command as 23:15. UNIX uses the 24-hour clock, also known as military time, to help distinguish a.m. from p.m.

RESET THE DATE

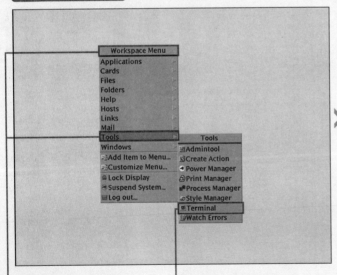

■1 Open a new UNIX terminal by right-clicking anywhere on the open desktop.

■ The Workspace Menu appears.

■2 Choose Tools.

■3 Click on Terminal in the submenu that appears.

■ When you select Terminal, the pop-up menu disappears and a new Terminal window appears on the desktop.

■4 For the current the date and time on the system, type **date** at the system prompt.

■5 Press Enter.

Extra

Why UNIX uses the military time set instead of using a.m. and p.m.

This is because it was easier for the early UNIX designers to program a machine that worked with numbers more easily than letters. A time of 23:00 is easier for a machine to work with than 11p.m.

Reasons to keep your time and date accurate

Keeping your machine's time and date accurate is helpful in two other situations. First, if you run into problems, the system will normally log when it sees an error. Showing what time the error took place is normally a good clue to find out what went wrong. Second, accurate time and dates allow you to note when you send important e-mails to other users. This is especially helpful if you send out time-critical information, such as when you plan to bring the system down for maintenance.

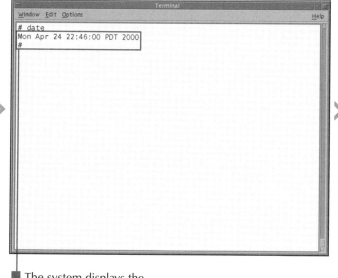

■ The system displays the current system date.

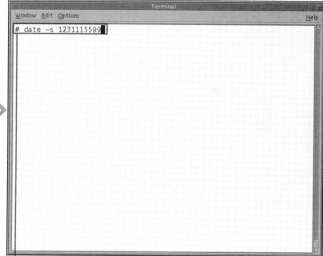

■6 To change the date, type in **date –s** and the desired date and time in month/day/time/year format at the command prompt.

■ For example, to change the date to December 31, 1999 at 11:55 p.m., type **date –s 1231115599**.

■7 Press Enter to accept the date.

WORK WITH THE CALCULATOR PROGRAM

You can use the Calculator program on the UNIX operating system's desktop to perform calculations without having to leave your work on the computer. By default, all current releases of Solaris that come with the Common Desktop Environment also have the useful Calculator utility.

At first glance, this utility is similar to the Calculator program that comes as a standard accessory on Microsoft Windows 95, 98, NT 4.0, and 2000. However, the Calculator program in UNIX is much more powerful and flexible than its Windows counterpart.

The Calculator program in Windows allows you to complete the most basic mathematical functions, such

as addition, subtraction, multiplication, and division. The Calculator program in UNIX, on the other hand, is equivalent to having a full-fledged scientific calculator at your fingertips.

This makes the UNIX version of the Calculator program highly desirable if you are working on derivatives, integrals, higher forms of calculus, or problems in probability and statistics. However, while you can use many more sophisticated operations with the UNIX version of the Calculator program, entering in operations via the keyboard or by clicking the graphic keys of the Calculator window is always a simple task.

WORK WITH THE CALCULATOR PROGRAM

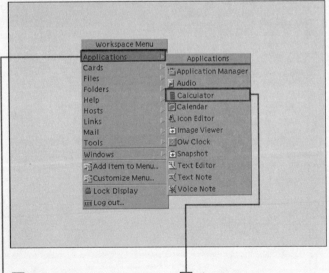
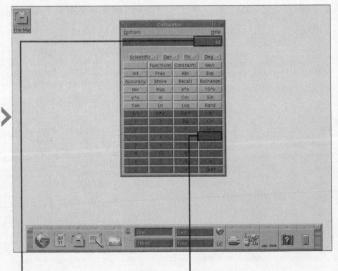

1 Right-click anywhere on the desktop.

■ The main pop-up menu appears.

2 Choose Applications.

3 Click Calculator.

■ The Calculator window opens on the desktop.

4 Type any number on either the numeric keypad or the numbers in the top row of your keyboard.

5 Select an operation by clicking the mouse pointer on any key displayed on the calculator screen.

Note: You can also type your selected operation on the keyboard (most mathematical operations are located on the numeric keypad).

Extra

Perform multiple mathematical operations at once with the Calculator program

You really have two choices when it comes to performing multiple mathematical operations with the Calculator program. For example, if you want to solve the equation 6 + 10 - 4, you could do the following. First, enter 6 +10, then click the equals sign. Next, click the minus sign followed by the 4, then click equals again, giving you the answer 12.

Another option is to simply enter in the whole string of symbols and numbers at one time: type 6, +, 10, -, 4 and click the equals sign to get the answer. Whichever method you choose depends on which is more comfortable to you.

Use the more sophisticated logarithmic and scientific functions of the Calculator program

The steps described in this section are designed to show you how to enter in basic information, such as numbers and operational symbols, and completing the operation you've selected. To gain more information on using the complex mathematics functions, click the Help menu listed on the upper right corner of the Calculator window. You'll be able to select the topic of your choice by clicking on the selection of the pop-up menu that appears.

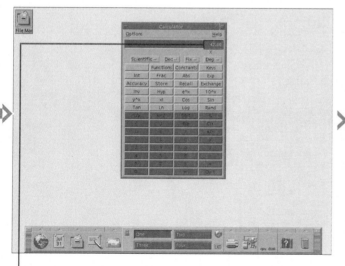

■ The number automatically switches to decimal form; for example, if you enter 42, the number will now appear as 42.00.

Note: This decimal form does not change the values that will result from any operation you select.

6 Type the second number you wish to use in the operation.

■ This number appears in the main display area in the Calculator window.

7 Press the equals sign to complete the operation.

■ You can either press the = key or use your mouse to click the sign in the Calculator window.

CONTINUED ▶

WORK WITH THE CALCULATOR PROGRAM (CONTINUED)

A major benefit of using the Calculator program in UNIX over the similar application in Microsoft Windows is the ability to change the method by which the number you are working with is displayed. The standard method of displaying the numbers you input into the Calculator program is in the default Decimal form.

The decimal form equates any number as the whole number you input, plus its amount to the hundredths place. Thus, entering the number 100 will appear as 100.00 once you begin to perform an operation on the number. This does not affect the result of the operation you perform; it's simply a form of

mathematical shorthand that the computer uses to perform the calculation.

If you build programs, or code in UNIX, then on occasion, you may need to know what a given number looks like in hexadecimal, or hex form for short. This form is used in UNIX, among other things, for determining the setting of permissions. (Most people use the easier alphabetic form of permission setting, discussed in detail in Chapter 4.) However, if you want to view the number in hex form in the Calculator program, you can do so with a single click on the Display button.

WORK WITH THE CALCULATOR PROGRAM (CONTINUED)

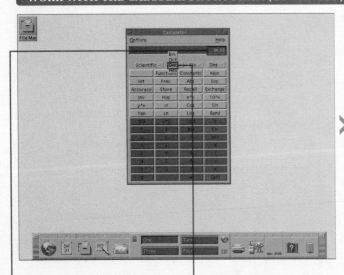

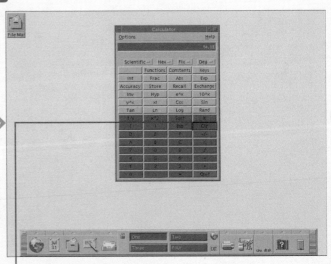

■ After you select the equals sign, the result of your operation appears in the Calculator's main display area in the default DEC (decimal) format.

■ To change the way the result is displayed, click on the display button, then make a selection from the small pop-up menu that appears.

For example, Hex displays the answer in hexidecimal form.

8 To return the Calculator's main display area back to zero, simply use your mouse pointer to click on the Clr button.

Extra

Closing the Calculator window

You have two other options for closing the Calculator window besides using the Quit key. First, you can select the box marked with a - sign in the upper left hand corner of the Calculator window, then click Close in the resulting pop-up menu.

Also, on some versions of UNIX, you may be able to shut the Calculator program down by simply pressing Ctrl-C.

Saving results

Unfortunately, the Calculator application is more of a desktop utility than a program in its own right. Therefore, you aren't given the option of saving the results of your work. You should write down the answer to a given problem you've calculated in the Calculator so you don't lose your work. Also, if you shut the Calculator program down, you will have to redo your calculations when you restart it the next time.

The availability of Calculator if you're working in CDE in a different version of UNIX, such as HP-UX

The Calculator application is native to the Common Desktop Environment, so you should be able to use it so long as your version of UNIX uses CDE.

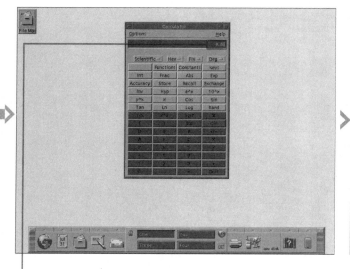

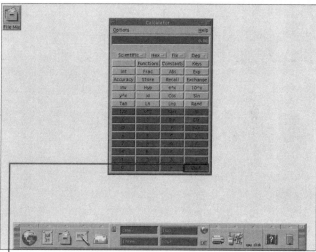

■ The Calculator's main display area returns to 0.00.

9 To close the Calculator application, use the mouse pointer to click the Quit button at the lower-right corner of the Calculator window.

OPEN THE CALENDAR PROGRAM

You can use the calendar program to create detailed schedules for appointments and "to do" tasks on a daily, weekly, monthly, and every yearly basis. While you may consider using a more sophisticated project management program if you need to plan out complex scheduling for groups of people or project tasks, the calendar program is perfectly acceptable for most mundane scheduling needs.

Where the UNIX operating system's version of the calendar program is vastly superior to the standard calendar utility that comes with Windows 95, 98, NT 4.0, and 2000 is in the ease of implementing detailed schedules that stretch for months or even years. Also, the related ease of being able to manipulate time frames by jumping from a daily or weekly schedule to a year-long one is a prime benefit of using the calendar program in the UNIX common desktop environment.

OPEN THE CALENDAR PROGRAM

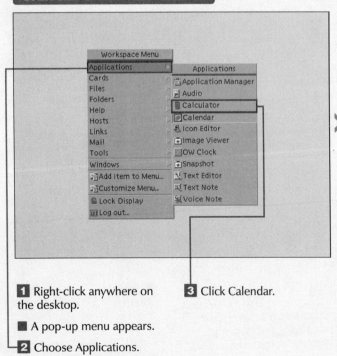

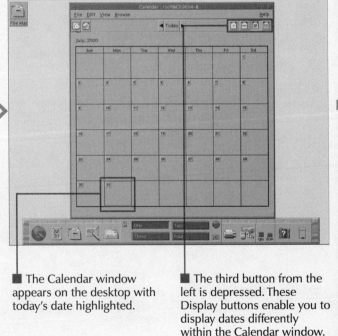

1 Right-click anywhere on the desktop.

■ A pop-up menu appears.

2 Choose Applications.

3 Click Calendar.

■ The Calendar window appears on the desktop with today's date highlighted.

■ The third button from the left is depressed. These Display buttons enable you to display dates differently within the Calendar window.

Using Calendar with other versions of UNIX

Luckily, the Calendar application that you're working with is available as part of the CDE (Common Desktop Environment) by default. If you're using an older form of Solaris that comes with CDE, or even a different flavor of UNIX that utilizes CDE as the desktop environment, you should have no problems using the Calendar program.

Using a calendar without CDE

If you're using a different kind of graphical desktop, such as OpenWindows, you may be able to use a different Calendar utility. Which one you have available depends on the flavor of the UNIX operating system you are using and how old it is. Keep in mind that other, more esoteric forms of graphical desktops may not come with a calendar utility at all.

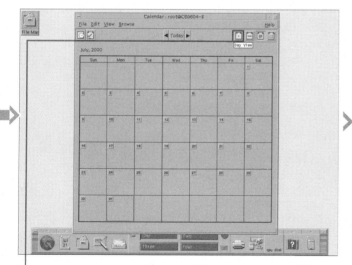

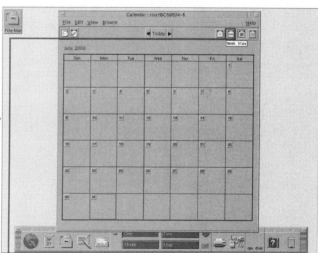

4 Move your mouse pointer over the first Display button from the left.

■ A tip displays informing you that this button activates the Day View. Clicking this button changes the display screen to show only one day at a time on the calendar.

5 Alternatively, move your mouse pointer over the second Display button from the left.

■ A tip displays informing you that this button activates the Week View. Clicking this button changes the display screen to show only one week at a time on the calendar.

SET APPOINTMENTS WITH THE CALENDAR'S DAY VIEW

A major benefit of using the Calendar application on the CDE in UNIX is that you can literally plan out a day on an hour-by-hour basis. This is especially helpful in today's business environment for two major reasons.

First, the average committee-style meeting is now intended to last no longer than 60 minutes, as this is the determined upper limit for an average attention span. Second, with the average business day becoming more filled with appointments, meetings, and reports, it is

essential that any daily planner be broken down into hour-long blocks for concise order.

The most common use of the Day View in the Calendar application is to take full advantage of the splitting of the day into one-hour slots that you can add appointments to. By taking these appointments and displaying them in either the daily or a monthly screen format, you can keep your schedule easier than if you had to switch back and forth between a daily planner and a month-long desktop calendar.

SET APPOINTMENTS WITH THE CALENDAR'S DAY VIEW

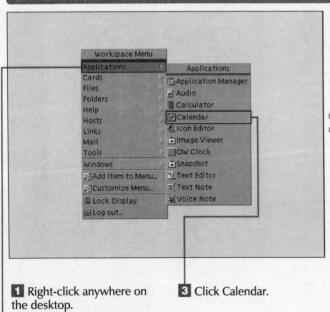

1 Right-click anywhere on the desktop.

■ A pop-up menu appears.

2 Choose Applications.

3 Click Calendar.

■ The Calendar window appears on the desktop with today's date highlighted.

4 Click the Day View button to start adding entries to a particular day on the calendar.

5 To add entries to a given day, double-click the day's square.

■ Alternatively, click the day and then click the Day View button.

Extra

Appointment limits

There is no limit to the number of appointments you can add to any day. However, due to space constraints, you will have difficulty reading the text of any appointment if you add more than five or six appointments per day.

Viewing extra appointments on the day

If a given day has several appointment entries (or one appointment entry that is described with a lot of text), then the text will trail off the slot that displays the date on the Month View screen. You can view the appointments that do not show up on the Month View screen by shifting to the Daily View screen. You can do this by double-clicking the date in question or choosing the date and then clicking the Daily View button.

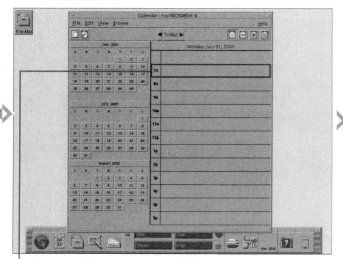

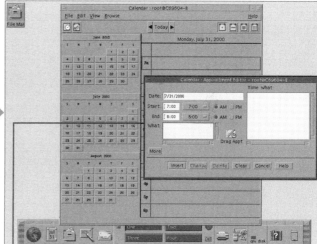

■ However you choose to select the Day View, the calendar screen changes so that the day divides into hourly slots on the right-hand side of the screen.

Note: The program automatically selects the earliest time of 7 a.m.

6 Double-click any hour slot.

■ The Calendar appointment editor appears in a separate screen that notes the date, end of the time slot, and any entries you made earlier.

CONTINUED ▶

SET APPOINTMENTS WITH THE CALENDAR'S DAY VIEW (CONTINUED)

You can add all sorts of extra detail about the appointments you create and insert into your calendar with the Calendar application. This is done through the Appointment Editor screen. You can add even further detail by expanding the Appointment Editor screen when you click the More button on the left-hand side of the screen.

The expanded screen also allows you to save unnecessary duplication of effort on the part of someone who is trying to add a regularly

scheduled appointment to a calendar on a yearly, monthly, or even more frequent basis. For example, if you plan to have a department meeting every Monday at 10 a.m., you don't have to go through each page month by month, writing in the appointment, the way you would on a paper calendar. Instead, you can simply add the appointment to your calendar schedule one time, then *stretch* or *duplicate* the appointment for each week in the Appointment Editor screen.

SET APPOINTMENTS WITH THE CALENDAR'S DAY VIEW (CONTINUED)

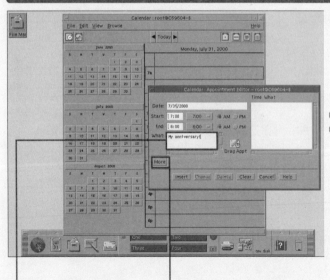

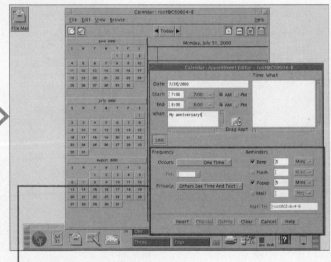

7 Click the What field.

■ This is where you type the nature of the appointment.

■ If you want to add more details about an appointment, click the More button.

■ The Appointment Editor window expands to give you additional options.

Hiding the Expanded Appointment Editor screen and restoring the editor screen to its original size

The More button that you click to expand the Appointment Editor window changes to a Less button.

Clicking the Less button returns the Appointment Editor window back to its original size.

Saving the information in the Expanded Appointment Editor

There is no need to perform a save command on the information that you enter in the Expanded Appointment Editor. All information you add, such as the frequency of the appointment in the Occurs field, is implemented whether you click the Less button or not.

On the other hand, if you want to discard the information that you add in the expanded area, you need to return the selections back to the way they were before you started editing them.

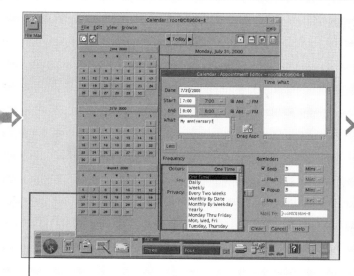

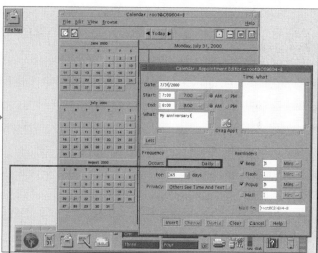

■8 Click the Occurs button for a pop-up menu with which you can set the frequency of the appointment.

■ The new setting displays in the Occurs field.

CONTINUED ▶

SET APPOINTMENTS WITH THE CALENDAR'S DAY VIEW (CONTINUED)

In addition to being able to set the frequency of a given appointment in the Calendar application, you can also set its duration. This feature is not only convenient, it also enables you to save unnecessary duplication of effort via the Appointment Editor screen. Whether you add a regularly scheduled appointment to a calendar on a yearly, monthly, or other frequency, you can tailor exactly how long you want the appointments to continue.

For example, if you plan to have a certification board meeting every Wednesday afternoon for the next nine or ten months, you don't have to go through each page of a paper calendar for the next nine or ten pages.

Instead, you can simply add the appointment to your calendar schedule one time, then *stretch* or *duplicate* the appointment for the allotted span of nine or ten months in the Expanded Appointment Editor screen.

SET APPOINTMENTS WITH THE CALENDAR'S DAY VIEW (CONTINUED)

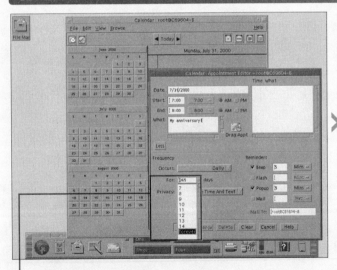

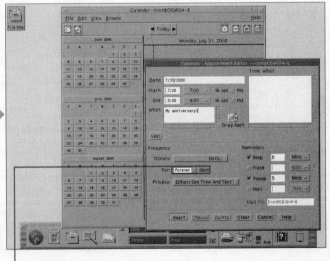

■**9** If you set the frequency of the appointment to anything besides Once, you can select the duration of the appointments by clicking the For button.

■ A pop-up menu appears where you can select the number of days the appointment runs, including Forever.

■ After you choose a duration by clicking it, the pop-up window disappears and the new setting is displayed in the For. . .days field.

Extra

Deciding to use the Privacy settings

You should use the Privacy settings only when it makes sense to do so. While setting a calendar for maximum privacy has no drawbacks to system speed, it may add an unnecessary step when you're working in the Appointment Editor.

For example, if your machine is not hooked up to a network (known as a *stand-alone* machine), then no one else can view your Calendar application.

Similarly, if your appointments are not particularly private, or if your machine is on a network that few users work on, then you don't usually need added privacy.

Adding repeating appointments to your calendar indefinitely

As the option name says, your appointments can repeat *forever*. Some people think this means until the end of the year, but in the Calendar application, until you switch the frequency to some other setting, it is set for all time.

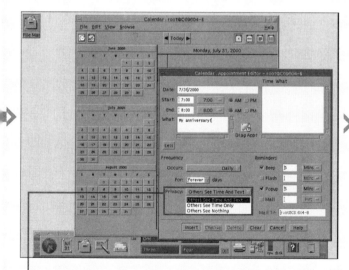

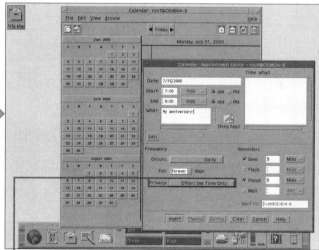

■ If you're running Calendar on a machine that several people use, you can select a Privacy setting so that only you can view your Calendar entries by using the Privacy button.

10 Click on the Privacy button to display a pop-up menu, from which you can set the level of privacy you desire.

■ After you choose a Privacy setting by clicking one, the pop-up window disappears and the new setting displays in the Privacy field.

CONTINUED ▶

SET APPOINTMENTS WITH THE CALENDAR'S DAY VIEW (CONTINUED)

You can insert appointments into the Calendar via the Day View screen after you add all of the details on a given appointment that you want. The Insert process marks the information that you enter in the What section of the Appointment Editor screen and places it in the Time What section of the Appointment Editor screen.

After you insert an appointment into the Calendar via the Appointment Editor, the appointment displays in three of the four available Date screens.

In the Daily View screen, the appointment displays in its appropriate hour slot on the right-hand column of the screen. In the Weekly View screen, the appointment's time and additional information appears in the box that displays the date of the appointment. Similarly, the box indicating the date of the appointment also appears with the time and additional information in the Monthly View screen, though the print is smaller than if you choose the Weekly View screen.

SET APPOINTMENTS WITH THE CALENDAR'S DAY VIEW (CONTINUED)

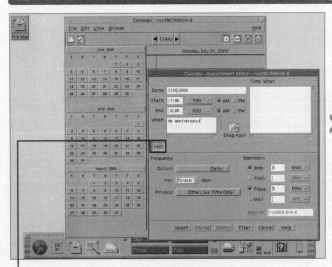

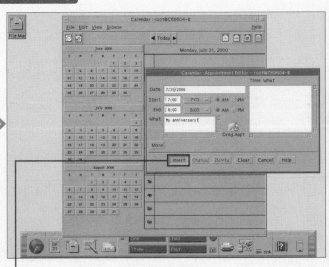

11 Click the Less button to return the Editor window to original size.

12 If you're satisfied with the appointment and want to enter it on the Calendar, click the Insert button.

Extra

Hidden information in the Yearly View Calendar screen

When you change to the Yearly View screen, all 12 months of a given year appear. At this great scale, notes on an individual day are too small to appear, including appointment times. To view appointments, you should return to Weekly, Monthly, or Daily View.

Creating appointments that do not fit into a one-hour slot of time

Begin by going to the Daily View screen for a particular date. Click the time slot where the appointment will begin to get to the Appointment Editor screen. Click the time buttons by Start and End on the Editor screen, choosing the starting and ending times from the resulting pop-up menus. These times that you choose appear in the Calendar after you enter them.

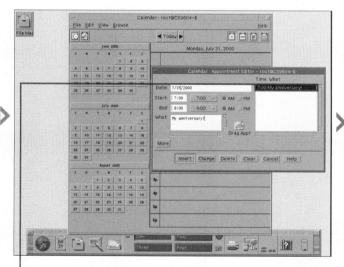

■ The entry appears in the Time What field as it appears on the Calendar.

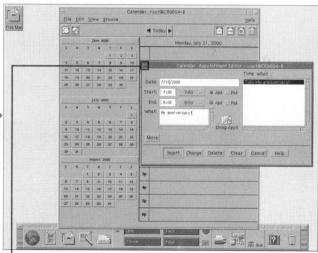

13 After you finish editing the appointment, click the – button to close the window and return to the Calendar screen.

REMOVE APPOINTMENTS IN THE CALENDAR'S DAY VIEW

You can easily remove a previously inserted appointment from the Calendar application. You can only perform this operation via the Calendar application's Day View screen. However, if you need to remove an appointment that is repeated in frequency or duration, the flexibility of the UNIX Calendar application enables you to save time and reduce repetitive effort.

For example, your organization decides to cancel the budget committee council that met every week at noon on Thursday for the next three weeks, but plans to resume these councils afterwards. Luckily, you're not limited to either removing the meetings for the next three weeks one at a time. Nor do you have to remove all the council meetings, then go back and replace the remaining council meetings after the three-week hiatus. Instead, the application is flexible enough to allow you to remove the three meetings one by one and leave the rest untouched.

REMOVE APPOINTMENTS IN THE CALENDAR'S DAY VIEW

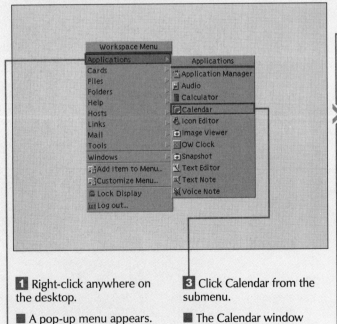

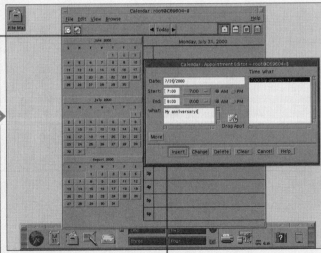

1 Right-click anywhere on the desktop.

■ A pop-up menu appears.

2 Choose Applications.

3 Click Calendar from the submenu.

■ The Calendar window appears on the desktop.

4 Click the date of the appointment you want to remove.

5 Click the Day View button.

■ Calendar screen changes so that the day divides into hourly slots on the right-hand side of the screen.

6 Double-click any hour slot to bring up the Calendar Appointment Editor.

Extra

Using the highlighted Cancel button on the Confirmation screen when you attempt to delete an appointment

As with most applications in UNIX, the Cancel operation is highlighted as the default action should you simply choose to press the Enter key to complete your choice. This is a built-in safeguard to keep you from accidentally completing an action that could result in deleting or damaging a given file or calendar.

Rescheduling meetings to different time slots

You have two choices available. First, you can simply delete all these appointments by choosing All in the Deletion Confirmation Screen, and Insert a new appointment later. A second option is to simply change the time by clicking the Start and End buttons in the Appointment Editor screen, and selecting different times from the resulting pop-up menus.

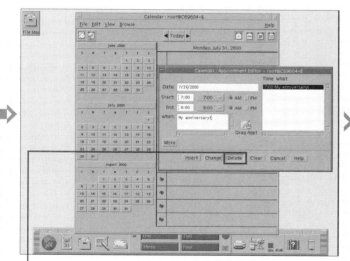

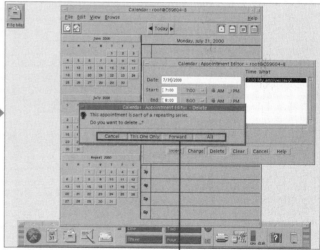

7 To delete the appointment, click the Delete button.

■ A confirmation screen appears.

8 Choose an option by clicking the proper button at the base of the Calendar Appointment Editor screen.

GET HELP IN THE CALENDAR

Even though the Calendar application in UNIX's Common Desktop Environment is designed to be extremely easy to use, you can get additional documentation to help you work with adding, editing, or deleting appointments. You can access the additional help documents directly from the Calendar application with the click of a button.

After you start the Calendar application, you can locate the Help area by activating the Calendar Editor screen. On this screen's lower right-hand corner is the Help button. The Help

button in the application links directly to the stored Help documents that come with the current UNIX installation.

From there, you can either select Help topics by clicking them, or by browsing the available index of topics in the Help Document screen. If you do not work with a flavor of UNIX that comes with the Common Desktop Environment, these help options may not be available to you, or they may be in a different form and location.

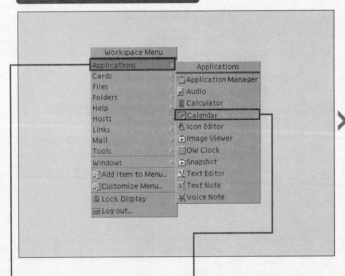

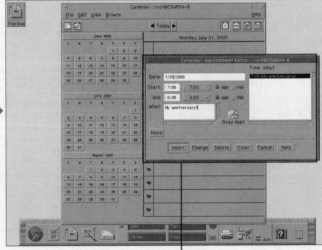

1 Right-click anywhere on the desktop.

■ A pop-up menu appears.

2 Choose Applications.

3 Click Calendar from the submenu.

■ The Calendar window appears on the desktop.

4 To remove an entry, click the date and then click the Day View button.

■ The Calendar screen changes so that the day divides into hourly slots on the right-hand side of the screen.

5 Double-click any hour slot to start the Calendar Appointment Editor.

Extra

Exiting the Help screen and returning to the Calendar application

You have a couple of different options to leave the Help menus and return to the Calendar application. First, you can click the – button in the upper left-hand corner to close the window and return to the Calendar screen. Second, you can click the File menu and choose Exit from the drop-down menu. Either method works when leaving Help.

Other resources for answers

On rare occasions, you may find that the Help documents in the Calendar application don't answer your questions. In these cases, begin by looking through any UNIX documentation you have available in book format. After you exhaust these resources, consider going online to your UNIX vendor's Web site and searching for the answer there.

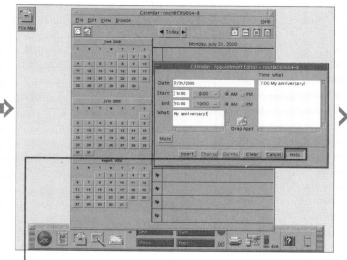

6 To view Calendar Help, click the Help button.

■ The Help window appears.

■ By clicking the topics that appear in the upper portion of the Help screen, you can read more about how to perform tasks in the Calendar utility.

MOVE BETWEEN MONTHS IN CALENDAR

You can easily move between several different months in the Calendar application due to its flexible system of Daily, Weekly, Monthly, and Yearly Views. This system allows you to move more quickly by not forcing you to scroll through each individual period, month-by-month or week-by-week until you reach your intended destination. Instead, you can bypass weeks or months at a time by changing the different View modes.

Moving between months on your calendar is especially useful if your schedule is not one

that lends itself to routine. For example, a structured, regular schedule may be one that a lab administrator could enter into the Calendar application by noting meetings that happen on a weekly or monthly basis.

By contrast, a division manager or sales rep may only have a regular semi-annual marketing meeting, while needing to enter in the dates of various seminars or trade shows that he must attend at irregular intervals. In this case, the ability to move between different months to add these appointments is very important.

MOVE BETWEEN MONTHS IN CALENDAR

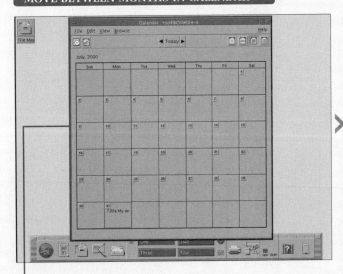

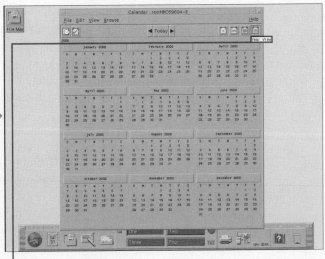

1 Open the Calendar as I describe in "Open the Calendar Program" earlier in this chapter. By default, the calendar displays the Month View.

2 Click the Year View button.

Extra

Moving month to month in the Calendar application

While in the majority of cases, the ability to move several months in a click of the mouse is helpful, you may want to move purely on a month to month basis without moving from the Year View screen. This can be done from the Month View screen by clicking either the left or right arrows next to the Today notation at the top center of the Calendar screen. Clicking once on the left arrow moves you back one month, while clicking the right arrow moves you ahead one month.

Moving between days on the Month View screen

This can be done from the Month View screen by clicking either the left or right arrows next to the Today notation at the top center of the Calendar screen. Clicking once on the left arrow moves you back one day, while clicking the right arrow moves you ahead one day.

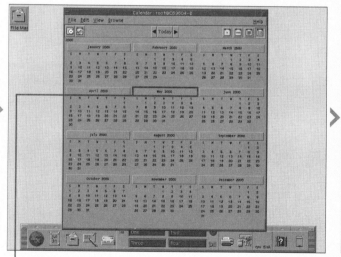

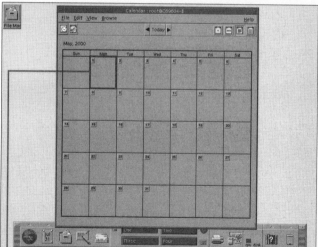

3 Select a different month by clicking its title bar in the Year View screen.

■ You return to the Month View screen. By default, the first day in the month highlights.

CHANGE A CALENDAR ENTRY

You can change a previously inserted entry in your calendar by starting the Calendar application and navigating to the Appointment Editor screen. After you're on this screen, you can change any aspect of the Appointment entry that you were able to enter in the first place. First, you can change the start time, stop time, and duration of a given appointment. You can also change what the appointment is about, by editing the text in the What field.

In addition, you can change appointment characteristics in the Appointment Editor screen that are only available in the expanded version of the Editor that you open by clicking on the More button. These extra characteristics include the frequency of repeated appointments, the duration of the appointment schedule, and the level of privacy you want to grant the entire appointment itself. In any of these cases, all you need to do is make your changes and be sure Insert the new entry into the calendar.

CHANGE A CALENDAR ENTRY

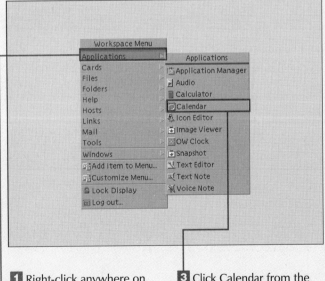

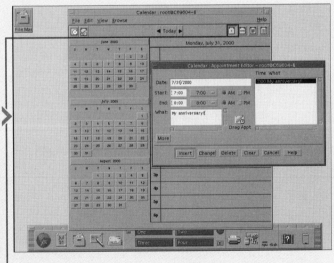

1 Right-click anywhere on the open desktop.

■ A pop-up menu appears.

2 Choose Applications.

3 Click Calendar from the submenu.

■ The Calendar window appears on the desktop.

4 To remove entries to a given day, click the date.

5 Click the Day View button.

■ The Calendar screen changes so that the day divides into hourly slots on the right-hand side of the screen.

6 Double-click any hour slot to bring up the Calendar Appointment Editor.

Choosing to edit only certain selected appointments in the Appointment Editor screen

After you make changes to a given appointment in your Appointment Editor, you can choose to only edit one appointment and move on to the next scheduled one by clicking the Forward button.

For example, if your weekly research and development meeting changes to a company party for the next two weeks, you edit the next appointment with the Appointment Editor, then click the Forward button to move to the next instance of the appointment.

You then click Forward button again to edit the appointment a second time. When you get to the third appointment, which is where the party time reverts to a regular research and development meeting, you click the Cancel button to cancel any more editing operations.

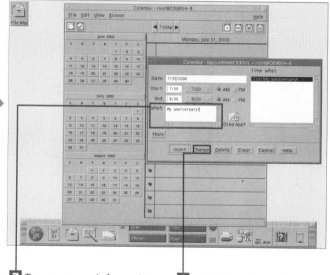

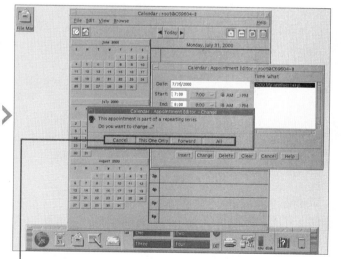

7 Type any new information in the What field of the Editor screen.

8 Click the Change button to complete the edit.

■ A Confirmation screen appears. You can select an option by clicking the proper button at the base of the Editor screen.

ADD A TO DO IN THE CALENDAR

You can choose to add a To Do entry into your calendar rather than a standard Appointment in the Common Desktop Environment Calendar application. The difference between a To Do entry and an Appointment is really very slim, except of course that a To Do entry denotes a task that you need to complete by a certain time or date, rather than an appointment, which you need to meet or keep. A To Do appears much the same on screen as an Appointment, with two main differences.

First, a To Do task has its own Editor screen, called the To Do Editor as opposed to the Appointments Editor screen. Second, the To Do Editor screen has an additional option for you to choose — the Completed button. By default, this button is left blank, or unselected. After you complete the task, you can return to the Editor and mark the task as completed by clicking the button so that your calendar is up-to-date.

ADD A TO DO IN THE CALENDAR

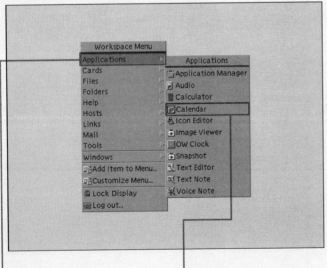

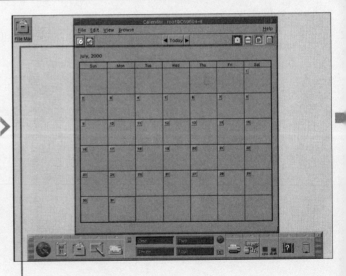

1 Right-click anywhere on the desktop.

■ A pop-up menu appears.

2 Choose Applications.

3 Click Calendar from the submenu.

■ The Calendar window appears on the desktop.

4 Click the Day View button.

Apply It

Differences between the To Do Editor and Appointment Editor screen

The majority of the settings available in the To Do Editor screen are similar or the same as in the Appointment Editor screen. Instead of a Start and End time field for an appointment, you have a Time Due field that you can manipulate by clicking a pop-up menu, just as in the Appointment Editor screen. The Completed button is only found in the task-oriented To Do Editor screen.

Similarity between the To Do Editor and Appointment Editor screen

Most notably, the More button that expands the Editor screen and the options in the expanded area are the same in the To Do and the Appointment Editor screens. This is because both tasks and appointments can be set up identically when it comes to the areas of frequency, duration, and privacy.

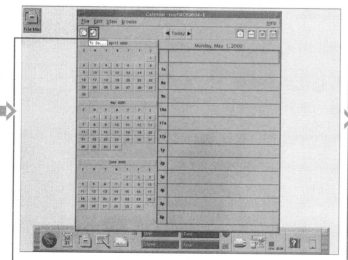

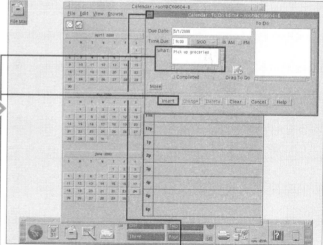

■ The Calendar screen changes so that the day divides into hourly slots on the right-hand side of the screen.

5 Click the To Do button.

■ The To Do Editor screen appears.

6 Type the task that you want to note in the What box.

7 Click the Insert button.

8 Exit the screen by clicking the – button, if you're finished editing this To Do item.

■ You return to the Calendar screen.

PRINT THE CALENDAR

If you decide that you want to have a hard copy of your calendar after you finish editing and inserting all of your tasks for the day, week, or month, you can print out a copy of the schedule directly from the Calendar application. This is especially useful to take with you into a meeting where you expect your schedule to change drastically. Any notes that you make on your printout can easily be added into your Calendar program after the meeting.

The printer or printers you have hooked up to your UNIX machine will treat your calendar like any other text file. This means that when you select your calendar for printing, it will print onto 8.5 by 11-inch paper on a standard laser, inkjet, or dot-matrix printer. If you need more information on setting up or adding printers, see Chapter 11.

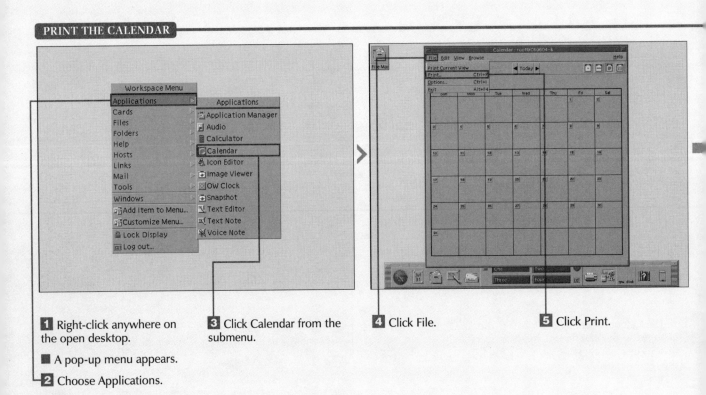

1 Right-click anywhere on the open desktop.

■ A pop-up menu appears.

2 Choose Applications.

3 Click Calendar from the submenu.

4 Click File.

5 Click Print.

Apply It

Changing output for other page sizes

This varies depending on what kind of printer you use to handle your print jobs. For example, on some printers, you may need to change the print mode to landscape instead of portrait. With other printers, you may not be able to even use legal size (11 by 14-inch) paper. Your best bet is to view the documentation that came with your printer to figure out how to perform this special form of printing.

Adjusting print quality

Problems in print quality cannot be solved in the Calendar program. Check out other sections of this book on printing or troubleshooting. You may also want to check to be sure that your ink ribbon or cartridge is in good working order and is not leaking or getting clogged with dust.

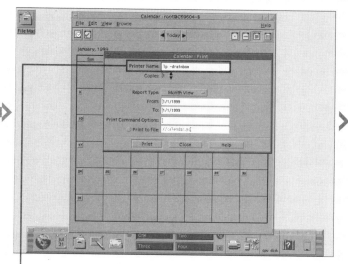

■ The Print window appears with your default printer in the Printer Name field.

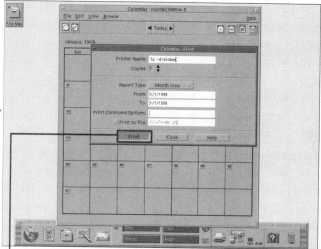

6 Click the Print button to send this job to the printer.

FINGER ANOTHER USER

The `finger` command enables you to find out whether or not a particular user is currently logged on. The odd name *finger* was given to this command because in a sense it points to the person's account that you are looking for.

This command is similar to the `who`, or `w`, command, which tells you the identity of each and every person logged onto the UNIX system. By contrast, the `finger` command only displays data on one user account, and you must know the user's account name in order to perform `finger` successfully.

The advantage of using `finger` over `who` or `w` is that it is slightly quicker, particularly on systems where there are dozens of users. The `finger` command is also more common on some versions of UNIX than `w` or `who` but `finger` is almost universal on all UNIX platforms and flavors.

FINGER ANOTHER USER

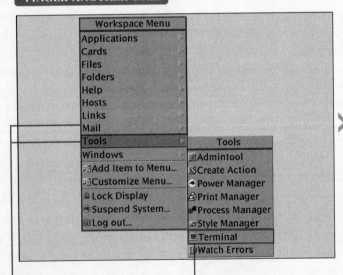

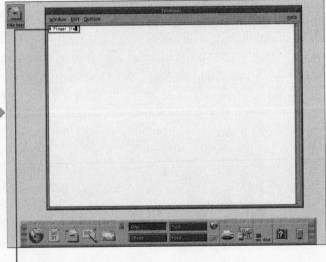

■1 Open a new UNIX terminal by right-clicking anywhere on the open desktop.

■ The main pop-up menu appears.

■2 Click Tools.

■3 Click Terminal.

■ The pop-up menu disappears and a new Terminal window is displayed on the desktop.

■4 At the command prompt, type: `finger <username>`.

■5 Press Enter.

Apply It

Limitations to the Search aspect of the `finger` command

Finger allows you to perform a limited search function to locate a person who is logged on to the system. However, you cannot use the `finger` command to search for a person's name or a group of people the way you search with, say, the `grep` command. For example, if you want to locate the users jjones, jsmith, and jwhite, you cannot finger all of them together by typing `finger j*`. Instead, you need to finger each account individually.

Applying user account names

You need to type in the user's account name to successfully use the `finger` command. Finger is designed to search for users only by their account names, not by their real names. Therefore, you finger bsmith on your computer, not Bob Smith.

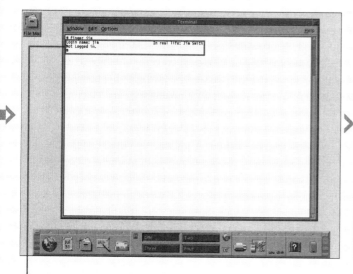

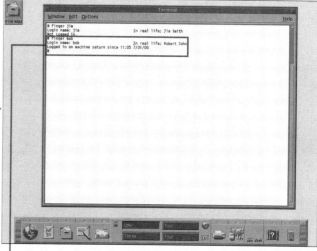

■ UNIX tells you whether or not the person is logged on. If the person is not logged on, you get a message similar to the one above.

■ In contrast, if the person is logged on, you get a message similar to the one listed above.

REVIEW AND REPEAT COMMANDS

The `history` command enables you to review the list of commands executed in a given UNIX session, repeat a command that you have already issued earlier without having to type it in again. The `history` command's first function is useful for trying to remember a complex command string that you used previously but cannot recall. Unless the command is so long again that it is beyond history's recall, you can see exactly what you typed in at the command prompt.

The history command's second function is also extremely useful. By being able to duplicate a command out of the history command's list, you save yourself a lot of typing. For example, if a given command to list an obscure file is `ls/etc/tmp/filename`, you instead type the bang (!) sign and the task's number under the history list, press Enter, and repeat the task without typing in the full command again.

REVIEW AND REPEAT COMMANDS

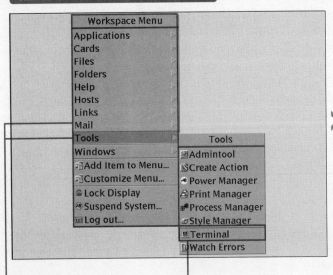

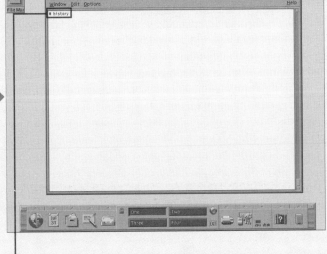

1 Open a new UNIX terminal by right-clicking anywhere on the open desktop.

■ The main pop-up menu appears.

2 Click Tools.

3 Click Terminal.

■ The pop-up menu disappears and a new Terminal window is displayed on the desktop.

4 At the command prompt, type `history`.

5 Press Enter.

Extra

I do not see a command I used in the list of commands displayed by history

Remember that history only displays commands that have been entered during your current UNIX session. A UNIX session is the period of time between logging in to the system and logging out of it. So, if you logged in to the system, performed the *copy* command cp, logged out, and then logged in again a couple hours later, history does not display the cp command you used because you are now in a new UNIX session.

I cannot see any commands listed when I use the history command

If you just logged in to your UNIX machine without performing any extra actions, you may see nothing on the history command list. You have not entered any commands in this particular session, so there isn't anything to display yet.

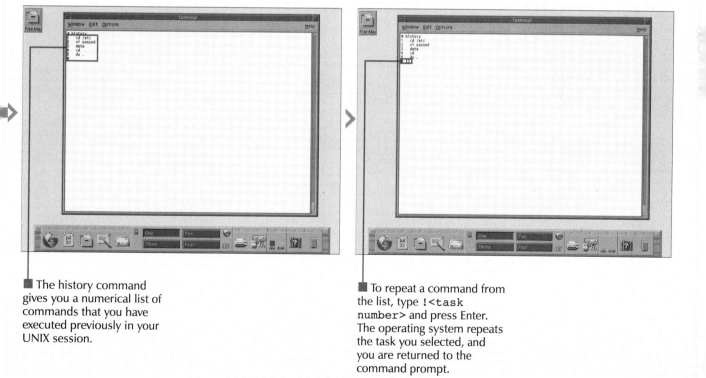

■ The history command gives you a numerical list of commands that you have executed previously in your UNIX session.

■ To repeat a command from the list, type !<task number> and press Enter. The operating system repeats the task you selected, and you are returned to the command prompt.

READ FILES WITH THE MORE COMMAND

The `more` command enables you to view text- and numerically based files in the UNIX terminal window. *More* is not a true word processing utility, because it does not allow you to edit text at all, let alone copy, delete, or save it. *More* is a limited tool, devoted to only one thing: displaying text or numbers.

This limitation is more useful than most people appreciate. When you use *more*, what you give up in word processing power, you more than make up in speed and safety. The primitive `more` command is very fast, because it does not have to work with formatting or spacing functions. When you use a command that does not allow you to edit a document, it protects the document from accidental changes that could take place in, say, a vi editor session. Because of this, *more* is especially useful if you want to view a sensitive system file, such as `/etc/system` or `/etc/passwd`.

READ FILES WITH THE MORE COMMAND

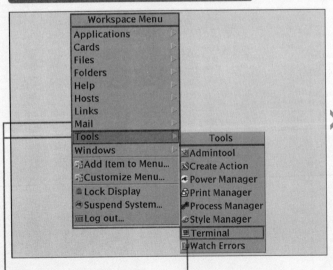

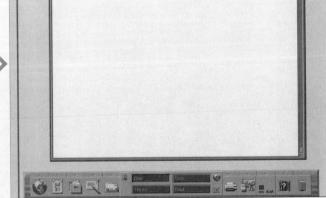

1 Open a new UNIX terminal by right-clicking anywhere on the open desktop.

■ The main pop-up menu appears.

2 Click Tools.

3 Click Terminal.

■ The pop-up menu disappears and a new Terminal window is displayed on the desktop.

4 At the command prompt, type `more <filename>` to view the contents of a given file.

5 Press Enter.

Apply It

Reversing in a document displayed on screen with the `more` command

Actually, there is nothing you can or should do. The primitive display capabilities of the `more` command do not allow you to manipulate a cursor to move to the left or right, or even to move back up in a document.

Your only option is to use the space key to move down through the document. If you want to return to a specific place, your best bet is to press the space key to move down page by page, then use the `more` command a second time to begin again.

Other options to paging down through a long document

Pressing the Q key instead of pressing the space bar multiple times to get to the ends of a long document breaks you out of the `more` command and returns you to the command prompt.

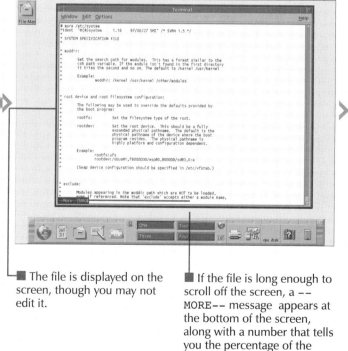

■ The file is displayed on the screen, though you may not edit it.

■ If the file is long enough to scroll off the screen, a `--MORE--` message appears at the bottom of the screen, along with a number that tells you the percentage of the document that has been displayed. Press the space bar to continue scrolling.

■ When *more* has finished displaying the file, it returns you to the command prompt.

TIME YOUR SYSTEM

The `time` command allows system administrators and users of a UNIX system to check the speed at which the system is working. This command measures the speed at which a given job is completed on the computer in three distinct parameters: actual, user, and system time.

Actual time is the amount of chronological time the computer takes to finish a task. The task is normally measured in seconds down through hundredths of seconds, although many jobs (such as listing files) often take only a fraction of that time.

User and system time are measured in milliseconds. User time is the amount of processing time that the machine takes to convey and display the information to the user. System time is the amount of time the computer actually needs to process and calculate the information.

TIME YOUR SYSTEM

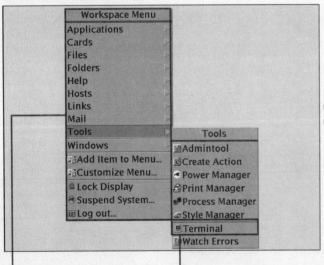

1 Open a new UNIX terminal by right-clicking anywhere on the open desktop.

■ The main pop-up menu appears.

2 Click Tools.

3 Click Terminal.

■ The pop-up menu disappears and a new Terminal window is displayed on the desktop.

4 To time a typical command, type **time** and the command name.

5 Press Enter.

■ The time the job took and the amount of time it took the user and system to complete the job are posted. If the job is simple and the time spent is effectively zero, the time is displayed as such on the screen.

Zero time can elapse for simple tasks

Your computer, no matter how old or slow, was designed to handle and transmit data via incredibly fast electrical impulses. When a relatively simple job, such as listing files, is performed on a machine with no heavy activity, the amount of time is measured in as little as a single millisecond — an amount so small that it is effectively zero.

System slowdown causes

Systems slow for a number of reasons. Possibly, the machine is currently under heavy activity, such as handling several dozen print jobs at once. Or, there may be too many people on the system, or a lack of an appropriate amount of RAM to keep things moving efficiently. For more information, check out this book's chapter on troubleshooting problems on the system.

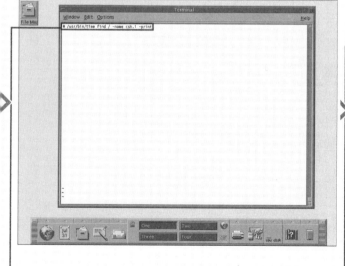

■ A common use of the `time` command is to time a print job, which is done by typing the `time` command, followed by the `print` command at the command prompt.

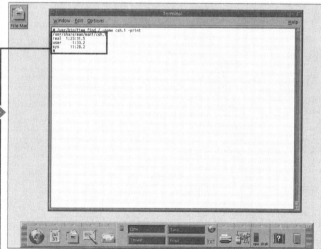

■ Press Enter. The time spent by the system to complete the job is displayed.

LOWER A JOB'S PRIORITY

The `nice` command enables you to lower a job's priority at times when a heavily-used system is starting to queue or schedule jobs, so that it processes them more efficiently. The `nice` number associated with a job, normally ranging from +20 to -20, is a method that your computer uses to prioritize jobs in a priority-based scheduling process.

On most systems (and almost all stand-alone systems) changing the nice number of a

process does not significantly speed up or slow down a process. However, if you are on a heavily-used machine at a peak time, you may want to downgrade a job you give your computer until the other more important jobs have completed and exited.

The lower the job priority, the more important the system considers the job. To reduce the job's importance, you need to add to the default `nice` level.

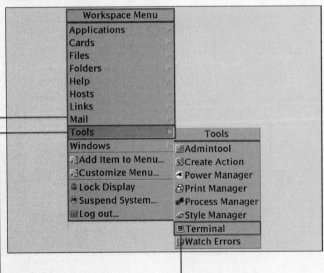

1 Open a new UNIX terminal by right-clicking anywhere on the open desktop.

■ The main pop-up menu appears.

2 Click Tools.

3 Click Terminal.

■ The pop-up menu disappears and a new Terminal window is displayed on the desktop.

4 At the command prompt, type nice + <number> <job name>.

5 Press Enter.

Apply It

Default nice value for most jobs

There is actually more variation in this than you may think. For example, the garden-variety job given to the system from a user is at level 20. However, most jobs that are requested by the root account, or are run automatically by the system are usually given lower (more important) priority.

Maximizing system performance by minimizing your actions

Again, spending the time typing in the `nice` command does not, as a rule, affect the speed of a completed job more than 99.9 percent of the time. Therefore, you do not need to reduce the priority of your job unless it is not very important, and it takes up significant computing resources at peak time.

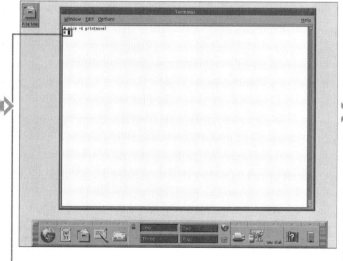

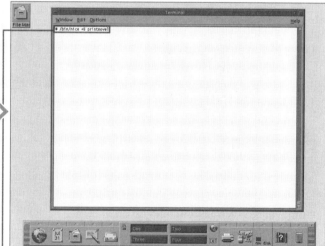

■ The priority of the job you specified is lowered by the number you indicated, and you are returned to the command prompt. Note that UNIX does not provide any additional screens or messages telling you the job is complete.

■ On some earlier versions of UNIX, the `nice` command does not work unless you type in the full path name. If this is the case on your machine, be sure to type `/bin/nice` to use the command at the command prompt.

RAISE A JOB'S PRIORITY

You use the `nice` command to raise a job's priority at times when a heavily-used system is starting to fall behind and schedules jobs so that it processes them in order of priority. The nice number associated with a job, normally ranging from +20 to -20, is a method that your computer uses to prioritize job requests.

On most small networks or stand-alone systems, changing the nice number of a process will not significantly speed up or slow down a process. However, you may be

accustomed to working on a heavily-used server at a peak time where people are sending large print jobs to the printer, or they are working with graphics and text. If this is the case, you may want to upgrade the priority of your job before less important jobs have completed and exited.

Because the computer considers high priority jobs more important at times, you may need to raise the job's importance by subtracting from the default `nice` level.

RAISE A JOB'S PRIORITY

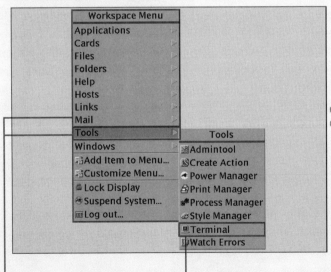

1 Open a new UNIX terminal by right-clicking anywhere on the open desktop.

■ The main pop-up menu appears.

2 Click Tools.

3 Click Terminal.

■ The pop-up menu disappears and a new Terminal window is displayed on the desktop.

4 At the command prompt, type `nice - <number> <job name>`.

5 Press Enter.

Apply It

Changing the *nice* priority in whole numbers

Because the nice priority is basically an order system, there are no levels of niceness, such as 16.1, 8.5, or -3.2. Running a `nice` command with a decimal or fraction causes the computer to ignore the request.

Primary impacts of changing the nice level

The only type of job that is affected by changing the *nice* level is a job that takes a computer more than a few seconds to finish, such as a printing job or transferring data during a time of peak use.

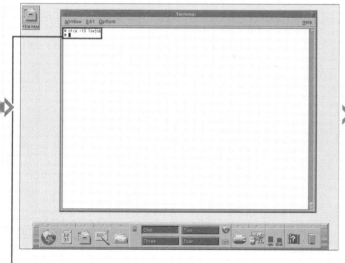

■ The priority of the job you specified is raised by the number you indicated, and you are returned to the command prompt. Note that UNIX does not provide any additional screens or messages telling you the job is complete.

■ On some earlier versions of UNIX, the `nice` command does not work unless you type in the full path name. If this is the case on your machine, be sure to type **/bin/nice** to use the command at the command prompt.

VIEW NICE PRIORITIES

You view the nice priorities assigned by your machine to various tasks by using the l command option with the ps, or process search command. The advantage of using this form of the process search command is that it allows you to view either all of the nice priorities on all of the processes currently running, or only one process at a time.

When using the ps command to view a particular task, you use only the pipe utility and the grep, (get regular expression) command together. This command combination is as potent as it is useful, which is why it is discussed in great detail in "Power Searches" in Chapter 7. It is particularly useful when you need to separate a command by process ID number or by process name in a sea of similar processes running on the UNIX network at the same time.

VIEW NICE PRIORITIES

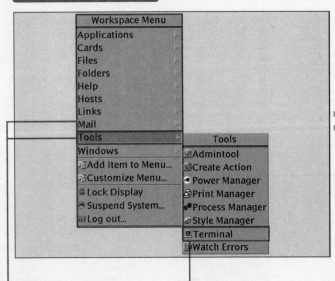

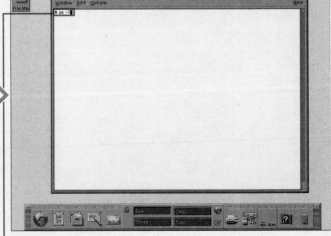

■1 Open a new UNIX terminal by right-clicking anywhere on the open desktop.

■ The main pop-up menu appears.

■2 Click Tools.

■3 Click Terminal.

■ The pop-up menu disappears and a new Terminal window is displayed on the desktop.

■4 To view the *nice* priorities of all jobs currently running on your system, type **ps -l** at the command prompt.

■5 Press Enter.

Apply It

Using the process search command with the -l option to search for a given type of process

If you have a rough idea of the name or nature of the process you are searching for, you can fine-tune the `ps` function to search for a given process. For example, if you need to search for processes like Netscape netstat and netcheck, you can view all of their nice priorities (assuming they are all running at the same time) by using `ps -l | grep net*`. This shows the nice priorities for all processes that start with net.

Processes are most likely to be found with the `ps-1` command

When searching for nice levels by the type of command, the most common form of command is an ongoing data transfer task. This might include a running Web browser like Netscape, or a telnet or FTP session.

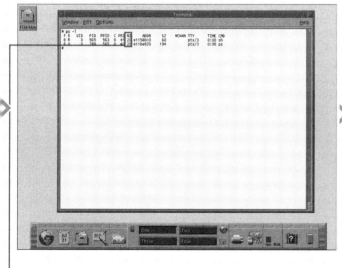

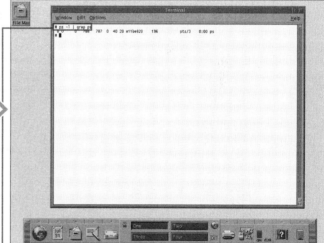

■ All running jobs are listed with their *nice* priority under the NI column, which is the 8th column from the left.

■ To view the *nice* priority of a specific job, you need to use the pipe utility and `grep` command with `ps`. At the command prompt, type **ps -1 | grep <job name>** and press Enter.

COUNT WORDS

You can quickly perform a count of the number of words, sentences, and characters in a given UNIX document with the wc (short for word count) command. This command is helpful if you are working on a document or report that has to be of a specific length, or starting to run short of disk space.

Running a wc command on a file is a good way to determine if any new information has been added to a file. For example, let's say that you run a word count on a critical system file and you get 100 words. After installing a complex piece of software on your system, you might run the same command to discover that the file now weighs in at 114 words, meaning that some editing took place to the file when you added the new software.

COUNT WORDS

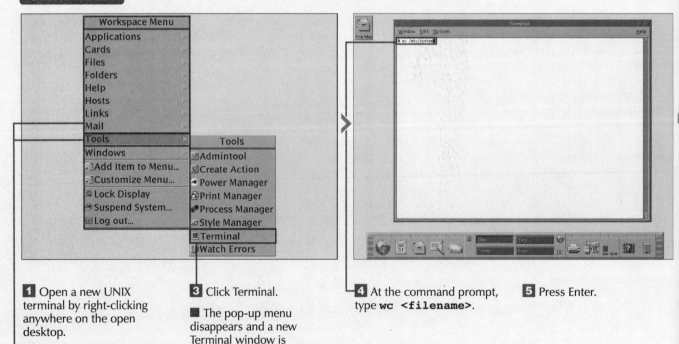

1 Open a new UNIX terminal by right-clicking anywhere on the open desktop.

■ The main pop-up menu appears.

2 Click Tools.

3 Click Terminal.

■ The pop-up menu disappears and a new Terminal window is displayed on the desktop.

4 At the command prompt, type **wc <filename>**.

5 Press Enter.

Apply It

Limited applications for wc

The word count command is a relatively primitive one, designed for maximum speed in execution. When you use wc, you get an accurate count and display of the components of a given document, but you cannot use wc to edit a file, let alone to tell you what new material has been deleted or added to a file if the word count is different. To perform a more thorough displaying of a file, use the more command. To actually edit the file, use the vi editor, as described in Chapter 5.

Counting spaces between words

A computer sees the blank space that is created between words as an electrical impulse that is recorded. Therefore, even a space, tab, or a hyphen is actually counted as a character by the wc program.

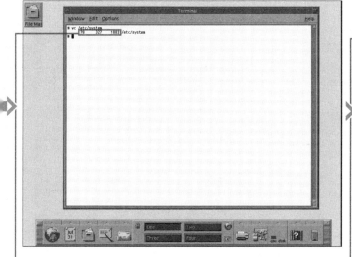

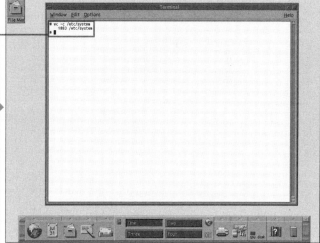

■ The results are given as a set of three numbers: the number of sentences in the document, the number of words, and finally the number of characters in the document.

■ If you just want to count the number of characters in the document, use the -c command option. At the command prompt, type **wc -c <filename>** and press Enter.

LIST RUNNING JOBS

You can list all jobs or tasks that are currently running on your UNIX machine with a single command: *jobs*. The jobs command is, like many of the older commands used in the UNIX terminal, a less flexible and sophisticated command. What it lacks in additional utilities, it makes up for in speed and general usefulness in its basic state.

The jobs command is, in some ways, similar to the history command discussed earlier in this chapter under the task spread, Using History to Review and Repeat Commands. However, there are some key differences. First, the jobs command lists only tasks that are still in progress; the history command lists only what has been run and completed. Second, the history command lists command names, while jobs actually lists the name of the job, regardless of the process name that is used to fulfill the task.

LIST RUNNING JOBS

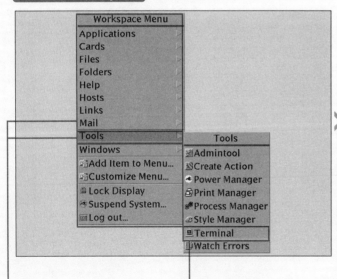

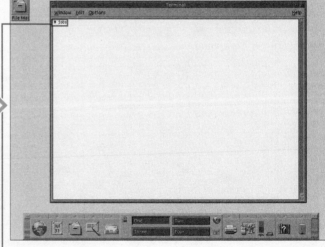

1 Open a new UNIX terminal by right-clicking anywhere on the open desktop.

■ The main pop-up menu appears.

2 Click Tools.

3 Click Terminal.

■ The pop-up menu disappears and a new Terminal window is displayed on the desktop.

4 At the command prompt, type **jobs**.

5 Press Enter.

Apply It

Uses for a job's Process ID number

The Process ID number gives you useful information on a process that is being used to complete a job. For example, it allows you to get the *nice* priority of the process with the p command, as shown in the earlier task "View Nice Priorities."

Limits to the number of jobs that can be displayed using the job command

There are technically no limits to the number of jobs that can be displayed in the job list of running tasks. However, executing jobs is much like taking a snapshot of jobs running on your computer at any time. After a job exits, the jobs command does not report it. You have to run jobs again to see if the task is still running.

■ The running jobs are listed by number in the left-hand column. You can see which job is running by looking at the listing in the right-hand column.

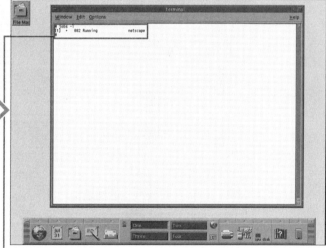

■ To view the running job's Process ID number, use the −l command option by typing **jobs −l** at the command prompt and press Enter.

BRING A JOB TO THE FOREGROUND

You can help bring a job to completion, or assist in speeding up it completion, by bringing it to the foreground for processing in UNIX. This is easily done with the fg (short for foreground) command.

In UNIX, all processes normally run in the foreground until they are completed. That is, the computer works on the task until it is completed, and you won't be returned to the command prompt until the job is completed. In the case of a long, slow job (such as printing

several dozen pages of text) you may decide to place the job in the background so that you may continue to work from the command prompt on other tasks. (See the task "Place a Job in the Background".)

Of course, a command like fg () is very helpful if you have completed what you needed at the command prompt, and want to bring a job out of the background so that additional processing power can be spent on it.

BRING A JOB TO THE FOREGROUND

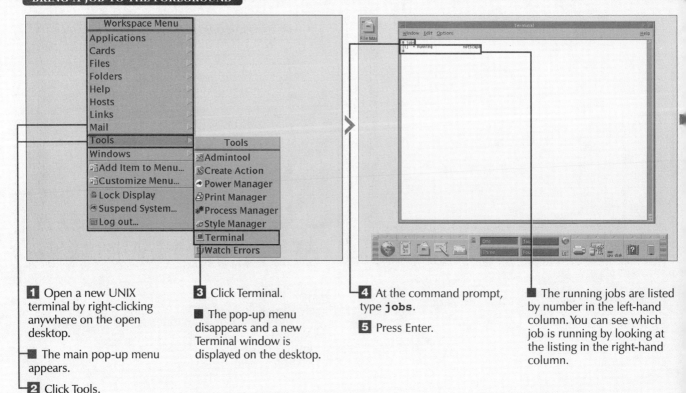

■1 Open a new UNIX terminal by right-clicking anywhere on the open desktop.

■ The main pop-up menu appears.

■2 Click Tools.

■3 Click Terminal.

■ The pop-up menu disappears and a new Terminal window is displayed on the desktop.

■4 At the command prompt, type **jobs**.

■5 Press Enter.

■ The running jobs are listed by number in the left-hand column. You can see which job is running by looking at the listing in the right-hand column.

Apply It

Types of jobs most commonly brought to the foreground

Any sort of job that is ongoing, long, and takes up significant amounts of processing power are candidates for being moved to the foreground for faster processing. Common examples are file transfers via the FTP (File Transfer Protocol) utility between networked computers, or other kinds of network connections, such as telnet.

Moving more than one job to the foreground at one time

You can bring only one job to the foreground at one time, because when you bring a job to the foreground, you are not returned to the command prompt until the job is completed. And of course, until you are returned to the command prompt, you cannot execute another fg command.

6 To move a job to the foreground, at the command prompt, type **fg**, followed by **%<job number>**.

7 Press Enter.

■ The job is brought to the foreground. You are not returned to the command prompt until the job is completed.

PLACE A JOB IN THE BACKGROUND

The bg command (background) enables you to get more work done by releasing the command prompt from an ongoing job. This command works by consigning an ongoing task to the background so that you can get more important tasks completed while you're busy working on other issues.

In the UNIX operating system, all processes normally run in the foreground until completed. As a rule, the computer works on the task until it is completed, and you will not be returned to the command prompt until the

job is completed. In the case of a long job (such as transmitting several pages of code across a network) you may place the job in the background so that you may continue to work from the command prompt on other tasks.

When a job is placed in the background, it is processed more slowly, because the system always allocates job priority to what is being run at the command prompt, or foreground of the UNIX system. Of course, this does not make much of a difference on any but the slowest or most busy systems.

PLACE A JOB IN THE BACKGROUND

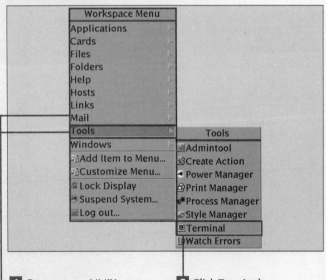

1 Open a new UNIX terminal by right-clicking anywhere on the open desktop.

■ The main pop-up menu appears.

2 Click Tools.

3 Click Terminal.

■ The pop-up menu disappears and a new Terminal window is displayed on the desktop.

4 You can see if a job is running in the foreground by typing **ps -aef | grep <job name>**.

5 Press Enter.

■ The process name and process ID numbers appear.

Note: For more information on this command string, see "Power Searches" in Chapter 7.

Extra

An alternative way to place a job into the background when the job is actually executed

You can actually specify that a process run as a background job from the start by adding an ampersand (&) after the command. For example, typing `netscape &` at the command prompt and pressing Enter allows you to run the Netscape Web browser, while at the same time keeping your command prompt available to run additional UNIX commands.

Limitations on placing multiple jobs into the background

Actually, unlike moving jobs to the foreground, where only one can be in the foreground at any time, multiple jobs can be running in the background at once. Whether you place these jobs in the background via the `bg` command or by starting them with an ampersand, they all run with less processing power while allowing you to retain the UNIX command prompt.

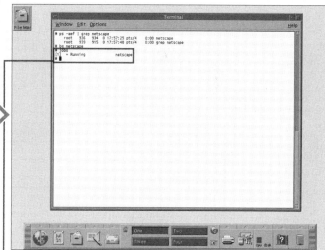

6 To move the job into the background, type **BG** followed by the job's name or process ID number at the command prompt.

7 Press Enter.

■ The job is backgrounded and you are returned to the command prompt.

■ To check whether or not the job is still running in the background, type **jobs** at the command prompt and press Enter. The job is listed.

TABLE A-1: VI MOVE COMMANDS

Command Option	What It Does	Command Option	What It Does
h	Move the cursor one character to the left	F<number>	Move the cursor a specified number of characters to the left
j	Move the cursor one line downward	w	Move the cursor one word forward
l	Move the cursor one character to the right	b	Move the cursor one word backward
K	Move the cursor one line upward	e	Move the cursor forward to the end of the next word
$	Move the cursor to the end of the current line	M	Move the cursor to the middle line of the screen
^	Move the cursor the first character in line	}	Move the cursor a paragraph forward
f<number>	Move the cursor a specified number of characters to the right (find)	{	Move the cursor a paragraph backward
		n	Repeat last action

TABLE A-2: APPENDING COMMANDS

Command Option	What It Does
a	Append text after the cursor
A	Append text at the end of line
i	Insert text before the cursor
o	Open a new line below the current one
O	Open a new line above the current one

TABLE A-3: DELETING COMMANDS

Command Option	What It Does
x	Delete characters under and after the cursor
X	Delete characters before the cursor
dd	Delete an entire line
D	Delete the rest of the line after the cursor

TABLE A-4: TEXT CHANGE COMMANDS

Command Option	What It Does
r<character>	Replace one character with another
R	Overwrite the rest of the line
s	Substitute characters
S	Substitute lines

TABLE A-6: UNDO COMMANDS

Command Option	What It Does
u	Undo the latest change
U	Undo all changes on a line
:u	Undo the last substitution on the line
:q!	Quit vi without writing (Linux-speak for 'saving')
:e!	Re-edit file. Useful if you've accidentally added or deleted lines from a file

TABLE A5: COPY TEXT COMMANDS

Command Option	What It Does
y<number>	Yank (copy) from begin to endpoint of a specified number of lines
yy	Yank (copy) a line of text
m<a-z>	Mark the cursor position with a letter

TABLE A-7: WRITING & EDITING COMMANDS

Command Option	What It Does
:q	Quit vi
:q!	Quit vi without writing
:w	Write to the file
:w <name>	Write to the file with a different file name
:w >> <name>	Append your changes to the file <name>
:w! <name>	Overwrite the file <name>
:x,y w <name>	Write lines x through y to the file <name>
:wq	Write the file and quit vi

WHAT'S ON THE CD-ROM

The CD-ROM included with this book contains many useful files and programs. Before installing any of the programs on the disc, make sure that a newer version of the program is not already installed on your computer. For information on installing different versions of the same program, contact the program's manufacturer.

SYSTEM REQUIREMENTS

To use the contents of the CD-ROM, your computer must be equipped with the following hardware and software:

- A PC with a Pentium or faster processor.

- Microsoft Windows 95 or later.

- At least 16MB of total RAM installed on your computer (we recommend at least 32MB).

- At least 300 MB of hard drive space.

- A double-speed (2x) or faster CD-ROM drive.

- A sound card for PCs.

- A monitor capable of displaying at least 256 colors or grayscale.

- A modem with a speed of at least 14,400 bps.

INSTALLING AND USING THE SOFTWARE

For your convenience, the software titles appearing on the CD-ROM are listed alphabetically.

Diskcheck

For UNIX systems and Windows machines running UNIX. Diskcheck looks for errors on your hard disk, such as corrupted files, and fixes these errors without the need to manually run the program. For more information regarding Diskcheck, check out `http://www.kaybee.org/~kirk/html/linux.html`.

Logwatch

For UNIX systems and Windows machines running UNIX. Logwatch monitors the size of your system logs and notifies you if the portion of the disk storing the logs is in danger of filling up, which could cause your machine to crash. For more information regarding Logwatch, check out http://www.kaybee.org/~kirk/html/linux.html.

Tripwire

For UNIX systems and Windows machines running UNIX. Tripwire 2.0 provides network security for your machine by preventing unauthorized access of your machine over the Internet or from your local area network. For more information on Tripwire, visit `www.tripwiresecurity.com/prodintro.html`.

For UNIX machines.

These files contain all the sample code from the book. You can browse these files directly from the CD-ROM, or you can copy them to your hard drive and use them as the basis for your own projects. To find the files on the CD-ROM, click on the arrow above the Files button on your desktop toolbar.

Choose Open CD-ROM from the drop-down menu. To copy the files to your hard drive, click and drag the files you want to your File Manager on your CDE desktop.

For Windows 95 or 98 machines running UNIX.

In each of the folders you find a file that contains the license agreement for that particular software. The filenames are either `gpl.txt` (General Public License) or `IDG_Eula.txt`. These files contain the licenses that you agree to when you use the CD. When you are done reading each license, close the program (most likely NotePad) that displayed the file.

1. Double-click the file called `Readme.txt`.

   This file contains instructions about installing the software from this CD. It can be helpful to leave this text file open while you are using the CD.

2. Double-click the folder for the software that you are interested in.

Be sure to read the descriptions of the programs in the next section of this appendix (much of this information also shows up in the Readme file). These descriptions give you more precise information about the programs' folder names and about finding and running the installer program.

Troubleshooting

I tried my best to compile programs that work on most computers with the minimum system requirements. Your computer, however, may differ and some programs may not work properly for some reason.

The two most likely problems are that you don't have enough memory (RAM) for the programs you want to use, or you have other programs running that are affecting the installation or running of a program. If you get error messages like `Not enough memory` or `Setup cannot continue`, try one or more of these methods and then try using the software again:

- Turn off any anti-virus software.

- Close all running programs.

- In Windows, close the CD-ROM interface and run demos or installations directly from Windows Explorer.

- Have your local computer store add more RAM to your computer.

If you still have trouble installing the items from the CD-ROM, please call the IDG Books Worldwide Customer Service phone number: 800-762-2974 (outside the U.S.: 317-572-3342).

USING THE E-VERSION OF THE BOOK

You can view *Unix: Your visual blueprint for building dynamic Web pages* on your screen using the CD-ROM disc included at the back of this book. The CD-ROM disc allows you to search the contents of each chapter of the book for a specific word or phrase. The CD-ROM disc also provides a convenient way of keeping the book handy while traveling.

You must install Adobe Acrobat Reader on your computer before you can view the book on the CD-ROM disc. This program is provided on

the disc. Acrobat Reader allows you to view Portable Document Format (PDF) files, which can display books and magazines on your screen exactly as they appear in printed form.

To view the contents of the book using Acrobat Reader, display the contents of the disc. Double-click the PDFs folder to display the contents of the folder. In the window that appears, double-click the icon for the chapter of the book you want to review.

USING THE E-VERSION OF THE BOOK

FLIP THROUGH PAGES

1 Click one of these options to flip through the pages of a section.

- [◄] First page
- [◄] Previous page
- [►] Next page
- [►] Last page

ZOOM IN

1 Click 🔍 to magnify an area of the page.

2 Click the area of the page you want to magnify.

■ Click one of these options to display the page at 100% magnification (□) or to fit the entire page inside the window (□).

Extra

To install Acrobat Reader, insert the CD-ROM disc into a drive. In the screen that appears, click Software. Click Acrobat Reader and then click Install at the bottom of the screen. Then follow the instructions on your screen to install the program.

You can make searching the book more convenient by copying the .pdf files to your own computer. Display the contents of the CD-ROM disc and then copy the PDFs folder from the CD to your hard drive. This allows you to easily access the

Acrobat Reader is a popular and useful program. There are many files available on the Web that are designed to be viewed using Acrobat Reader. Look for files with the .pdf extension. For more information about Acrobat Reader, visit the Web site at www.adobe.com/products/acrobat/readermain.html.

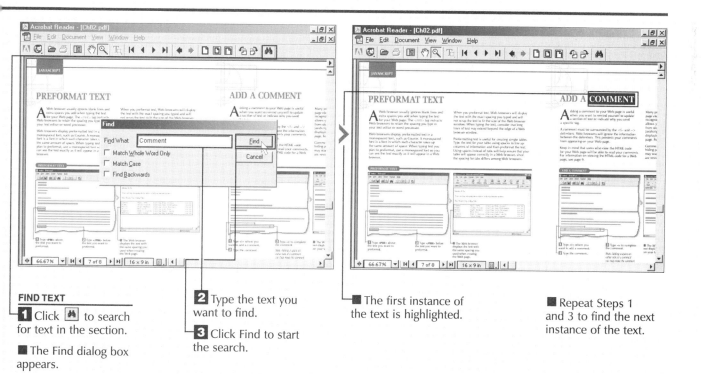

FIND TEXT

1 Click 🔍 to search for text in the section.

■ The Find dialog box appears.

2 Type the text you want to find.

3 Click Find to start the search.

■ The first instance of the text is highlighted.

■ Repeat Steps 1 and 3 to find the next instance of the text.

INDEX

Numbers and Symbols

& (ampersand), 120, 215, 313
* (asterisk), 5, 6, 59, 117, 158
: (colon), 57
, (comma), 242, 247, 249
{} (curly braces), 77
- (dash), 44
$ (dollar sign), 18, 142
! (exclamation point), 97
/ (forward slash), 49, 53, 57, 75, 84
> (greater-than sign), 122–123, 124
(hash sign), 7, 18
- (hyphen), 57
< (less-than sign), 122–123, 124
% (percent sign), 18
. (period), 156, 231
| (pipe symbol), 108
-1 command option, 44–45, 61, 204–205, 207, 209, 309
-8 command option, 261
-9 command option, 260–261, 263

A

-a command option, 156, 209
About Managing Users option, 165
access control. *See* ownership; permissions
Add Bookmark command, 219
Add command, 195
Add Local Printer screen, 195
Add User screen, 163
Admintool
    adding printers with, 194–195
    adding user groups with, 176–177
    basic description of, 160–161
    changing user accounts with, 166–169
    creating user accounts with, 162–165
    deleting printers with, 196–197
    deleting user accounts with, 170–171
    deleting user groups with, 177, 178–179
    disabling user accounts with, 172–173
    finding more information about, 161
    getting basic host information with, 198–199
    listing user groups with, 174–175
alerts, 42–43. *See also* warning messages
aliases
    basic description of, 138
    checking for, 138–139
    creating, 139
    naming, 139
ampersand (&), 120, 215, 313
anti-virus software, 315
append command, 124–125
applications

closing, 28–29
    launching, 2, 20–21, 34
    utilities and, distinction between, 21
Applications button, 2
Applix, 225
Appointment Editor screen, 274–279, 286–287
appointments. *See also* Calendar accessory
    changing, 286–287
    removing, 280–281
    rescheduling, 281
    setting, 272–279
    stretching/duplicating, 276
archiving, 236–239, 248–249. *See also* compression
arrow keys, 76, 83, 122–124
ASCII (American Standard Code for Information Interchange), 50
asterisk (*), 5, 6, 59, 117, 158
attachments, 223, 225
Auto Save feature, 90

B

-b command option, 98–100
Back button, 218, 219
Backdrop option, 36
background
    executing scripts in the, 136–137
    placing jobs in the, 312–313
    running processes in, 120–121
Backtrack button, 35
backups
    through archiving, 236–241, 248–249
    to floppy disks, 184–185
    made before performing troubleshooting procedures, 257
    system, 240–249
banners, 195
Beep option, 42
bg command, 312–313
biff (program), 226–227
binary files, 30–33, 50–51, 242–243
/bin/bash file, 133
/bin/csh file, 133, 134
bitmap (BMP) files, 37, 57, 185. *See also* graphics
    archiving, 236–237
    sending, as e-mail attachments, 225
Bookmark utility, 219
bookmarks, 219
booting
    basic description of, 16–17
    login and, 4
    fixing device problems when, 256–257
borders, of windows, 22, 24, 25
bottlenecks, 189
Bourne Again shell, 132–135
Bourne shell, 130–134, 163, 164
break points, links as potential, 61

UNIX:
Your visual blueprint to
the universe of UNIX

INDEX

command prompt
    appearance of, after login, 5
    starting applications from, 21
commands (listed by name). *See also* command options
    Add Bookmark command, 219
    Add command, 195
    append command, 124–125
    bg command, 312–313
    cat command, 98–100, 104, 108–109, 121, 123
    cd command, 48–49, 61, 136
    chmod command, 63, 65, 71, 156–157
    chown command, 69, 71
    Close command, 29, 211, 269
    cmp command, 104–105
    copy command, 32, 54–55
    cp command, 54–55, 139
    date command, 264–265
    Delete command, 179, 197
    df command, 180–181
    du command, 258–259
    echo command, 130–131, 133, 135, 142–143, 145
    eject command, 186–187, 190–191
    env command, 140–141
    exit command, 135, 233–234, 283
    fg command, 310–311
    find command, 46–47
    Find Process command, 114, 116, 118, 121
    finger command, 292–293
    force command, 96–97
    grep command, 99, 110–112, 115–116, 125
    halt command, 14–15, 17
    head command, 99–102
    history command, 294–295, 308
    init command, 17
    jobs command, 308–309
    kill command, 121, 126–127, 260–263
    killall command, 262–263
    ln command, 60–61
    Log File command, 119
    Log Out command, 9
    Logout command, 8
    lp command, 109
    lpc command, 193
    ls command, 44–45, 51, 53, 108–109, 125, 139, 150–153
    M command, 77
    man command, 150–151
    mkdir command, 52
    Modify command, 172, 197
    more command, 296–297
    mount command, 188–189
    mv command, 56–57
    nice command, 300–305, 309
    Open Floppy command, 182–184
    passwd command, 166–167
    ping command, 252–255
    pipe command, 99, 125, 200–201, 305
    Print command, 211, 290

    ps command, 106–107, 112–113, 115–116, 125–127, 304–305
    pwd command, 49, 61
    :q command, 93
    q command, 95, 234
    :qw command, 95
    reboot command, 17
    redirect command, 141
    rlogin command, 202–205, 207, 209
    rm command, 58–59, 171
    rsh command, 206–207
    Save As command, 37
    Search command, 35
    Set View Options command, 183
    setenv command, 144, 145
    shutdown command, 12–14, 16–17
    sort command, 258–259
    su command, 6–7, 146–149
    sync command, 15, 17
    tail command, 99, 102–103
    telnet command, 126
    time command, 298–299
    touch command, 50–51
    u command, 87
    uncompress command, 246–247
    undo command, 94
    Update command, 185
    :w command, 91
    w command, 62–63, 95, 292
    wc command, 306–307
    :wq command, 95, 97 257
    x command, 62–63, 82–83
Comment field, 165
comments, entering, 165
compilers, 80–81
Completed button, 288, 289
Compose screen, 223
compression, 185, 236–249
    with the compress utility, 242–245, 248–249
    dual-, schemes, 248–249
    restoring files after, 246–247, 250–251
Configuration Location field, 217
Confirmation screen, 281, 287
connectivity, checking, with the ping command, 200–201
consoles, using, instead of terminals, 19
copy command, 32, 54–55
copying and pasting. *See also* copying
    e-mail text, 228
    with the mouse, 89
    with the vi editor, 88–89
copying. *See also* copying and pasting
    files between windows, 23, 32–33
    files from CD-ROMs, 188–189
    files to/from floppy disks, 184–185
    files to new directories, 55
core files, 129, 261
corruption, data, 15, 17

UNIX:
Your visual blueprint to
the universe of UNIX

o command, 54–55, 139
PUs (central processing units), 47, 114–116, 118
    ejecting CD-ROMs and, 191
    e-mail and, 222
    kill command and, 128
    mailx and, 234
    speed of, required for the CD, 314
ashes, 180, 244, 314
eation dates, 45
on utility, 50, 158–159
ontab file, 158–159
-Shell, 130–133, 135
urly braces ({}), 77
vf command option, 237, 239, 248, 250

D

aemons, 129, 175
    print, 193, 263
    telnet, 208–209, 263
    viewing the status of, 193
aily View, 272–283, 288–289
ish (-), 44
ita compression. See compression
ita corruption, 15, 17
ite command, 264–265
ites
    creation, 45
    system, resetting, 264–265
EC (decimal format), 268
ef command option, 113
fragmentation, 175
elete command, 179, 197
elete Home Directory option, 171
leting
    directories, 58–59, 171
    e-mail, 232–233
    files, 58–59, 119
    log files, 119
    print jobs, 197
    printers, 196–197
    in progress, stopping, 59
    recovering text after, 83
    text, 82–83, 87
    user accounts, 170–171
    user groups, 177–179
eletion Confirmation screen, 281
sktop
    accessing, 3
    background, customizing, 36–38
    basic description of, 2–3
    buttons, 3
    configuring, 3, 36–38
    help system and, 34–35
    locking your screen from, 10
    in Microsoft Windows, 60
    moving files to a window on, 31

moving windows across, 22–23
opening terminals from, 18
shutdown from, 11
sounds, 42–43
starting applications from, 20–21
Desktop Style option, 36, 38, 40
Destination Folder text box, 33
device
    busy message, 256
    problems, fixing, 256–257
df command, 180–181
Direct Connection to the Internet button, 217
directories. See also home directory; root directory
    changing, 48–49
    copying, 54–55
    copying files to/from, 32–33, 55
    creating new, 52–53
    deleting, 58–59, 171
    moving, 56–57
    moving files between, 30–31, 33
    ownership of, altering, 68–69
    permissions for, 64–65
    renaming, 54, 56–57
    searching for files in, 46–47
    storing log files in, 119
    temporary, 119, 238
disk bound, 189
disk defragmentation, 175
disk hogs, finding, 258–259
Diskcheck, 314
diskettes. See floppy disks
Display button, 268, 271
documents. See also file(s); text file(s)
    archiving, 236–239, 248–249
    going the end of, 296
    printing, 81
    saving, 185
    sending, as e-mail attachments, 225
    viewing, with the more command, 296–297
dollar sign ($), 18, 142
domain names, 230
DOS (Disk Operating System) prompt, 18
drive bound, 189
du command, 258–259
dual-compression schemes, 248–249
dummy accounts, 67

E

-e command option, 106, 158
echo command, 130–131, 133, 135
    determining variables and, 142–143
    $PATH variable and, 145
Edit menu
    Add command, 195
    Delete command, 179, 197
    Modify command, 197

UNIX:
Your visual blueprint to
the universe of UNIX

UNIX:
Your visual blueprint to
the universe of UNIX

Microsoft Windows, 18, 60
    accessories and, 266, 268, 270
    copying/pasting text and, 88–89
    executable files and, 72
    Force Quit action, 128
    GUI, 2
    remote shells and, 206
    running the CD with, 314–315
    telnetd daemon and, 208
    wizards, 212
Microsoft Word, 90, 185, 225, 228
military time, 265
Min Change field, 168
Minimize button, 26–27
mkdir command, 52
Modify command, 172, 197
monitors, 37–39. *See also* screen(s)
Monthly View, 273, 278–279, 284–285
More button, 274, 275
more command, 296–297
more detailed mode, 101
Motif, 4, 89
mount command, 188–189
mouse
    cut and paste with, 89
    right-handed/left-handed, 40–41
    settings, 3, 40–41
move to... option, 30
MP3 sound files. *See also* sound
    archiving, 225
    downloading, 43
    playing, 43
mv command, 56–57

N

-n command option, 258
-r command option, 102–103
nesting, 132, 134, 148
netcheck, 305
Netscape Communicator browser
    bg command and, 313
    configuring, to connect to the Internet, 216–217
    installing, 210–213
    nice command and, 305
    receiving e-mail with, 220–221
    running processes and, 120
    sending e-mail with, 222–223
    starting, 21, 214–215
    using, for browsing, 218–219
Netscape Messenger, 222–223, 232
Netscape Web site, 218
netstat, 305
network(s)
    access speed, 217
    Calendar accessory and, 277
    connections, testing, 200–201, 252–255
    job priority settings and, 300–303

    printers and, 194
    remote shells and, 206–207
    shutdown and, 11, 12–13
nice command, 300–305, 309
"No space left on device" message, 251
Notepad, 315
notifications, 17, 195
    shutdown, 13
    sounds for, 42–43
Novell, 206
numbers/numerical patterns, searching for, 85, 110–111

O

Occurs button, 275
Occurs field, 274, 275
octothorp symbol. *See also* hash sign (#)
Open CD-ROM utility, 188–189
Open Floppy command, 182, 183, 184
Open Floppy utility, 182
OpenSound Web site, 43
OpenWindows, 271
options, basic description of, 44
Options menu, 3
output
    appending, 124–125
    redirecting, 122–123
Owner button, 115
Owner text box, 67
ownership
    altering, 66–69
    group, configuring, 70–71
    root file, finding, 152–153
    taking back, 66
    transfers, 66–67

P

packets, 200–201
padlock icon, 10
paper sizes, 290–291
parallel ports, 195
partitions, 119, 124, 180
passwd command, 166–167
password(s). *See also* /etc/passwd file
    accessing desktops with, 3
    changing, 7, 166–169
    entering, 4–5
    locking, 172–173
    login, 4–7, 203, 205
    restricting terminal access and, 156
    root accounts and, 146–149, 156
    su command and, 146–149
    telnet and, 209
    unlocking your screen with, 10
    user accounts and, 146–149, 156, 166–169, 172–173

INDEX

UNIX:
Your visual blueprint to
the universe of UNIX

(continued)

UNIX:
Your visual blueprint to
the universe of UNIX

U

V

(continued)

APPENDIX

IDG BOOKS WORLDWIDE, INC.
END-USER LICENSE AGREEMENT

READ THIS. You should carefully read these terms and conditions before opening the software packet(s) included with this book ("Book"). This is a license agreement ("Agreement") between you and IDG Books Worldwide, Inc. ("IDGB"). By opening the accompanying software packet(s), you acknowledge that you have read and accept the following terms and conditions. If you do not agree and do not want to be bound by such terms and conditions, promptly return the Book and the unopened software packet(s) to the place you obtained them for a full refund.

1. **License Grant.** IDGB grants to you (either an individual or entity) a nonexclusive license to use one copy of the enclosed software program(s) (collectively, the "Software") solely for your own personal or business purposes on a single computer (whether a standard computer or a workstation component of a multiuser network). The Software is in use on a computer when it is loaded into temporary memory (RAM) or installed into permanent memory (hard disk, CD-ROM, or other storage device). IDGB reserves all rights not expressly granted herein.

2. **Ownership.** IDGB is the owner of all right, title, and interest, including copyright, in and to the compilation of the Software recorded on the disk(s) or CD-ROM ("Software Media"). Copyright to the individual programs recorded on the Software Media is owned by the author or other authorized copyright owner of each program. Ownership of the Software and all proprietary rights relating thereto remain with IDGB and its licensers.

3. **Restrictions on Use and Transfer.**

(a) You may only (i) make one copy of the Software for backup or archival purposes, or (ii) transfer the Software to a single hard disk, provided that you keep the original for backup or archival purposes. You may not (i) rent or lease the Software, (ii) copy or reproduce the Software through a LAN or other network system or through any computer subscriber system or bulletin-board system, or (iii) modify, adapt, or create derivative works based on the Software.

(b) You may not reverse engineer, decompile, or disassemble the Software. You may transfer the Software and user documentation on a permanent basis, provided that the transferee agrees to accept the terms and conditions of this Agreement and you retain no copies. If the Software is an update or has been updated, any transfer must include the most recent update and all prior versions.

4. **Restrictions on Use of Individual Programs.** You must follow the individual requirements and restrictions detailed for each individual program in the "About the CD" section of this Book. These limitations are also contained in the individual license agreements recorded on the Software Media. These limitations may include a requirement that after using the program for a specified period of time, the user must pay a registration fee or discontinue use. By opening the Software packet(s), you will be agreeing to abide by the licenses and restrictions for these individual programs that are detailed in the "About the CD" section and on the Software Media. None of the material on this Software Media or listed in this Book may ever be redistributed, in original or modified form, for commercial purposes.

5. **Limited Warranty.**

IDGB warrants that the Software and Software Media are free from defects in materials and workmanship under normal use for a period of sixty (60) days from the date of purchase of this Book. If IDGB receives notification within the warranty period of defects in materials or workmanship, IDGB will replace the defective Software Media.

Unix®
Your visual blueprint to
the universe of Unix

(b) IDGB AND THE AUTHOR OF THE BOOK DISCLAIM ALL OTHER WARRANTIES, EXPRESS OR IMPLIED, INCLUDING WITHOUT LIMITATION IMPLIED WARRANTIES OF MERCHANTABILITY AND FITNESS FOR A PARTICULAR PURPOSE, WITH RESPECT TO THE SOFTWARE, THE PROGRAMS, THE SOURCE CODE CONTAINED THEREIN, AND/OR THE TECHNIQUES DESCRIBED IN THIS BOOK. IDGB DOES NOT WARRANT THAT THE FUNCTIONS CONTAINED IN THE SOFTWARE WILL MEET YOUR REQUIREMENTS OR THAT THE OPERATION OF THE SOFTWARE WILL BE ERROR FREE.

(c) This limited warranty gives you specific legal rights, and you may have other rights that vary from jurisdiction to jurisdiction.

6. Remedies.

(a) IDGB's entire liability and your exclusive remedy for defects in materials and workmanship shall be limited to replacement of the Software Media, which may be returned to IDGB with a copy of your receipt at the following address: Software Media Fulfillment Department, Attn.: *Unix Blueprints*, IDG Books Worldwide, Inc., 10475 Crosspoint Blvd., Indianapolis, IN 46256, or call 800-762-2974. Please allow three to four weeks for delivery. This Limited Warranty is void if failure of the Software Media has resulted from accident, abuse, or misapplication. Any replacement Software Media will be warranted for the remainder of the original warranty period or thirty (30) days, whichever is longer.

(b) In no event shall IDGB or the author be liable for any damages whatsoever (including without limitation damages for loss of business profits, business interruption, loss of business information, or any other pecuniary loss) arising from the use of or inability to use the Book or the Software, even if IDGB has been advised of the possibility of such damages.

(c) Because some jurisdictions do not allow the exclusion or limitation of liability for consequential or incidental damages, the above limitation or exclusion may not apply to you.

7. U.S. Government Restricted Rights. Use, duplication, or disclosure of the Software by the U.S. Government is subject to restrictions stated in paragraph (c)(1)(ii) of the Rights in Technical Data and Computer Software clause of DFARS 252.227-7013, and in subparagraphs (a) through (d) of the Commercial Computer–Restricted Rights clause at FAR 52.227-19, and in similar clauses in the NASA FAR supplement, when applicable.

8. General. This Agreement constitutes the entire understanding of the parties and revokes and supersedes all prior agreements, oral or written, between them and may not be modified or amended except in a writing signed by both parties hereto that specifically refers to this Agreement. This Agreement shall take precedence over any other documents that may be in conflict herewith. If any one or more provisions contained in this Agreement are held by any court or tribunal to be invalid, illegal, or otherwise unenforceable, each and every other provision shall remain in full force and effect.

Read Less, Learn More™

Visual

with these two-color Visual™ *guides*

The Complete Visual Reference

For visual learners who want an all-in-one reference/tutorial that delivers more in-depth information about a technology topic.

"Master It" tips provide additional topic coverage

ORDER FORM

TRADE & INDIVIDUAL ORDERS

Phone: **(800) 762-2974**
or **(317) 572-3993**
(8 a.m.–6 p.m., CST, weekdays)
FAX : **(800) 550-2747**
or **(317) 572-4002**

EDUCATIONAL ORDERS & DISCOUNTS

Phone: **(800) 434-2086**
(8:30 a.m.–5:00 p.m., CST, weekdays)
FAX : **(317) 572-4005**

CORPORATE ORDERS FOR 3-D VISUAL™ SERIES

Phone: **(800) 469-6616**
(8 a.m.–5 p.m., EST, weekdays)
FAX : **(905) 890-9434**

Qty	ISBN	Title	Price	Total

Shipping & Handling Charges

	Description	First book	Each add'l. book	Total
Domestic	Normal	$4.50	$1.50	$
	Two Day Air	$8.50	$2.50	$
	Overnight	$18.00	$3.00	$
International	Surface	$8.00	$8.00	$
	Airmail	$16.00	$16.00	$
	DHL Air	$17.00	$17.00	$

Subtotal _____

CA residents add
applicable sales tax _____

IN, MA and MD
residents add
5% sales tax _____

IL residents add
6.25% sales tax _____

RI residents add
7% sales tax _____

TX residents add
8.25% sales tax _____

Shipping _____

Total _____

Ship to:

Name _____

Address _____

Company _____

City/State/Zip _____

Daytime Phone _____

Payment: □ Check to IDG Books (US Funds Only)
 □ Visa   □ Mastercard   □ American Express

Card # _____ Exp. _____ Signature _____

***maranGraphics*™**